Ultimate AWS Certified Solutions Architect Associate Exam Guide

Master Designing Resilient, Scalable Architectures with Core and Advanced AWS Services to Crack the SAA-C03 Certification

Venkata Sasi Kanumuri

Otieno Ododa

www.orangeava.com

First Published: September 2024

Published By: Orange Education Pvt Ltd, AVA™

Address: 9, Daryaganj, Delhi, 110002, India

275 New North Road Islington Suite 1314 London,

N1 7AA, United Kingdom

ISBN (PBK): 978-81-97953-41-5

ISBN (E-BOOK): 978-81-97953-43-9

Scan the QR code to explore our entire catalogue

www.orangeava.com

Dedicated To

To Mom, my inspiration
You taught me to dream big and
strive with determination
Everything I've achieved, I owe to you
This book is for you

- Sasi

To Johnny Ray Richard,

who was always engineering things

This book is for you

- Oates

About the Authors

Venkata Sasi Kanumuri is a renowned Cloud Strategy and FinOps/Cloud Economics expert, specializing in cloud efficiency, cost savings, and successful cloud migrations.

Sasi's thought leadership in FinOps has significantly shaped the industry, driving efficiency programs and lasting partnerships through vendor management and deal strategy.

As a pioneer in cloud economics, Sasi bridges the gap between finance, procurement, operations, and engineering, setting new standards for efficiency programs and redefining industry norms.

Sasi Kanumuri's unique "#Piggy-bank" framework for cost governance promotes cost awareness and productive discussions on cloud expenditure. His expertise in cloud infrastructure, effective cost governance, and vendor deal analysis drives efficiency and optimization.

Additionally, Sasi is passionate about mentoring and continuous learning. He has led educational sessions, workshops, and internal meetups, sharing expertise and empowering engineering teams to flourish and succeed.

Otieno Ododa is a senior engineering leader with over 20 years of experience in Site Reliability Engineering (SRE), DevOps, and Infrastructure Engineering, contributing to companies like Twitch, Patreon, Zeta Global, and Opendoor. He specializes in building, nurturing, and scaling high-performing platform and infrastructure engineering teams across domestic and international landscapes, driven by an "automate first" philosophy for efficiency and consistency.

Otieno's leadership emphasizes building tight-knit teams, prioritizing continuous learning and mentorship, and balancing cost with performance, focusing on the impact of engineering on architecture, customers, and the broader business.

His hands-on experience at companies like Friendster, Chomp, and Apple, where he managed data centers and large distributed systems, keeps him closely connected to the technical challenges his teams face.

Outside of work, Otieno enjoys spending time with his three kids and indulging his creative side through hands-on projects.

About the Technical Reviewer

Karan Vichare is an experienced Data Engineer with a demonstrated history of working in the information technology and services industry. He is skilled in Python (Programming Language), Google Cloud Platform, Data Warehousing, SQL, and Linux. Karan holds a Bachelor of Engineering in Information Technology from Mumbai University.

He is the Lead Data Architect at Ganit Business Solutions Private Limited with over 6 years of experience. Karan has worked in various areas, including data engineering, data analytics, web app development, and cloud migration. He is experienced in setting up ETL pipelines, data warehouses, web applications, governance, and security practices for clients to manage the facade of data deluge.

Acknowledgements

There are a few people I want to thank for the continued and ongoing support they have given me during the writing of this book. First and foremost, my wife and daughter deserve my deepest thanks. Their love and unwavering belief in me made all the difference during this journey.

I want to thank my uncle, Laxmikanth Malladi, who ignited my passion for cloud solutions architecture. Your inspiration continues to shape my path.

I want to thank Otieno Ododa (Oates), the co-author of the book for his support and expertise throughout the process.

I want to thank my parents, friends and family for their encouragement and belief. Their constant support meant the world to me. I appreciate you acknowledging all my accomplishments and being there to support me during difficult times.

My gratitude also goes to the Orange AVA team for the support and their belief in us to publish the book.

Preface

Cloud computing today encompasses an extensive reach, impacting every sphere of modern life. The march to the cloud has been fast-paced. This book introduces the background knowledge and required skills to handle the complexity of cloud infrastructure focused on Amazon Web Services. This book is for anyone seeking to transform their career in cloud computing. It combines detailed explanations with practical exercises to offer a comprehensive approach to mastering AWS solutions architecture. With dedication and effort, you can achieve your certification goals and unlock new opportunities in cloud computing.

In the eleven chapters, we will progress from a general overview to important specialized areas of cloud computing. Each chapter is well-designed to allow you to view it with a practical vision, bringing real-life examples. This approach will help you understand the theoretical concepts and develop the capability to apply them confidently in real-world scenarios using AWS services.

Let's embark on this journey together and hope that this guide serves as a valuable resource in your path to success.

Chapter 1. Introduction to Cloud Computing, AWS, and AWS SAA C-03: The chapter will introduce you to the basics of cloud computing by studying different cloud service models and types. You will learn the benefits and challenges of adopting cloud solutions, understand the role of the Cloud Solutions Architect, and how AWS works regarding its global infrastructure and fundamental account management.

Chapter 2. Identity and Access Management in AWS: This chapter will focus on AWS's security features, especially Identity and Access Management (IAM). You will learn how to construct sturdy security practices with IAM. The chapters will teach you authentication, authorization, and management of users, groups, roles, and policies. The focus of this chapter is granular access control. You will get a blueprint for mastering IAM in AWS.

Chapter 3. Networking in AWS: Every cloud professional should have a sound networking background. This chapter will teach you about the OSI model, key networking protocols, and other critical concepts like IP Addressing and

Subnetting. It will cover in detail all the AWS Networking Services, including Virtual Private Clouds, Load Balancers, DNS, and the Content Delivery Services offered by Route 53 and CloudFront.

Chapter 4. Cloud Storage: The chapter elaborates on how AWS offers different storage solutions, from block storage with EBS to file storage with EFS and FSx and object storage with S3. It also includes data transfer options provided by AWS Storage Gateway and the Snow family and cost optimization strategies for managing storage in the cloud.

Chapter 5. Deep-Dive into AWS Compute: This chapter will explore AWS compute services–EC2 instances, containers, and serverless computing with AWS Lambda–in depth. It will also examine how to use reservations and savings plans to optimize costs so your cloud infrastructure remains scalable and cost-effective.

Chapter 6. Deep Dive into AWS Databases: Databases are part of any application. This chapter will examine relational databases using RDS and Aurora, NoSQL databases using DynamoDB, and other big data and analytics services. You will also master techniques for database performance optimization and cost-effective data management.

Chapter 7. AWS Application Services: This chapter will explain some AWS services for front-end web and mobile, application integration, machine learning, and migration, and provide an overview of advanced AWS capabilities that can be leveraged to realize innovative, scalable solutions.

Chapter 8. AWS Management and Governance Services: The second most important aspect of cloud computing is managing its infrastructure. This chapter will review the process of provisioning and managing infrastructure on AWS and show how to monitor and log services. You will learn about security and compliance tools, such as CloudTrail, and explore further management and governance services through real-world use cases.

Chapter 9. AWS Cloud Security: Security is the prime concern of any cloud environment. This chapter presents an overview of cloud security in general and then explores AWS security services in-depth, such as AWS Shield, WAF, KMS, and others. You will learn how to consolidate the security of a multi-subscription setup within AWS Organizations and use other tools for added security in real-world scenarios.

Chapter 10. Cloud Architecture and AWS Framework: It covers the aspects to consider when designing cloud applications, including the 12-factor Methodology and famous Cloud Architecture Patterns. You will gain good input about the AWS Well-Architected Framework and in-depth views into its five pillars, which are needed for developing cloud applications with excellent availability, scalability, and safety.

Chapter 11. AWS SAA C-03 Certification Preparation: The final chapter covers how to prepare for the AWS Certified Solutions Architect–Associate (SAA-C03) exam. It provides an in-depth guide to certification, tips for booking and taking the exam, sample questions, and FAQs. It comprises the best practices to keep you fully prepared and ensure you achieve the much-needed certification.

With this book, begin your journey towards mastering AWS and the skills that will set you apart in cloud computing. Whether for certification, career development, or simply broadening your knowledge spectrum, this book provides the tools and insights you need to succeed.

This book is a valuable resource on your way to mastering the cloud.

Get a Free eBook

We hope you are enjoying your recently purchased book! Your feedback is incredibly valuable to us, and to all other readers looking for great books.

If you found this book helpful or enjoyable, we would truly appreciate it, if you could take a moment to leave a short review with a 5 star rating on Amazon. It helps us grow, and lets other readers discover our books.

As a thank you, we would love to send you a free digital copy of this book, and a **30%** discount code on your next cart value on our official websites:

www.orangeava.com

www.orangeava.in (For Indian Subcontinent)

☑ **Here's how:**

Leave a review for the book on Amazon.

Take a screenshot of your review, and send an email to **info@orangeava.com** (it can be just the confirmation screen).

Once, we receive your screenshot, we will send you the digital file, within 24 hours.

Thank you so much for your support – it means a lot to us!

Downloading the code bundles and colored images

Please follow the links or scan the QR codes to download the ***Code Bundles and Images*** of the book:

https://github.com/ava-orange-education/Ultimate-AWS-Certified-Solutions-Architect-Associate-Exam-Guide

The code bundles and images of the book are also hosted on ***https://rebrand.ly/cdb0e5***

In case there's an update to the code, it will be updated on the existing GitHub repository.

Errata

We take immense pride in our work at **Orange Education Pvt Ltd,** and follow best practices to ensure the accuracy of our content to provide an indulging reading experience to our subscribers. Our readers are our mirrors, and we use their inputs to reflect and improve upon human errors, if any, that may have occurred during the publishing processes involved. To let us maintain the quality and help us reach out to any readers who might be having difficulties due to any unforeseen errors, please write to us at :

errata@orangeava.com

Your support, suggestions, and feedback are highly appreciated.

DID YOU KNOW

Did you know that Orange Education Pvt Ltd offers eBook versions of every book published, with PDF and ePub files available? You can upgrade to the eBook version at **www.orangeava.com** and as a print book customer, you are entitled to a discount on the eBook copy. Get in touch with us at: **info@orangeava.com** for more details.

At **www.orangeava.com**, you can also read a collection of free technical articles, sign up for a range of free newsletters, and receive exclusive discounts and offers on AVA™ Books and eBooks.

PIRACY

If you come across any illegal copies of our works in any form on the internet, we would be grateful if you would provide us with the location address or website name. Please contact us at **info@orangeava.com** with a link to the material.

ARE YOU INTERESTED IN AUTHORING WITH US?

If there is a topic that you have expertise in, and you are interested in either writing or contributing to a book, please write to us at **business@orangeava.com**. We are on a journey to help developers and tech professionals to gain insights on the present technological advancements and innovations happening across the globe and build a community that believes Knowledge is best acquired by sharing and learning with others. Please reach out to us to learn what our audience demands and how you can be part of this educational reform. We also welcome ideas from tech experts and help them build learning and development content for their domains.

REVIEWS

Please leave a review. Once you have read and used this book, why not leave a review on the site that you purchased it from? Potential readers can then see and use your unbiased opinion to make purchase decisions. We at Orange Education would love to know what you think about our products, and our authors can learn from your feedback. Thank you!

For more information about Orange Education, please visit **www.orangeava.com**.

Table of Contents

Chapter 1
Introduction to Cloud Computing, AWS, and AWS SAA C-03

Introduction

Cloud computing delivers IT resources (storage, servers, databases) over the internet. This eliminates physical data centers. This lets you adjust resources as needed, optimizing costs. You can work from any internet-connected device and only for what you utilize. Virtualization technologies (like Xen and KVM) split servers into virtual machines (VMs) for the most excellent efficiency. Cloud services come in three forms- IaaS (building blocks to manage your IT infrastructure), PaaS (a development platform letting you focus on applications), and SaaS (ready -to-use applications accessible over the internet)

Cloud Solutions Architects design, build, and secure cloud environments. They protect data and applications in the cloud, design and configure cloud resources for specific needs, and transition applications and data to the cloud securely. AWS Solutions Architect Associate Certification: Confirm Your Expertise- This certification validates your ability to design and deploy solutions on AWS, the leading cloud platform. Earning it demonstrates your skills in selecting the right AWS Services, building cost-effective solutions and securing resilient AWS Architecture Design. This chapter guides you to mastering cloud computing fundamentals and excelling in the AWS Solutions Architect Associate Certification. This will cover the core cloud concepts (deployment and service models), cloud's advantages and limitations, cloud storage and data management, deep dive into AWS Global Infrastructure and AWS SAA-03 Certification blueprint.

By mastering these topics, you will gain a solid foundation in cloud computing and be well-prepared for the AWS Solutions Architect Associate Certification.

Structure

In this chapter, we will cover the following topics:

- Diving into the World of Cloud Computing
- The Cloud and its Offerings
- Cloud Development Models
- Types of Cloud
- Benefits and Challenges
- The Cloud Solutions Architect Role
- The Four key domains
- An Introduction to AWS
- An Introduction to AWS Global Infrastructure
- A Brief introduction to AWS Accounts

Diving into the World of Cloud Computing

The digital world is witnessing a revolution. Cloud computing, a network of interconnected servers and software, delivers on-demand services. It's like having an infinite pool of computing resources available.

Forget bulky hard drives. Cloud computing offers agility and scalability. Data transcends borders and is accessible from anywhere via the internet, fostering collaboration and innovation.

The magic of cloud computing is that it democratizes access to technology. Startups can compete globally without massive upfront costs. Cloud computing levels the playing field, letting ideas and ingenuity flourish.

Now, let us explore the cloud's scalability and security arsenal.

Imagine a young entrepreneur with a brilliant idea. Cloud computing lets them start small and scale resources as their business grows. Need more storage for customer data? The cloud provides it. Need more processing power? The cloud adjusts in real-time. You only pay for what you use, eliminating wasted resources.

Security is a significant concern in the digital age. Cloud providers offer robust, multi-layered security that surpasses most individual setups. Data encryption, intrusion detection, and geographically dispersed data centers safeguard your information. Automatic backups and disaster recovery ensure business continuity.

The cloud is a platform for innovation. Cloud-based platforms offer readily available development tools, analytics engines, and AI services. Businesses can experiment with cutting-edge technologies without substantial infrastructure investments.

Imagine developers prototyping an app using the cloud's processing power. Marketers are leveraging AI to understand customer behavior. The cloud fosters agility and experimentation, accelerating innovation and propelling businesses forward.

Cloud computing is more than a trend; it's a transformative force. Its scalability, security, and innovation potential empower businesses to thrive in the digital age.

The Cloud and its Offerings

Cloud service providers maintain the infrastructure hosting a business's applications and services. This infrastructure stores vast amounts of data and efficiently executes computing tasks. Instead of being limited to storing files on local devices, users entrust their data to this infrastructure and the utility services built on them, granting the users accessibility and flexibility.

This is like storing your belongings in a secure vault. The vault is accessible from anywhere globally, as long as you have an internet connection.

The Cloud Computing Development Models

Let us explore the cloud computing development models that power modern applications.

Beyond the Pizzeria: Explore a Development Model Buffet

While our pizza analogy is a delicious way to grasp core concepts, the development world offers diverse models to cater to every project's needs. Let's explore it with *Figure 1.1*:

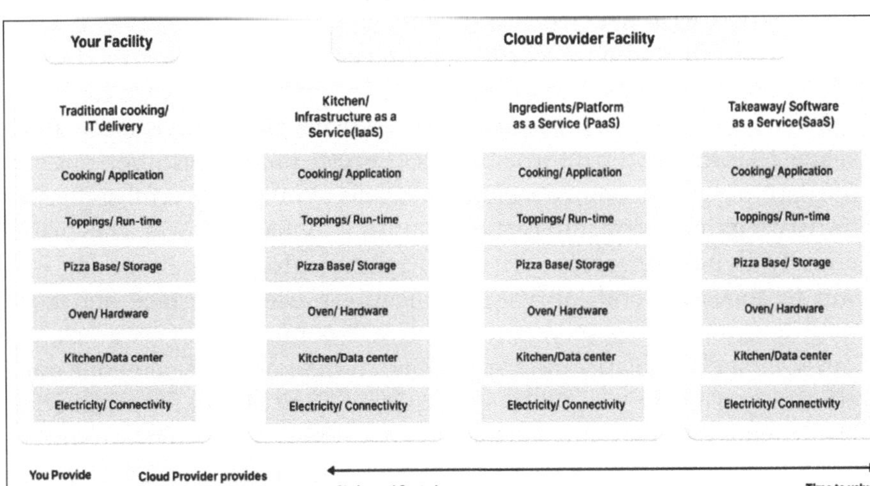

Figure 1.1: *The Development Model Buffet*

- **Platform as a Service (PaaS):** Suppose you are a pizza chef and have devised a recipe to bake the tastiest pizza ever. But you lack the tools to bring your envisioned pizza to life. This is when PaaS comes into the picture. It provides you with the essential infrastructure and tools to build and deploy your custom application (in this case, a pizza) without needing to manage the underlying hardware or software. The oven and kitchen space required for baking a pizza is analogous to programming languages and deployment tools in the cloud world, which let you craft your application (pizza) according to your code (recipe). Pre-built services such as databases and payment processing gateways play the roles of ingredients. These can be incorporated into your application (your pizza) to increase its functionality. The way a fridge lets you store your pizza, PaaS provides secure storage for your application data to preserve its integrity. Do you know the best thing about PaaS? These are designed to scale with your application's growth!
- **Software as a Service (SaaS):** Suppose you are craving a pizza but lack the resources or time to bake it from scratch. You need not knead the dough, buy ingredients, or preheat your oven; this is what SaaS offers. The functioning of SaaS is as simple as ordering a pizza from a pizza outlet. The pizza dough translates to the core functionality of the SaaS application, which is the pre-built foundation for addressing specific needs. Similarly, just as a regular margherita pizza comes with sauce and cheese, SaaS applications have standard features that cater to general needs within the core functionality. Customizing your pizza toppings is the same as customizing your application to meet specific needs in the SaaS world. Moreover, with SaaS, you do not have to install software and manage servers; the application is readily available and accessible from any device with a stable internet connection. Isn't this similar to having a delicious pizza delivered to your doorstep?
- **Information as a Service (IaaS):** Imagine you feel the urge to bake a lip-smacking pizza and have all the necessary ingredients, such as dough, sauce, cheese, and toppings. But to bake the pizza and satiate your taste buds, you will need the essential infrastructure - an oven, electricity supply, and kitchen space. Likewise, in the Information as a Service (IaaS) world, you might possess the data, algorithms, and development skills to build powerful applications, yet translating that vision into reality requires a robust platform. IaaS provides the underlying infrastructure – virtual machines, storage, networking – allowing you to focus on crafting your application's user interface and core logic. With IaaS, managing servers and network configurations is a cakewalk; you can leverage the platform's capabilities to deploy and scale your application efficiently. This layer provides the basic building blocks for cloud computing, like storage, compute resources, and networking. Users have control over the underlying infrastructure but are still responsible for managing it.

The preceding image depicts a layered architecture of a cloud computing system.

Here's the breakdown of the layers mentioned:

- **Application**: This is the top layer where users interact with the software. It includes the user interface (UI) and the source code that defines the application's functionalities.
- **Compute**: This layer refers to the processing power that runs the application. It can be a physical server in a data center or a virtual server in the cloud.
- **Hardware**: This layer consists of the physical components, such as CPUs, memory, and storage devices, that make up the compute resources.
- **Data Center**: This layer is a physical facility and the system's backbone. It houses the computing hardware and provides the necessary infrastructure and environment to run the servers and other networking equipment, making it a vital part of the system's operation.
- **Power:** This layer refers to the electricity that powers all the components in the data center, from the servers to the cooling systems.

The Final Fermentation: Choose the Perfect Recipe for Success

The ideal development model depends on your project's unique requirements, such as the perfect pizza catering to your taste buds. Here are some key factors to consider when making your choice:

- **Project Complexity:** Highly intricate projects enjoy Agile methodologies and CI/CD for continuous refinement and feedback.
- **Team Size and Expertise:** Smaller teams with diverse skill sets might succeed with the DIY model or IaaS for more control. Larger teams with specialized developers could leverage PaaS or SaaS for faster development cycles.
- **Budget and Resource Constraints:** On-premises development requires a significant upfront investment in hardware and software. SaaS offers a more budget-friendly, pay-as-you-go approach.

Remember, there's no single "holy grail" solution. You can choose the perfect recipe for your software development project by understanding these development models and their strengths and weaknesses. Now code confidently and create software as delicious (and functional) as the perfect pizza!

Types of Cloud

Let us explore the three cloud options and choose which suits your needs.

Public Cloud

Spread applications across providers such as AWS, Azure, and GCP to gain flexibility, leverage best features, and negotiate pricing. Yet, managing separate consoles can be complex.

Private Cloud

A secure enclave for your organization. It offers dedicated resources, enhanced data security, and compliance control. But it requires significant upfront investment and ongoing management expertise.

Hybrid Cloud

Blend public and private clouds. Keep sensitive data private and leverage public cloud scalability for specific workloads. It offers flexibility but requires robust orchestration tools.

Benefits and Challenges of Cloud Computing: A Strategic Advantage

- **Scale effortlessly**

  Adapt storage and compute resources to fluctuating demands, eliminating upfront hardware costs.

- **Boost disaster recovery**

  Leverage geographically distributed data centers for automatic backups and seamless access during disruptions. This minimizes downtime and ensures business continuity.

- **Enhance security**

  Enjoy leading cloud providers' robust security infrastructure with encryption, access controls, and regular threat monitoring.

- **Free IT resources**

  Free internal IT from managing infrastructure, allowing them to focus on core initiatives and innovation.

- **Streamline collaboration**

  Helps in real-time project collaboration and data sharing across dispersed teams, boosting productivity and communication.

Considerations for Implementation

- **Assess Security:** Conduct thorough evaluations of potential cloud providers' security protocols, compliance certifications, and data residency regulations.

- **Optimize Costs**: Put in place cost-monitoring tools and use flexible pricing models to optimize cloud resource allocation and avoid exceeding budgets.
- **Mitigate Vendor Lock-in**: Adopt open-source cloud solutions and maintain data portability to ensure flexibility in switching providers if necessary.

Strategic integration of cloud computing delivers significant cost savings, enhances operational efficiency, and grants a competitive edge through improved scalability, security, and collaboration.

The Cloud Solutions Architect Role

Cloud Architects are the masterminds behind secure, scalable cloud solutions. Let us dive deeper into their role.

Decoding the Cloud Solutions Architect: Navigating the Digital Landscape

Imagine someone really into tech who knows the various technical know-how of the cloud. Well, there's this person who's immersed in it. They're on a mission to become an AWS Certified Solutions Architect - Associate. But for them, it's not just about getting a fancy title. It's about diving deep into the world of cloud computing and mastering it.

Every day, they immerse themselves in AWS, learning and absorbing information. They diligently explore AWS guides, experiment with various services, and strive to optimize performance while managing costs. Although it can be challenging, they persevere. Each obstacle they overcome drives them, fueling their determination to succeed further.

As they dive into the Well-Architected Framework, they find a treasure of the best strategies. They're learning to build solid and reliable digital structures in the cloud. They're improving at thinking ahead, seeing problems before they happen, and coming up with lasting solutions.

But getting certified isn't about passing a test. It's about showing everyone–potential employers, clients, you name it–that you know your stuff. Once you've got that certification, you'll be the go-to person for advice on cloud computing. It's like a stamp of approval for your skills and opens up many job opportunities.

Even with all the technical stuff, they always remember the human side. Every line of code they write and every solution they develop is about helping others succeed in the digital world. They're problem solvers, trusted advisors, and champions of innovation.

Looking back on their journey, it's like a thrilling adventure novel–full of ups and downs and unexpected twists and turns. And they know that getting certified is just the start of it all. There are always new challenges, new things to learn, and endless ways to make a real difference in cloud computing.

Architecting Digital Transformation

Cloud Solution architects are digital wizards. They use their tech to solve problems and make companies run smoothly.

Imagine them sitting in a cozy office surrounded by screens and gadgets. Their job is to ensure everything in the company's digital world works right. It's like building a virtual city where every piece fits together perfectly.

These architects are detectives. They figure out what the company needs and how technology can help. They're always looking for ways to make things better and faster.

Security is a big deal for them. They're like knights guarding a castle, keeping out the bad guys and the company's secrets safe. They work hard to keep everything running smoothly without surprises or interruptions.

But they're not all serious business. They're also dreamers and inventors, creating significant new ideas to make work more accessible and fun. They love finding ways to automate tasks and improve the lives of everyone in the company.

Even though they're experts in all things tech, they're also great communicators. They talk to everyone in the company–from the IT folks to the sales team–to ensure everyone's on the same page.

But the best part of their job is that it's constantly changing and growing. They're always learning new things and finding better ways to do things. It's like being on a never-ending adventure, with new challenges around every corner.

Becoming a Cloud Wizard with AWS

Welcome to a world of cloud computing ruled by the ethereal Amazon Web Services (AWS). To master this realm, start by learning the secrets of AWS services. A Cloud Solutions Architect is a sage who navigates the labyrinthine pathways of the AWS ecosystem with the familiarity of a well-worn spellbook.

Charting Your Course

Embarking on the path of a Cloud Solutions Architect is like setting forth on a grand odyssey. Knowledge is your treasure, and accolades are your badges of courage. Certifications such as the AWS Certified Solutions Architect–Associate are your maps. They guide you through AWS's uncharted territories.

To embark on this quest, you must forge a sturdy groundwork in cloud computing.

Explore the mysteries of virtualization, unravel the secrets of networking, storage, and security, immerse yourself in the elemental lore of AWS, and acquaint yourself with its core services such as EC2, S3, and RDS. Though the journey may seem daunting, each stride you take brings you closer to enlightenment.

As you advance, remember to sharpen your practical skills. Establish your sanctum within the AWS realm and begin or start your experiments. Summon instances, craft repositories, and weave security enchantments. The more hands-on experience you gain, the more adept you will wield AWS's arsenal.

Conquering the Cloud Behemoth

The cloud is a massive, multi-headed beast with various moods and behaviors. And as a Cloud Solutions Architect, you're the brave hero wrangling this beast. Your job is to dive into the AWS Well-Architected Framework.

This framework has five main principles:

- Being good at operations
- Ensuring everything is secure
- Ensuring things run smoothly all the time
- Making everything work efficiently
- Saving money wherever possible

Each of these principles acts like a shield. They protect your cloud fortress and keep everything running smoothly. You'll learn to build fault tolerance, elasticity, and cost-effective cloud solutions.

But it's not all about playing defense; you'll also go on the offensive. You'll use tools such as AWS CloudFormation and AWS Elastic Beanstalk to automate and organize tasks. This will help you create whole virtual worlds with a few clicks, saving time and reducing the chance of mistakes.

Let's remember security. It's like putting up magical barriers around your kingdom. As a Cloud Solutions Architect, you'll become an expert in managing identities and access, encrypting data, and ensuring everything meets regulations. You'll also build strong defenses to protect your data from prying eyes and cyber-attacks.

Unleashing Digital Sorcery

Imagine having the power to transform businesses into unstoppable forces in the digital world. That's what Cloud Solutions Architects do. With their expertise, they help organizations tap into the vast potential of the cloud.

Think of Cloud Solutions Architects as modern-day guides. They lead companies through the sometimes-confusing journey of digital transformation. They study a business's needs, create plans for celestial cloud structures, and oversee every step of the process from start to finish. Organizations can use cloud technologies with their guidance to smooth their operations, spark new ideas, and fuel growth.

Cloud Solutions Architects encourage teams to embrace change. They adopt agile methods and DevOps principles. They foster a culture where trying new things and learning from mistakes are essential for progress.

Success isn't measured by how fancy the cloud setup is but by how much it helps the business succeed. Cloud Solutions Architects work closely with everyone involved. They ensure the technological choices align with the company's bigger goals. Their achievements aren't counted by the number of servers they set up but by their impact on the bottom line.

So, if you're ready to dive into a world of discovery and change, grab your metaphorical wand and join the community of AWS wizards. The cloud is calling, and the possibilities are endless.

Reasons to Opt-in for AWS

Amazon Web Services (AWS) is a guiding star in the web world. Imagine you're on a journey, searching for a trustworthy vessel to carry your dreams across the boundless seas of the internet. AWS is that sturdy ship, ready with unfurled sails. It invites you to embark on a voyage of innovation and growth.

Whether you're a small startup reaching for the stars or a big corporation exploring new territories, AWS welcomes all. Its promise of scalability is a real possibility. With AWS, the whole world becomes accessible, and spreading your digital creations to distant corners is as easy as a gentle breeze.

However, AWS provides a wealth of tools and technologies still waiting to be explored. Imagine diving into the fascinating world of machine learning or navigating the intricate web of the Internet of Things. With AWS as your guide, you're a pioneer, leading the way into unexplored realms of potential.

Now, let's talk about security. It's the fortress protecting your digital assets from cyber threats. In a time when breaches are common, AWS stands as a stronghold fortified with advanced security measures. Your data is safe within its walls, shielded from prying eyes and malicious attacks.

The most appealing aspect of AWS is its versatility. It's a whole ecosystem offering various services tailored to modern enterprises. Whether you need to store large amounts of data, analyze it, or innovate, AWS provides the canvas for your ambitions to flourish.

Choosing AWS is a partnership, a bond formed between explorers and guides in the vast world of cyberspace. So, why choose AWS? The real question isn't why, but why not? AWS is a beacon of opportunity, lighting the way to a future limited only by your imagination.

AWS Solutions Architect Associate Certification Exam Roadmap

The AWS Certified Solutions Architect Associate (SAA) certification validates your skills in building secure, resilient, high-performing, cost-effective architectures on AWS. This guide equips you with the knowledge to ace the exam, regardless of your experience level.

Benefits of Certification

- Proven Cloud Expertise
- Enhanced Career Opportunities
- Increased Earning Potential

The exam covers four key domains depicted in *Figure* 1.2:

- **Design Secure Architectures (30%)**
    - **Master IAM:** Lock down your AWS environment with granular IAM permissions.
    - **Secure Your Data:** Protect your data using encryption and KMS.
    - **Control Network Traffic:** Put security groups and ACLs in place for network control.
    - **Identify Weaknesses:** Use Inspector to find and fix security vulnerabilities.
- **Design Resilient Architectures (26%)**
    - **Build Fault Tolerance:** Leverage Availability Zones to keep your apps running during outages.
    - **Distribute Traffic:** Use Elastic Load Balancing to ensure high availability.
    - **Scale Automatically:** Configure auto-scaling groups to handle fluctuating workloads.
    - **Recover Quickly:** Develop a disaster recovery plan using AWS backup and restore solutions.
- **Design High-Performing Architectures (24%)**
    - **Track Effectively:** Use CloudWatch to track your AWS resources and identify performance issues.

  - **Reduce Latency:** Configure CloudFront distributions for global content delivery.
  - **Choose the Right Storage:** Select between EBS and EFS based on performance needs.
  - **Explore NoSQL Databases:** Consider DynamoDB for high-performance applications with massive datasets.
- **Design Cost-Optimized Architectures (20%)**
  - **Save with Spot Instances:** Learn to use Spot Instances for cost-effective workloads.
  - **Reduce Predictable Costs:** Use Reserved Instances and Savings Plans for predictable workloads.
  - **Track Your Spending:** Install cost allocation tags for granular cost analysis.
  - **Optimize Your Costs:** Usc AWS billing and cost management tools to identify and put in place cost-savings opportunities.

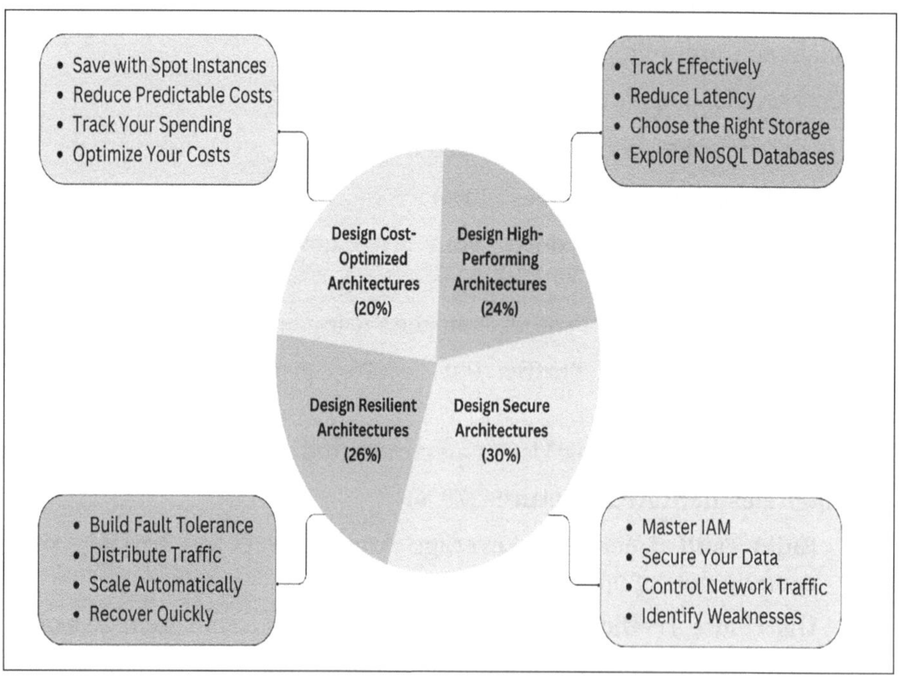

***Figure 1.2**: The four key domains*

Traditional Data Center versus AWS

Do you wish to know the need for switching from Traditional Data Centers to AWS? That is exactly what the next section explains!

Traditional Data Centers: Costly and Complex

Organizations used to build their own data centers, filled with servers, storage, and networking equipment. This required a substantial upfront investment in money and expertise to manage. Scaling up or down to meet changing needs took time and effort.

AWS: Cloud-Based Agility

AWS offers a cloud-based alternative. Users access computing resources over the internet, eliminating the need to manage physical infrastructure. This frees IT staff to focus on innovation, not maintenance. AWS uses a pay-as-you-go model, so users only pay for what they use.

Traditional Data Centers: Technical Challenges

The technical challenges faced in traditional data centers are:

- IT staff need server management, networking, and security expertise.
- Disaster recovery plans need extra infrastructure and planning.
- Scaling resources up or down takes time and effort.
- Initial setup costs associated with this project are significant.

AWS: On-Demand and Scalable

Here's why you need to switch to AWS:

- Users provision resources (servers, storage) via a web portal in minutes.
- AWS infrastructure scales up or down to meet real-time needs.
- Users only pay for the resources they consume.

Choosing Between Them

The best option depends on your specific needs. Consider:

- **Data Sensitivity**: Although AWS offers robust security features, susceptible data might be better suited for an on-premises data center.
- **IT Expertise**: If you have a skilled IT staff experienced in data center management, you might prefer an on-premises solution. AWS offers a managed service if expertise is lacking.
- **Scalability Needs**: Businesses with fluctuating workloads enjoy AWS's on-demand scalability.

By understanding both options, you can make an informed decision about your IT infrastructure strategy.

AWS Global Infrastructure - An Introduction

In this section, we will demystify the cloud and have a look at its Global Infrastructure depicted in *Figure 1.3*:

AWS Regions and Availability Zones: Optimizing for Uptime

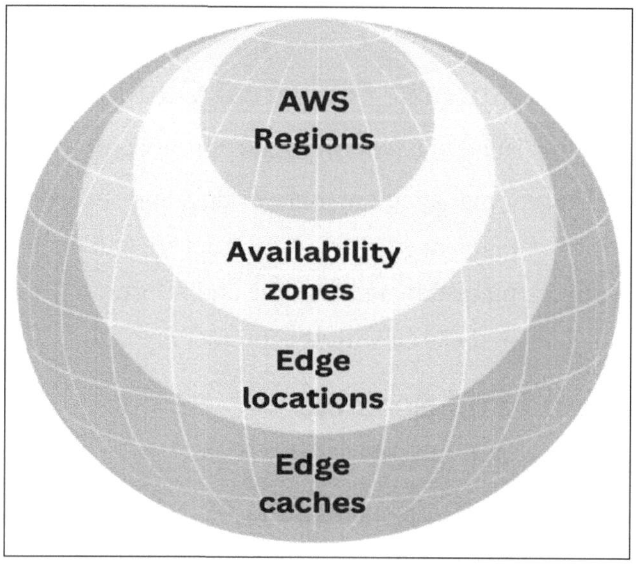

Figure 1.3: *AWS Global Infrastructure*

Let us look at some key concepts to understand AWS regions and optimization of uptime with availability zones:

- **Global Infrastructure**: AWS's global data center network is organized into Regions and Availability Zones (AZs) for optimal service delivery.
- **Regions:** These distinct areas (for example, US East (N. Virginia), and Asia Pacific (Tokyo) house many AZs and function as self-contained units.
- **Availability Zones (AZs):** Located within Regions, AZs are isolated data centers designed for exceptional fault tolerance and high availability. For redundancy, each AZ is likely to comprise several close data centers.

  AWS is expanding its global footprint with 105 Availability Zones across 33 regions. The company plans to add another 18 Availability Zones and establish six new AWS Regions in Malaysia, Mexico, New Zealand, Saudi Arabia, Thailand, and for the European Sovereign Cloud.

- **Isolated for Resilience**: AZs operate with independent power and network connectivity, even while connected by high-bandwidth, low-latency fiber links to a nearby peer AZ. This minimizes impact if one AZ encounters an issue.
- **Low-Latency Replication**: These inter-AZ connections enable data replication for superior high availability. For example, RDS uses synchronous replication between primary and secondary databases within a Region for immediate failover during disruptions.
- **Regions**: Building Blocks of Resilience: A Region consists of many interconnected AZs (3-5), forming a localized group with significant data processing power. This strategic grouping allows you to build available applications.
- **Multi-AZ Deployments**: You reduce downtime risks from isolated AZ outages by distributing resources across many AZs within regions. Leveraging at least two AZs is an industry best practice to ensure high availability.
- **Expertise Matters**: While anyone can deploy resources in the cloud, true architectural expertise lies in optimizing for stability, availability, and disaster recovery. Understanding Regions and AZs is crucial to achieving this.

Edge Locations and Regional Edge Caches

AWS offers a global network of Edge Locations and Regional Edge Caches to accelerate content delivery and enhance user experience. Let's explore their functionalities.

Edge Locations: Distributed Delivery Points

Edge Locations are extensively deployed in major cities worldwide, bringing physical content closer to users. They serve as the foundation for AWS's CDNs such as CloudFront, caching frequently accessed data for lower latency. These locations are not for deploying core infrastructure like EC2 instances; they focus on content delivery.

Imagine Edge Locations as a global network of access points for your end users. CloudFront can leverage a nearby Edge Location to serve cached content, minimizing latency for geographically distant users.

Regional Edge Caches: Enhanced Storage Layer

Introduced in 2016, Regional Edge Caches sit between your origin servers and Edge Locations.

They boast a larger cache capacity than individual Edge Locations, allowing for more content storage for extended periods. Due to cache policies, content might get evicted from individual Edge Locations. Regional Edge Caches are a backup, retaining evicted data for faster retrieval by Edge Locations if needed. Fulfilling requests from Regional

Edge Caches minimizes the load on your origin servers, improving performance and scalability.

In summary, Edge Locations is the frontline for content delivery, while Regional Edge Caches is a secondary storage layer. This combined approach ensures fast and reliable user experiences globally.

Deep Dive into AWS Local Zones: Bringing the Cloud Closer

AWS Local Zones bring cloud services closer to users, enhancing performance and reducing latency, let us have a deeper look at these.

Local Zones: Mini AWS Data Centers

Imagine an AWS data center close to your users. That's Local Zones - core AWS services (compute, storage, networking, databases) positioned near populated areas. This offers benefits for specific use cases:

- **Ultra-low Latency**: Single-digit millisecond latency for real-time applications such as gaming, live streaming, AR/VR, and high-frequency trading
- **Data Residency Compliance**: Keeps data within compliant geographic boundaries
- **Technical Architecture**: Connected Yet Separate

Local Zones are connected to a nearby parent Region via a secure, high-speed connection. This allows access to all services offered in the Region.

Deployment and Management: Simple and Familiar

Enable Local Zones in your AWS account.

Local Zones appear alongside Availability Zones when deploying resources (VPC subnets, EC2 instances, and more).

Current Status and Future: Expansion and Dedicated Options

As of April 2024, Local Zones span 33 metro areas globally, with 19 planned additions.

Dedicated Local Zones (new in August 2023) offer fully managed, single-tenant infrastructure for:

- Public sector organizations
- Industries with strict governance

Key Takeaways: Local Zones = Big Benefits

The benefits of local zones are:

- **Exceptional Performance**: Ultra-low latency optimizes real-time applications
- **Regulatory Adherence**: Local Zones ensure data residency compliance
- **Seamless Integration**: Access all AWS services via the parent Region
- **Simplified Management**: Use your existing AWS account for Local Zones
- **Enhanced Security (Dedicated)**: A managed, single-tenant environment for strict compliance

Businesses leverage the AWS cloud using Local Zones while achieving top performance and regulatory adherence. Understand the core concepts, architecture, and deployment to unlock the potential of Local Zones for your applications.

Getting Started with Your AWS Account: Costs and Budgets

Welcome to the exciting world of AWS! This guide will equip you with the basics of setting up your AWS account, understanding costs, and creating budgets to keep your spending under control.

Signing Up for AWS

Follow these steps to sign up for AWS:

1. Head to the AWS website and click the big, friendly button that says **`"Create an AWS Account".`**
2. Follow the steps to enter your email, create a strong password (think complex and unique), and provide some basic account information.
3. Don't worry–you won't be charged right away. AWS offers a free tier for new users, letting you explore their services for a while. However, remember that there are limits, so be mindful of what you use.
4. Please verify your account using the method they provide. This is to make sure it's you!

Accessing Your AWS Console

Once your account is set up, you'll use the AWS Management Console to manage your resources. Think of it as your mission control center for the cloud! Just log in with your email and password.

Exploring for Free with the Free Tier

AWS offers a free tier for new users. This lets you experiment with various services without paying a dime–perfect for getting your feet wet. Remember, though, that there are limits to what you can use for free, so stay within those boundaries.

No Longer Need Your Account? Delete It!

If you decide AWS isn't for you, you can quickly delete your account to avoid future charges. Before hitting the delete button, back up any critical data or resources.

Keeping an Eye on Your Spending: AWS Billing

AWS uses a pay-as-you-go billing system. This means you only pay for the resources you use, which is fair. Here's how to stay on top of your spending:

- **Creating Budgets**: This is your secret weapon for cost control. Budgets let you set spending limits and receive alerts if your spending gets close to those limits. Think of it like a speed limit for your cloud usage!
- **Cost Explorer**: This handy tool gives you a detailed breakdown of your AWS spending. You can see exactly where your money is going, which helps you identify areas to save and make smarter resource choices.

Setting Up a Budget in AWS

Now that you know the importance of budgets, let's create one step-by-step:

1. Log in to your AWS account (remember, don't use the root user!).
2. Use the search bar at the top of the console to find **`"AWS Budgets"`**.
3. Click the bright **`"Create budget"`** button to get started.

Here, you have a few options to choose from, depending on your needs:

- **Are you trying Things Out? Zero Spend Budget**: If you're experimenting, pick this option. It sets your spending limit to zero, so you won't be charged unless something unexpected happens. Remember to enter a name for your budget and an email address for alerts.
- **Monthly Cost Budget (Pre-configured):** This option is a good starting point for

regular users. It comes with pre-set alerts to notify you when your spending reaches 85% or 100% of your budget or your projected spending is about to hit your limit. Name it, enter your email, and specify your desired monthly spending amount.

Customized Budget: Choose "Customize (advanced)" for more Control

Here's a breakdown:

- Select **"Cost budget"** and click **"Next"**.
- Give your budget a name.
- Choose your billing period (monthly is the default).
- Enter your desired spending limit.
- Click **"Next"** and **"Add an alert threshold"** to set up notifications. You can choose percentages or specific amounts to trigger alerts. When you're done, click **"Next"** again.
- The next page lets you attach additional actions to alerts (optional). For now, click **"Next"**.
- On the final page, review all the details of your budget. If everything looks good, click **"Create budget"** to activate it.

Creating a budget prevents charges. It's a tool to keep you informed and in control. However, you'll still need to monitor your spending and be mindful of what resources you're using to avoid surprises on your bill.

Conclusion

Congratulations! You've conquered the critical concepts of this chapter. Level up your AWS knowledge by turning this guide into your weapon for the AWS SAA-C03 exam.

This chapter explored the essence of cloud computing, the cloud landscape, the role of a Cloud Solutions Architect, the AWS Global Infrastructure, and AWS accounts. Cloud computing refers to the on-demand delivery of IT resources over the internet, with scalability, flexibility, and cost-effectiveness. The Cloud Landscape refers to the various deployment models, including public, private, and hybrid. The AWS Global Infrastructure is a widely spread network that supports AWS for your applications to scale and remain in operation in case of a failure. While AWS accounts are the building blocks for your AWS cloud venture.

With this knowledge, you can explore AWS cloud computing further and utilize its capabilities to reach your objectives.

The next chapter will explore IAM, a fundamental service for securing your AWS resources. Stay tuned! Understanding IAM is essential for any AWS professional, and it's a core topic you will likely encounter on the SAA-C03 exam.

References

- https://www.spiceworks.com/tech/cloud/articles/what-is-cloud-computing/#:~:text=Security%20Best%20Practices-,Types%20of%20Cloud%20Computing,service%20the%20cloud%20model%20offers.
- https://aws.amazon.com/types-of-cloud-computing/
- https://engineering.dunelm.com/pizza-as-a-service-2-0-5085cd4c365e
- https://aws.amazon.com/about-aws/global-infrastructure/
- https://m.oursky.com/saas-paas-and-iaas-explained-in-one-graphic-d56c3e6f4606
- https://d1.awsstatic.com/training-and-certification/docs-sa-assoc/AWS-Certified-Solutions-Architect-Associate_Exam-Guide.pdf
- https://www.google.com/url?q=https://www.techtarget.com/searchcio/opinion/Cloud-A-disruptive-technology-thats-worth-the-disruption&sa=D&source=docs&ust=1714712147809233&usg=AOvVaw0PQk42zScZlXsh_oALYRbJ
- https://cloudacademy.com/blog/disruptive-technology-and-cloud-computing/

CHAPTER 2
Identity and Access Management in AWS

Introduction

Do you wish to conquer the IAM basics? Let us unlock some advanced tactics to make your cloud security impenetrable.

Imagine your team as a group of knights, each with unique strengths. An archer wouldn't need access to the armory like a web developer wouldn't need permission to manage databases. IAM user groups come in here. They let you categorize similar roles and assign specific permissions to each group. This simplifies permission management and ensures everyone has the right tools for the job without unnecessary access.

Adopt the mindset of a wise king. You wouldn't entrust the crown jewels to just anyone, would you? That's the 'Principle of Least Privilege' in action. Grant users only the minimum permissions they need to perform their tasks. A data analyst shouldn't be able to modify server configurations, and a junior developer shouldn't have access to production environments. This approach ensures the damage is limited even if someone gains unauthorized access, providing a strong sense of security and reassurance.

Multi-factor authentication (MFA) is like your loyal royal guard dog. It adds an extra layer of security by requiring a unique code from your phone on top of your username and password to access sensitive resources. Think of it as having a double lock on the treasure vault! This additional step significantly raises the bar for attackers, making it much harder for them to break in, even if they steal your login credentials. It's a comforting shield of protection for your cloud security.

Finally, be your cloud detective! Review IAM policies and user activity regularly, like a detective investigating crime scenes. This helps identify any suspicious behavior or weaknesses in your security. Imagine checking your cloud logs for strange activity. Are there unusual login attempts at odd hours? Are users accessing resources they shouldn't? Regular monitoring helps you stay ahead of potential threats.

Structure

In this chapter, we will cover the following topics:

- IAM Fundamentals
- Forge Your AWS Security with IAM
- Conquering Authentication and Authorization with IAM
- Unleash IAMs Arsenal: Users, Groups, Roles, and Policies
- Empowering Granular Access Control in AWS
- Decoding the IAM Policy Blueprint
- Claim Your AWS Throne: Mastering Access

CloudTrail: Your All-Seeing Eye

CloudTrail is a built-in service that acts like a network of royal spies, keeping a log of every action happening in your cloud environment. So, if someone tries to access something they shouldn't, CloudTrail will catch them red-handed! This detailed log helps you investigate any suspicious activity and identify potential security breaches before they cause any damage.

Following these tactics and mastering IAM can transform your cloud environment into a secure fortress. Remember, security is an ongoing quest, so keep these tips in mind to keep your valuable data and resources safe! In the upcoming chapters, we'll cover CloudTrail, a powerful AWS service for auditing and compliance.

Authentication: Verifying Your Identity

When someone tries to enter a restricted area, they must show their ID. In AWS, this is called Authentication. IAM verifies the identity of the user or entity trying to access a resource through:

- **Username and Password**: Like your restaurant ID badge.
- **Temporary Security Credentials**: A unique code for temporary workers, like a temporary badge for a weekend chef.

Guarding the Gates: IAM Checks Permissions

We saw how IAM verifies identity, like checking a royal seal at the gate. Now, IAM decides who gets in!

- **Authorization: Permission Slips:** After confirming identity, IAM checks users' permissions (such as a digital permission slip) to see if they can do what they want. Imagine a guard checking your ID and a special pass before letting you into a specific castle area.

- **Least Privilege: Just What You Need:** The King wouldn't give the janitor the master key. IAM works the same way. Users and programs only get the permissions they need for their jobs. No more cooks tinkering with the royal library or guards messing with the treasury!

Example: John the Craftsman

John fixes the castle defenses. He needs access to the forge and armory. Here's how IAM grants access:

- **Authentication**: John shows his ID badge and warrant (username and password).
- **Authorization**: IAM checks John's permission slip (policy) to see if he can "Enter Armory" and "Use Forge."

  Access Granted! John can fix the defenses (access the needed areas).

  Access Denied! If John's slip doesn't allow access, he asks the King for more permissions.

IAM keeps your kingdom secure by ensuring only authorized people or programs access resources such as stockpiles and blueprints.

Key Terms

Actions/Permissions: Specific tasks users can do on resources, such as "View" for data or "Start" for a virtual machine.

- **Resources**: Things users interact with, such as storage buckets or virtual machines.
- **Identity Federation**: Users access the kingdom using trusted providers (like a company email login), improving security and access management.

IAM Fundamentals

Let us level up your cloud security game with the core principles of IAM. This section will explore various concepts such as identity toolbox, actions, resources, and security-must haves.

IAM: Your Identity Toolbox

Now is the time to unlock the power of managing access to AWS accounts by understanding some key terms:

- **Users**: Create individual users for specific tasks. Give them only the permissions they need (least privilege). Keep access keys and secret keys secure (use Secrets Manager).
- **Groups:** Bundle users with similar needs. For simpler management, assign policies to groups, not individual users.
- **Roles:** Applications need temporary credentials to access resources. No long-term credentials on machines means better security. Use Instance Profiles or STS to assign roles.

Principals Calling

Who should get the access? Users with strong passwords and MFA, or with temporary credentials?

- **Human Users**: Everyone needs an MFA! Enforce strong password policies (complexity, rotation) too.
- **Workload Identities**: For your applications, use roles with temporary credentials. This reduces the attack surface compared to long-term credentials. Configure workloads to assume roles with appropriate permissions.

Getting Access: Authentication and Authorization

It is important to authenticate and authorize, that is, double check before granting access.

- **Authentication**: Use MFA for users and temporary credentials with roles for workloads. This double-checks identity and credential possession.
- **Authorization**: IAM policies control access. These JSON documents say who (user/group) can do what (actions) to what resources (buckets, instances). Use identity-based policies for users/groups within your account and resource-based policies to grant access across accounts. Remember, all requests are denied by default!

Actions You Can Take

Each service has specific actions for its resources. Be granular! An S3 policy might allow uploading objects but deny deleting them.

Resources: Your AWS Stuff

Identify resources needing access control (buckets, instances, and tables). Use IAM policies to define who can do what to these resources.

Security Must-Haves

Follow these IAM security basics to improve the security of your AWS environment. Security is an ongoing process, so adapt your IAM policies as your needs change. *Figure* 2.1 gives an overview of these security basics that you must have:

- **Least Privilege**: Give only the least permissions needed.
- **Review Policies Regularly**: Ensure your policies align with your security needs.
- **Limit Root User Access**: Don't use the root user for everyday tasks. Create IAM users with appropriate permissions.
- **Use CloudTrail**: Log all IAM API calls for monitoring and troubleshooting.

Figure 2.1: *Security Must-Haves*

Forge Your AWS Security with IAM

Ascend the throne of your digital domain – your AWS kingdom! But beware, treachery lurks in the shadows. Unleash the power of IAM, your loyal Identity and Access Management champion. It acts as an impenetrable wall, guarding your treasure trove of AWS services. Only the worthy must pass! With IAM by your side, you'll become a legend – a security sovereign ruling over a digital utopia. Let's unlock IAM's true potential and forge your reign of supreme security!

Assemble Your IAM Champions

Meet the key players who control access to your AWS accounts:

- **Users:** These individuals – your employees and trusted applications – need long-term access to your AWS realm. Grant them entry with care!
- **Groups:** Organize your users into well-defined groups for efficient permission control. Think of them as specialized regiments, each with designated access levels.
- **Roles:** Enlist roles for temporary tasks with specific needs. Unlike long-term user credentials, roles grant access only for the mission duration, minimizing security risks. Consider them as special ops units deployed for targeted objectives.

- **Policies:** These edicts define what your users, groups, and roles can or can't do within your AWS domain. Craft clear IAM policies, such as a well-defined legal code, to establish boundaries for authorized actions.

Master Fine-Grained Access

IAM isn't a passive security guard. It empowers you with granular control over your entire AWS kingdom. Regulate access to individual APIs and resources, ensuring every corner of your digital domain is secured. Imagine assigning specific permissions for each user or group, granting access only to the file cabinets containing relevant documents, not the entire library.

Identity

Think of IAM identities as digital passports for anyone or anything seeking entry into your AWS domain. These passports can include details such as email addresses, passwords, or unique device IDs. You'll encounter three main types of identities. including:

- **Human Identities**: This represents your employees, valued customers, or trusted partners interacting with your AWS resources.
- **Workload Identities:** Software applications or services within your organization that need adequate AWS access. Imagine them as specialized tools needing access to specific resources to complete their tasks.
- **Device Identities:** These are the hardware devices such as computers, mobile phones, or even internet-connected sensors (IoT) that interact with your AWS environment.

By understanding these identities and how IAM manages them, you can create a layered security approach, ensuring only authorized entities gain access to your AWS kingdom. Stay tuned for further explorations into the exciting realm of IAM policies and how to craft them for optimal security!

Conquering Authentication and Authorization with IAM

Have you ever built a stunning AWS empire only to discover the gates wide open? Fear not! Here's your guide to wielding the mighty tools of Authentication (AuthN) and Authorization (AuthZ) to secure your cloud kingdom.

Authentication

Imagine a drawbridge. Authentication is the process of verifying whoever requests entry. It's like checking their ID – are they who they claim to be? You'll use passwords, robust multi-factor authentication (MFA), and even biometrics to ensure only authorized users approach your castle walls.

Increase your account security by enabling a virtual multi-factor authentication (MFA) device on your phone or other device. Here's how:

Install a mobile app that generates time-based one-time passwords (TOTP) according to the RFC 6238 standard. These apps will provide six-digit codes for login.

While virtual MFA offers convenience, it might be less secure than physical FIDO security keys since phones can be vulnerable. It's a great temporary solution while waiting for hardware or approval to purchase it.

Many virtual MFA apps let you create multiple devices within the same app, allowing you to manage various AWS accounts or users. Register up to eight MFA devices (any combination of supported types) for your root user and IAM users. With multiple devices, you only need one to sign in. We highly recommend registering multiple devices for redundancy.

If you choose an authenticator app, enable its cloud backup or sync feature to prevent losing access if your device is lost or damaged.

Find compatible virtual MFA apps by referring to the multi-factor authentication documentation. Remember that AWS requires a virtual MFA app that generates six-digit OTP codes.

Authorization

Now, let's say their identity checks out. Authorization is like the vigilant guard who decides what that person can do inside. Do they have permission to enter the armory, the kitchens, or the guest chambers? Secure your cloud by understanding that authentication is about who you are, while authorization is about what you can do.

Master IAM

This is where Identity and Access Management (IAM) becomes your master architect. IAM equips you with the tools to construct a robust security posture in your AWS environment. Only authorized entities get the keys to the kingdom (or, more precisely, your valuable AWS resources).

Unleash IAMs Arsenal: Users, Groups, Roles, and Policies

Now that we have had a brief look at our IAM champions, let us now have a deep dive into these.

IAM Users

Here is your team for managing AWS access:

- **Deploy IAM Users:** These are your permanent residents, ideal for long-term access. Equip them with usernames and passwords for the console and access keys for programmatic tools.
- **Organize IAM Groups:** Think of them as efficient access control commanders. Assign policies to groups for consistent access across teams.
- **Grant Temporary Access with IAM Roles:** Do you need temporary access for external, existing IAM users or applications? Roles are your guest passes. Grant temporary access with expiring credentials, minimizing damage if compromised.

Craft Policies: The Keys and the Rules

There are two types of policies that work in tandem:

- **Issue Trust Policies:** These are like keycards, deciding who can "wear the hat" of a particular role. Imagine a "Knight" role – only qualified users with proper training get the trust policy to assume that role.
- **Define Permission Policies:** These define what a role (and anyone assuming it) can do within the castle walls. They control the "what" and "how" of access. Imagine a policy that allows the "Knight" role to access the armory but restricts modifying weapon quantities.

IAM Policies

Think of IAM policies as the blueprints for access control. Construct these JSON documents and attach them to users, groups, roles, or resources to grant or deny access with pinpoint precision.

Fortify Your Cloud: Essential Security Measures

Here's how you can fortify your cloud:

- **Enforce Least Privilege:** Like a well-run castle doesn't give everyone full armory access; the principle of least privilege is critical. Grant users and roles only the bare minimum permissions they need to function. Less access equals less risk.
- **Activate Multi-Factor Authentication (MFA):** This adds an extra layer of

security, requiring more than a username and password to enter your digital domain. Think of it as a portcullis that strengthens your defenses.

- **Implement Role-Based Access Control (RBAC):** Align permissions with job roles. Define clear and consistent access control by creating roles like "Admin," "Developer," or "Read-Only User."

You can transform your AWS environment into a well-defended fortress by wielding the power of IAM and understanding the distinctions between Authentication and authorization. Security is an ongoing quest, so keep your IAM knowledge sharp and your security posture vigilant!

The Magic of RBAC and SSO Working Together

RBAC assigns permissions based on job roles. Imagine an accountant only seeing financial data, not marketing materials. Easy to manage, secure, and compliant!

SSO lets you log in once and access all approved apps. No more juggling multiple logins! This boosts productivity, reduces security risks, and simplifies IT management.

Together, RBAC and SSO are a powerful team. RBAC ensures the right access to SSO-approved apps. It's a win-win for security, convenience, and IT!

Empowering Granular Access Control in AWS

This section will help you understand granular access control in AWS.

Unleash the Power of Fine-Grained Access with IAM Entities

AWS Identity and Access Management (IAM) provides a powerful toolset for securing your cloud environment. At the core of IAM lies the concept of least privilege, enforced through IAM entities: users, groups, and roles. Let's dissect each entity to understand how they empower granular access control:

- **Users:** IAM creates individual identities representing human users or service accounts requiring direct access to AWS resources. Each user boasts a unique username, security credentials, password, and access key(s). For an extra layer of security, install Multi-Factor Authentication (MFA) as a secondary authentication step beyond the password. Access keys enable programmatic access via the AWS SDKs or CLI. Remember, passwords are only mandatory for users accessing the AWS Management Console.

- **Groups:** Simplify permission management by establishing logical user groupings. Attach policies to groups, and these permissions cascade down to all members within the group. This streamlines administration as you manage permissions at the group level rather than for each user. IAM groups shine in applying the least privilege principle - associate users with groups that mirror their specific job functions within the organization. A single user can belong to many groups, allowing for the application of appropriate permissions based on an individual's diverse roles. But remember that groups cannot be nested – they can only contain users, not other groups.
- **Roles:** IAM offers temporary security credentials that users, applications, or AWS services can assume. Unlike users, roles are not tied to a specific user identity. This makes them ideal for scenarios where on-running resources like EC2 instances require credentials. By assuming a role, an EC2 instance can be granted temporary, task-specific permissions to access AWS resources without storing long-term credentials on the instance itself. This approach significantly reduces the security risk associated with compromised credentials.

IAM Policies: Navigate the Labyrinth of AWS Permissions Like a Pro

Your AWS account is a treasure trove of resources, but managing access permissions can be frustrating without a precise map. Here's when IAM policies come in. Written in JSON format, these policy documents act as your compass and guide, actively defining the actions users and roles can take within your digital domain.

Upholding the principle of least privilege, IAM policies act as vigilant guardians. They explicitly specify which actions are allowed and on which specific resources. To navigate this permission labyrinth effectively, you have two critical tools at your disposal.

Managed Policies: Pre-Built Pathways for Common Access

Think of managed policies as pre-built trails blazed by AWS itself. They offer pre-defined permissions for various AWS services – ready-made pathways that get you up and running. Ideal for assigning frequently used permissions, managed policies save you time and effort crafting access controls from scratch.

Inline Policies: Craft Granular Access Controls

For situations demanding surgical precision, you can craft custom policies. These inline policies grant you granular control over user and role permissions. Meticulously tailor permissions to each user or role's needs, ensuring they have only the precise actions required for their tasks.

By effectively wielding managed and inline policies, you actively chart a course through your AWS account's permission labyrinth. Your destination is a secure and well-defined access landscape safeguarding your valuable resources.

Decoding the IAM Policy Blueprint

IAM policies are the blueprints for your AWS access control. Master these blueprints, and you'll lock down your cloud infrastructure. Let's explore how to keep your keys updated, craft access rules, and secure your digital domain.

Lock Down Your Cloud Fortress with IAM Policies

Your AWS infrastructure is a sprawling digital domain; IAM (Identity and Access Management) is your key security system. IAM policies are the blueprints that define who gets the keys and to which chambers. Master these blueprints, and you'll build a robust access control framework – the foundation of your cloud security.

Version Control: Keeping Your Keys Updated

Every policy has a version, just like software. This ensures you're always using the latest, most secure iteration. It's like regularly upgrading your fortress's locks to stay ahead of potential threats.

Craft Access with Statement Blocks

Policies are built from statements, each acting as a specific rule within your access control system. Here's how you define the rules:

- **Effect:** Allow or deny? You decide whether a particular action is authorized within your fortress.
- **Action:** Imagine actions as specific tasks users can perform within AWS services. Grant access to "StartInstance" to launch EC2 instances but without deleting them (another action).
- **Resource:** This defines the specific AWS resource to which the statement applies. It's like assigning a key to a particular vault within your fortress, not the entire complex.

Example:

Assume that John, who uses the username **`johnjacob`**, tries to save a file to the **`johnjacob-logs`** Amazon S3 bucket.

Also assume that the following policy is attached to the **`johnjacob`** IAM user.

```
{
        "Version": "2012-10-17",
        "Statement": [
        {
                "Sid": "AllowS3ListRead",
                "Effect": "Allow",
                "Action": [
                   "s3:GetBucketLocation",
                   "s3:GetAccountPublicAccessBlock",
                   "s3:ListAccessPoints",
                "s3:ListAllMyBuckets"
                ],
                "Resource": "arn:aws:s3:::*"
        },
        {
                "Sid": "AllowS3Self",
                "Effect": "Allow",
                "Action": "s3:*",
                "Resource": [
                "arn:aws:s3:::johnjacob/*",
                "arn:aws:s3:::johnjacob"
                ]
        },
        {
                "Sid": "DenyS3Logs",
                "Effect": "Deny",
                "Action": "s3:*",
                "Resource": "arn:aws:s3:::*log*"
```

```
        }
        ]
}
```

Evaluating Policies

Understanding the policy evaluation process in AWS is crucial for effective resource management and security. AWS evaluates policies to determine if a user has permission to act on a resource.

Request Context

When a request is made, AWS gathers information such as the action, resource, user, and environment data.

Policy Types

- Different policy types apply depending on the scenario (identity-based, resource-based, and more).
- Policies are evaluated in a specific order.

Allow versus Deny

- Policies contain Allow or Deny statements.
- An explicit Deny overrides any Allow statements.
- By default, all requests are denied unless explicitly allowed by a policy.

Evaluation Process

- AWS checks all applicable policies for Deny statements first.
- If no Deny is found, it checks for Allow statements.
- The request is allowed if at least one Allow is found and no Deny applies.

Permissions Boundaries and Additional Factors

Permissions boundaries and other factors (like SCPs in Organizations) can further restrict permissions even if a policy allows an action.

Assign Keys to Principals

The "Principal" element specifies who the policy applies to. This could be an individual user, a group of users, or even another IAM role within your AWS account. Imagine assigning keys to specific personnel or departments, ensuring only authorized individuals can access particular resources.

Least Privilege: The Key to a Secure Fortress

The core principle of IAM policies is the concept of least privilege. This means granting users only the minimum permissions necessary to perform their jobs. Think about it–why give a guard the master key when a key to the specific armory is enough? This minimizes potential damage if a key falls into the wrong hands.

Crafting IAM policies with these elements establishes granular access control within your AWS infrastructure. This ensures your fortress remains secure, with only authorized personnel accessing specific resources, keeping your valuable data and applications safe.

Ditch the Root User and Forge a Security Stronghold

The root user in your AWS account is powerful and convenient, but it's a security Achilles' heel. It's like giving everyone the master key to your entire digital kingdom! One compromise, and your whole AWS infrastructure crumbles. Let's dethrone the root user for daily tasks and implement battle-tested practices to make your account impenetrable.

Deploy IAM Users: Create a Granular Guard Force

Imagine your AWS account as a medieval castle. We wouldn't give everyone the master key, right? We create IAM (Identity and Access Management) users – custom keys for each knight (user) needing access. You craft these finely-tuned accounts to grant specific permissions, following the "least privilege" principle. Even if a bad actor snags a credential, they'll only access a pre-defined section of the castle, minimizing the damage.

Craft IAM Policies: Define Permission Parchments for Secure Access

Take control of your castle with IAM policies! Here, you define precisely what actions each IAM user can take within AWS. These intricately detailed parchments outline permitted services, actions, and resources. You can attach these to users or assign them through IAM groups for flexible control. This granular approach ensures users only have the specific permissions they need, solidifying your security posture.

Embrace Temporary Access with STS

IAM Security Token Service (STS) becomes your champion for fleeting access needs. STS grants temporary, limited-privilege credentials that self-destruct after a designated timeframe. Imagine a secret handshake that grants access for a brief period before vanishing – you proactively reduce the risk of long-term access keys falling into the wrong hands.

Enforce MFA: Add a Drawbridge for Enhanced Security

Multi-factor Authentication (MFA) is like adding a secondary drawbridge to your castle. Even with a username and password, an attacker would be thwarted by needing a one-time code from a dedicated hardware token or mobile app. To create a robust authentication barrier, enforce MFA on all IAM users, including the root user (yes, even the king needs an extra layer of protection!).

Forge Your Security Citadel: Build a Multi-Layered Defense

By leveraging IAM users, crafting granular IAM policies, and granting temporary credentials from STS, you construct a fortified security citadel around your AWS resources. Reserve the root user for critical tasks such as creating IAM users and crafting policies. Regularly rotate root user credentials, turn off unused services, and diligently track IAM activity logs – constant vigilance is critical to maintaining a secure AWS environment.

This revised version replaces passive voice constructions with active ones, making the text more engaging and emphasizing your actions to secure your AWS account.

Claim Your AWS Throne: Mastering Access

Do you dream of ruling a digital kingdom? AWS awaits! It's filled with computing workshops, storage vaults, and unique tools. But how do you get in safely? This guide reveals three keys to unlock AWS: IAM users, STS, and IAM Identity Center.

Forge Your IAM User Signets

Create IAM users, like personal signets for your AWS accounts. You define their permissions, like who can build new structures (launch VMs) or manage the royal treasury (S3 buckets). But be warned, these signs are powerful! If lost, your security is at risk.

Enter STS: The Royal Seal Provider

Wise advisors (security experts) recommend against using signets for long periods. That's where STS, the Security Token Service, steps in! Request temporary signets with limited power for your users or applications. Think of it as borrowing a carriage for a specific errand, not handing over the keys to the entire royal fleet. These temporary signets expire after a set time, minimizing damage from potential breaches.

Federate and Simplify: One Signet to Rule Them All

Managing many signets becomes a burden if you have a central login system like a council hall (Active Directory). Here's where the IAM Identity Center comes to the rescue. It acts as a bridge, allowing your users to sign in once with their existing council hall credentials and access all their assigned AWS accounts and tools. Single sign-on, a dream realized!

Choosing Your Ideal Royal Tool

You might wonder, "Which tool should I use?" As with most things in the AWS kingdom, the answer depends on your needs.

- **IAM Users:** These are ideal for more straightforward tasks, with a few requiring long-term access. But remember to enforce strong passwords and secure them with multi-factor authentication–like a reinforced gate on your signet.
- **STS:** Perfect for situations where temporary, controlled access is crucial. Think application access or automated tasks. Imagine lending your carriage for a specific errand, not an unrestricted journey.
- IAM Identity Center is a game-changer for organizations with existing council halls. It streamlines access management and offers a unified login experience for your users–a single signet that unlocks all your designated areas within the AWS kingdom.

Leverage SAML 2.0 for Streamlined AWS Access

This section outlines configuring SAML 2.0 federation between your organization's identity provider (IdP) and AWS. This approach simplifies user management, enhances security, and enables seamless single sign-on (SSO).

Benefits:

- **Reduced Management Overhead**: Eliminate individual IAM user creation for your organization. Users leverage existing IdP credentials for AWS access.
- **Robust Security**: Centralized authentication within your IdP, potentially leveraging stricter access controls and multi-factor authentication (MFA).
- **Effortless SSO**: Users sign in once to your organization's IdP and access the AWS Management Console or APIs without further authentication.

Supported Scenarios:

- **Federated API Access**: Utilize SAML assertions to obtain temporary security credentials for programmatic AWS access by users or applications within your organization.
- **Web-based SSO to AWS Management Console**: Allow users to sign in once to your organization's SAML 2.0-compatible IdP portal and then access the AWS console without further authentication.

Configuration Steps

Gather Requirements: Ensure your organization has an IdP supporting SAML 2.0 (such as Microsoft AD FS or Shibboleth) and an AWS account.

1. **Establish Trust:**
   a. **Register AWS in your IdP:** Use the regionalized AWS SAML metadata document (recommended) or the global document for improved resiliency.
   b. **Generate IdP Metadata**: Create a document describing your IdP as an IAM identity provider for AWS.
2. **Configure AWS IAM**:
   a. **Create a SAML Identity Provider**: Upload your IdP's metadata document in the IAM console.
   b. **Create IAM Roles**: Define roles with trust policies referencing the SAML provider and permission policies outlining user actions in AWS.
3. **Map Users/Groups in your IdP**:
   a. Define assertions mapping users or groups to corresponding IAM roles based on access control needs.

Optional:

- Configure SSO for Console (if supported): Set the maximum session duration for console access within your IdP.

Integrate with Applications

Use the **AssumeRoleWithSAML** API call to obtain temporary security credentials using the user's SAML assertion.

Want to share AWS resources across accounts? IAM offers two options depicted in *Figure 2.2*:

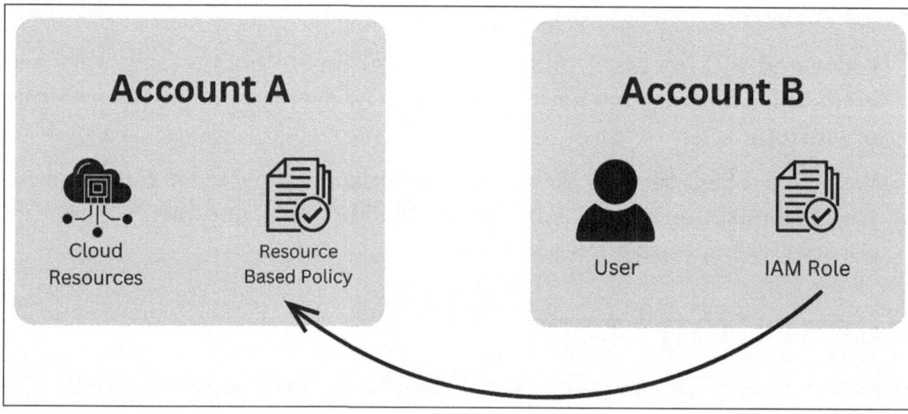

***Figure 2.2**: Sharing AWS resources across accounts*

Resource-Based Policies (Direct Sharing):

- Works for services such as S3 buckets, SNS topics, and SQS queues.
- Attach a policy to the resource, specifying who can access it.
- Grant full or any permissions allowed.
- Users keep their permissions while accessing the resource in a more straightforward setup.

Cross-Account IAM Roles (Proxy Access):

- Use this for services without resource-based policies or for more control.
- Create a role in the resource account.
- Set up a trust policy allowing specific users/roles from another account to assume the role.
- Attach a policy to the role defining permissions for those assuming the role.
- Grants permissions based on the role's policy.
- Offers centralized permission management and granular control.

Secure User Logins for Mobile Apps with Amazon Cognito

Build a secure login system for your mobile game with Amazon Cognito and OIDC federation.

Scenario

You're developing a mobile game. Player data such as scores and profiles will be stored in Amazon S3 and DynamoDB. Security is crucial, and you expect a large user base.

The Solution:

- **External Login Providers**: Register as a developer with providers like Login with Amazon, Facebook, or Google. Configure your app with each chosen provider.
- **IAM Roles and Identity Pool**: Create IAM roles in your AWS account that define permissions for your game using Cognito. If using an OIDC provider, create an IAM OIDC identity provider to connect your Cognito identity pool with the chosen provider.
- **Mobile App Integration**: The app calls the configured IdP's sign-in interface. The IdP handles user login, and the app receives an access or ID token. The app uses this token to get temporary AWS security credentials (access key ID, secret access key, session token) from Cognito. These credentials allow the app to access authorized AWS services based on permissions from the IAM role.

Benefits:

- Leverage trusted IdPs for secure user authentication.
- Manage user identities centrally in Cognito.
- Control access precisely with IAM roles.
- Scale quickly for a large user base.

Steps to Implement:

1. (Optional) Register with your chosen IdPs and configure your app.
2. Create an identity pool in Amazon Cognito using the AWS Management Console.
3. (Optional) Integrate AWS Amplify for easier Cognito integration in your app.
4. Create an Amazon Cognito credentials provider with the identity pool ID, AWS account number, and IAM role ARNs.
5. When accessing AWS resources, pass the credentials provider to the client object to get temporary security credentials.

Note:

- *Cognito also supports unauthenticated (guest) access.*
- *The Cognito wizard in the AWS Management Console provides sample code for a more straightforward setup.*

Conclusion

In this chapter, you gained the foundation to secure your AWS resources confidently. You learned about the building blocks of IAM-users, groups, roles, and policies, and how they work together to control access to your AWS resources. You also learned how to create a secure IAM strategy by following the principle of least privilege and leveraging IAM features like MFA. You've mastered IAM for user access control, ensuring only authorized users can access specific AWS resources with the necessary permissions. You can effectively define identities (users and roles) and assign granular permissions using groups for efficient access management. Besides, you can craft IAM policies to grant fine-grained access controls for your resources, ensuring users only have the permissions they absolutely need.

Now you can securely share AWS resources across accounts. IAM lets you collaborate securely without compromising security by providing temporary credentials or leveraging roles.

Remember, security is a continuous process. Stay tuned for the next chapter, where we'll explore the world of AWS networking and strategies to strengthen your cloud security further!

Multiple Choice Questions

1. You are new to AWS and looking to provide your team access. Which of the following best describes what IAM does in this scenario?
    a. IAM provides you with a firewall that protects your AWS resources.
    b. IAM is used to monitor and optimize AWS resource usage.
    c. IAM enables safe management of access to AWS services and resources.
    d. IAM is automated in deploying AWS infrastructure.
2. Your company wants to ensure that only particular IP addresses can access your AWS resources. Which feature of the IAM will you implement?
    a. IAM Policies
    b. IAM Roles

c. Multi-Factor Authentication (MFA)

d. IAM Groups

3. You have a third-party auditor. The auditor needs to perform some temporary audit-related tasks within your AWS environment. Which of the following IAM resources would you use to provide access?

a. IAM Users

b. IAM Roles

c. IAM Groups

d. IAM Access Keys

4. Several IAM users require similar permissions within your AWS environment. What is the best way to manage these permissions?

a. Apply separate individual policies to each user.

b. Create a group; attach users to the group, then attach policies.

c. Attach policies directly to each user.

d. IAM Roles for each User

5. A developer only has to access one specific S3 bucket. He doesn't require any other buckets. How would this be implemented using IAM?

a. Create a role with a policy that allows only access to that particular S3 bucket and assign the role to the developer.

b. Create an IAM user for the developer, but grant all S3 access.

c. IAM Groups for all S3 bucket access.

d. Enable MFA for the developer's IAM account.

6. Users have an IAM policy granting access to an S3 bucket; another policy is attached to a group denying the same bucket access. What will be the effective permission for this user to access the S3 bucket?

a. The user will have access to the S3 bucket

b. The user won't have access to the S3 bucket.

c. The user may access the bucket only via the AWS CLI.

d. The user will have to request temporary access from the administrator.

7. You want to delegate permission management to a team lead without giving full administrative privileges. What IAM feature should you use to achieve this?
   a. Create a custom policy with specific permissions and attach it to an IAM role, then assign the role to the team lead.
   b. Make the team lead an IAM Administrator.
   c. Attach the AdministratorAccess policy to the team lead's user account.
   d. Use the AWS account root user to manage permissions.
8. Your company wants to ensure that every action performed in the AWS environment is securely authenticated. Which of the following practices should be implemented for IAM users?
   a. Authentication must be done only via IAM access keys
   b. Multi-factor authentication must be enabled for all users.
   c. All your team members can share the same IAM user account.
   d. Use the AWS root account all the time.
9. You would like to allow an application inside an Amazon EC2 instance to access a specific Amazon S3 bucket. Which of the following will achieve this most appropriately without static credentials?
   a. Storing the AWS access and secret key inside the EC2 instance
   b. IAM roles with attached appropriate policies to the EC2 instance.
   c. Manually edit S3 Bucket permissions to allow access from the IP address of the EC2 instance
   d. Utilize the AWS root account credentials within the application.
10. Your organization must limit access to the AWS Management Console for IAM users concerning their job roles. For example, developers need access to EC2 and S3 but not to any information on billing. Which of the following is the best way to develop this access control?
   a. Create individual IAM users for every service and distribute the credentials.
   b. Attach the AdministratorAccess policy to all users and request that they only access the services they need
   c. Create specific permission sets using IAM policies and attach these permission sets to IAM groups that contain different users based on job roles
   d. Using the root account, manually restrict and allow access for each user

Answers

1. c
2. a
3. b
4. b
5. a
6. b
7. a
8. b
9. b
10. c

References

- https://docs.aws.amazon.com/IAM/latest/UserGuide/intro-structure.html
- https://docs.aws.amazon.com/IAM/latest/UserGuide/reference_policies_evaluation-logic.html
- https://learn.microsoft.com/en-us/entra/fundamentals/identity-fundamental-concepts
- https://learn.microsoft.com/en-us/entra/fundamentals/introduction-identity-access-management
- https://www.freecodecamp.org/news/aws-iam-explained/
- https://docs.aws.amazon.com/IAM/latest/UserGuide/id_roles_providers_saml.html
- https://docs.aws.amazon.com/IAM/latest/UserGuide/access_policies-cross-account-resource-access.html
- https://docs.aws.amazon.com/IAM/latest/UserGuide/id_roles_providers_oidc_cognito.html
- https://docs.aws.amazon.com/IAM/latest/UserGuide/tutorial_cross-account-with-roles.html
- https://www.google.com/search?q=aws+federation&source=lnms&tbm=isch&sa=X&ved=0ahUKEwjwgO6u57TjAhVROH0KHUs_CxUQ_AUIESgC&biw=1422&bih=721#imgrc=1_4ZG0kFOEm-qM:

- https://docs.aws.amazon.com/singlesignon/latest/userguide/manage-your-directory.html
- https://www.pingidentity.com/content/dam/ping-6-2-assets/Assets/ebooks/en/amazon-web-services-ebook.pdf
- https://docs.aws.amazon.com/IAM/latest/UserGuide/id_roles_use_switch-role-ec2.html?ref=wellarchitected

CHAPTER 3
Networking in AWS

Introduction

The cornerstone of modern cloud computing is a robust, secure, and scalable networking foundation. Within the dynamic world of Amazon Web Services (AWS) Cloud, a comprehensive suite of networking services empowers you to establish seamless communication between the diverse components of your cloud environment.

This chapter equips you with the knowledge to navigate and optimize your AWS network architecture. We begin by revisiting the fundamental building blocks of networking through the lens of the OSI model. Starting with a grasp of the basics, we move into the complexities of AWS networking. We break down the elements of a VPC, such as subnets, internet gateways, and security groups, examining how they manage secure and monitored network communication in your AWS setup.

Our exploration continues beyond there. We further equip you with best practices for designing and configuring your VPC to achieve optimal performance and security. Here, we provide tactical guidance on:

- **Subnet Sizing**: We explore strategies to define subnet sizes that align with your application's resource needs and potential future growth. This includes considerations for availability zones and resource placement within your VPC.
- **Security Group Configuration**: This guide discusses practices for configuring security groups, such as following the principle of least privilege and utilizing security group placement groups to streamline security rules management.

Furthermore, we introduce functionalities such as VPC peering, route tables, and Network Access Control Lists (NACLs) to help you construct secure cloud networks. We also present examples and scenarios for:

- **VPC Peering**: We demonstrate how to create network links between your VPC and a peering VPC within the same or different AWS region, which benefits situations requiring connections between resources in VPCs.

- **Route Tables**: We shed light on how you configure route tables to dictate the traffic flow within your VPC. You will gain insights into optimizing network communication and achieving specific routing goals.
- Network Access Control Lists (NACLs): We empower users to manage outgoing network traffic within subnets, enhancing VPC's security posture.

Upon completing this chapter, you will acquire the knowledge needed to navigate AWS networking complexities effectively and design scalable and budget cloud network solutions.

Structure

In this chapter, we will discuss the following topics:

- Networking Foundations
    - OSI Model Basics
    - Protocols You Should Be Familiar With
    - Other Key Networking Concepts
    - IP Addresses and Subnetting
- Networking in AWS
    - Deep Dive into VPC
    - VPC Best Practices and Enhancements
    - Load Balancers
- Domain Name System and Content Delivery
    - DNS Fundamentals
    - Route53
    - CloudFront

Networking Foundations

Networking foundations are the building blocks for connecting computers and devices. They allow the sharing of information, resources such as printers, and access to the Internet. They are like the invisible wires and rules that make the digital party happen. Let us delve deeper to obtain a thorough understanding.

The OSI Model: A Deep Dive into Network Communication

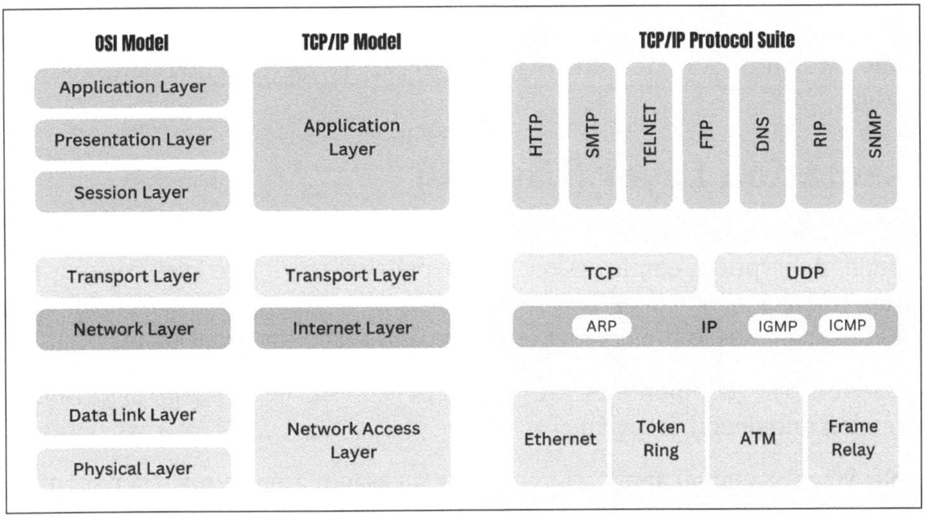

***Figure 3.1**: Comparing the OSI model with the TCP/IP model*

Figure 3.1 compares the OSI model with the TCP/IP model. It can be elaborated as:

TCP/IP, the older internet model, is more straightforward than OSI. It combines OSI layers for a more practical approach:

- The top 3 OSI layers become the TCP/IP Application layer.
- The bottom 2 OSI layers become the TCP/IP Network Access layer (without sequencing/acknowledgment).

TCP/IP is built for real-world problems with specific protocols, while OSI is a general blueprint for network communication.

The Open Systems Interconnection (OSI) model is a foundational framework in computer networking. It acts as a conceptual blueprint, dividing network communication processes into seven layers. Each layer has specialized functions that contribute to the process. This standardized approach fosters interoperability, ensuring diverse systems can communicate seamlessly.

Imagine the OSI model as a complex postal system, where each stage relies on the previous one to guarantee successful data transmission. Let us delve deeper into each layer:

Application Layer (Layer 7)

The application layer serves as the user interface for network services. It provides network functionalities directly to applications such as web browsing, email, file transfer, and video streaming. The user interacts with the content, either writing or reading the mail or interacting with the item being sent or received at Layer 7.

Components: Application protocols (HTTP, FTP, SMTP), user applications.

Example: A web browser interacts with a web server using HTTP to request and display a webpage.

Presentation Layer (Layer 6)

The presentation layer focuses on data formatting and presentation. It handles data encryption, decryption, compression, and expansion to ensure system compatibility. Preparing a letter or package before it arrives at a designated mail drop-off point involves ensuring it is in the correct envelope and ready for processing.

Components: The components are data encryption, decryption algorithms, and compression and decompression.

Example: When an email application sends a message, it encrypts it for security, and the recipient's email application decrypts it for readability.

Session Layer (Layer 5)

The session layer establishes, manages, and terminates sessions between applications. It facilitates data exchange and synchronization between communicating applications. This is like registering the mail and being able to track it. It starts and maintains the communication session, ensuring you can follow the mail's journey from sender to receiver.

Components: Session initiation and termination protocols.

Example: A file transfer application initiates a session with a remote server to transfer a file, ensuring a reliable and ordered data exchange.

Transport Layer (Layer 4)

The transport layer provides reliable communication between applications running on different hosts. It ensures that information reaches its destination in the sequence of mistakes and handles traffic control. It is similar to the methods of transportation (such as trucks, planes, and boats) that transport mail across distances. Its goal is to ensure the letter or package travels securely and reaches its destination without getting misplaced or harmed along the journey.

Components: The building blocks include port numbers and protocols such as Transmission Control Protocol (TCP) and User Datagram Protocol (UDP).

Example: When a website server interacts with a web browser, it relies on TCP to create a link, ensuring all the webpage content is transmitted properly without glitches.

Network Layer (Layer 3)

The network layer manages IP addresses for addressing and packet routing. It decides the route for data packets to travel through networks to reach their intended destination, much like how a letter is directed from one post office to another.

Components: It includes IP address routing protocols such as OSPF, BGP, and routers.

Example: A router examines the destination IP address in a data packet and directs it towards the network segment.

Data Link Layer (Layer 2)

This particular layer acts as a connection point between the layer and the network layer. Its primary focus is ensuring data is transmitted reliably and without errors among devices within the physical network segment. Think of it like arranging the timing for dropping off and picking up mail at different places. The aim is to synchronize the delivery and pickup schedules to ensure that the mail reaches its intended destination on time (using MAC addressing and framing).

Components: Media Access Control (MAC) addresses, Frame Check Sequence (FCS) for error detection and error correction protocols.

Example: When an Ethernet switch receives data frames, it verifies their MAC address to determine their destination and forwards them accordingly.

Physical Layer (Layer 1)

The foundation of network communication lies in the layer that handles transmitting data. This layer oversees the properties of the transmission medium, such as cables and wires, as well as the electrical or optical signals that convey data. Within this layer are individuals and machines involved in transporting mail, such as workers, sorting machines, and mail trucks, which ensure letters and packages are moved from one place to another.

Components: Network interface cards (NICs), cables, connectors, hubs, and repeaters.

Example: A network cable sends signals representing digits (1s and 0s).

The OSI model provides an approach to grasp and troubleshoot network communication problems. By identifying the layer where an issue occurs, network experts can effectively resolve connectivity or data transfer glitches. Although real-world network protocols may not align perfectly with each OSI layer, this model remains a tool for conceptualizing and analyzing network functions.

Essential Networking Protocols

Knowing protocols is essential for devices to communicate on networks. They create a shared way to exchange data, making interactions efficient and dependable.

Let us look at protocols grouped by their layers in the Open Systems Interconnection (OSI) model:

Layer 3 - Network Layer

- **Internet Protocol (IP):**

  IP serves as the backbone of any network, be it a LAN linking devices within a home, a business network, an office complex, or the extensive web of the Internet. Its role involves allocating identifiers (IP addresses) to devices on a network. Additionally, it sets the guidelines for packaging data into packets and directs them through networks according to their intended destinations.

  You can liken IP to a service that designates addresses to places and transports mail packets accordingly.

- **Internet Control Message Protocol (ICMP):**

  ICMP acts like a courier in IP networks. ICMP messages report errors (such as informing a sender that a destination cannot be reached) and serve diagnostic purposes (example, pinging a device to check connectivity). Think of ICMP as akin to notes within the service sharing details about failed deliveries or network problems.

Layer 4 - Transport Layer

- **Transmission Control Protocol (TCP):**

  TCP ensures that data is delivered reliably, in order, and without errors. It sets up a link between the sender and receiver, divides the data into segments, sends them, and confirms receipt for each segment. Additionally, it guarantees that segments reach their destination in the sequence and retransmit any damaged data. Imagine TCP as a delivery service that verifies the delivery of each parcel in the sequence and resents any misplaced ones.

- **User Datagram Protocol (UDP):**

  UDP provides a connectionless communication channel for best-effort data delivery. It prioritizes speed over reliability. It transmits data packets (datagrams) without establishing a connection and doesn't guarantee delivery or order. Imagine UDP as a fast-paced mail service that throws letters in a mailbox without confirmation– some might arrive quickly, some might get lost.

Layer 5 - Session Layer

- **Web Sockets:** Application Programming Interfaces (APIs) allow applications on different networked devices to establish communication channels. Sockets provide a standardized method for processes to exchange data over a network. Consider sockets as designated ports at a harbor where ships (applications) can dock and exchange cargo (data) following specific procedures.

Layer 6 - Presentation Layer

- **Secure Shell (SSH):** SSH securely allows users to log in, run commands, and move encrypted data between devices. By using public key cryptography, SSH verifies users and secures data during transit to prevent access and monitoring. Visualize SSH as a safeguarded passageway with controlled entry and encryption, enabling authorized individuals to access and oversee systems.
- **File Transfer Protocol (FTP):** It is a method for file transfer between a client and server over a network. It governs activities such as file listing, uploading, downloading, and navigating directories. Picture FTP as a truck specifically designed to transfer files between computers according to set procedures for initiating transfers and managing files.
- **Transport Layer Security (TLS):** The evolution from SSL (Sockets Layer); TLS is a protocol that ensures communication over networks by encrypting data exchanged between applications to maintain privacy and data integrity. TLS employs certificates for authenticating servers, thus thwarting man-in-the-middle attacks. Conceptualize TLS as a communication incorporating encryption measures and validation procedures similar to safeguarded packaging that secures the contents.

Layer 7 - Application Layer

- **HTTP:** HTTP, the acronym for Hypertext Transfer Protocol, is the backbone of Internet communication. It governs the way in which web browsers and servers share information, enabling the retrieval and display of web pages, multimedia content, and various resources on the World Wide Web. Picture HTTP as the communication bridge that allows web browsers to request and servers to deliver web content such as pages and images. This detailed explanation offers insight into each protocol's function in the network communication setup.
- **HTTPS:** It stands for HyperText Transfer Protocol Secure. Represents the secure iteration of HTTP. It encrypts data to protect it from access or alterations, dictating how information is securely exchanged between web browsers and servers. Imagine HTTPS as a language with built-in security measures that ensure safe communication between web browsers and

servers. This expanded explanation sheds light on HTTPS role in network communication by emphasizing its significance in securing interactions.

HTTPS enhances HTTP security by incorporating encryption to protect data. This encryption guarantees Confidentiality, Integrity and Authentication (CIA):

- **Confidentiality:** HTTPS encrypts data to keep information, such as passwords and payment details
- **Integrity:** HTTPS ensures that data remains unchanged during transmission, providing users with information.
- **Authentication:** HTTPS uses certificates to verify the identity of servers, preventing users from inadvertently accessing counterfeit websites

How HTTPS operates:

1. **Handshake:** When a user tries to access a website (identified by HTTPS in the URL) the browser and server initiate a handshake. The server shares its SSL/TLS certificate containing its key.
2. **Verification:** The browser validates the certificate by checking its expiration date and confirming it was issued by a trusted Certificate Authority.
3. **Session Key Establishment**: If the certificate is valid, the browser generates a private session key protected by the server's key. The server's private key can decrypt this key.
4. **Secure Communication**: All subsequent communication between the browser and server is encrypted using the session key, ensuring that authorized parties can understand the information.

Figure 3.2 explains how HTTPS works:

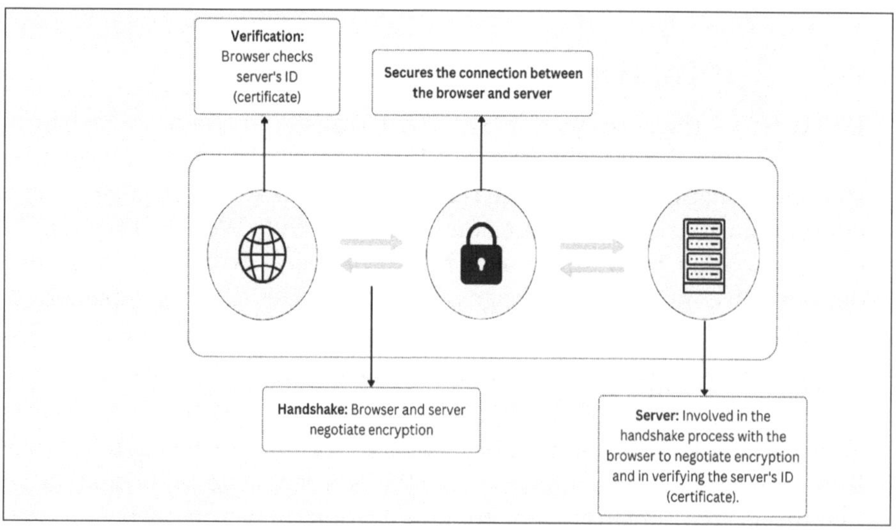

Figure 3.2: *How HTTPS works*

Core Networking Concepts: A Deeper Dive

A solid foundation of core networking concepts is essential for a clear picture of networking in AWS. This section will provide the foundation for networking.

IP Addressing: The Foundation of Network Communication

Imagine a small city. Every resident needs a unique identifier (IP address) to receive mail (data packets). We assign an IP address, a 32-bit logical address, to each device connected to a network. It is typically displayed in dotted-decimal format (example, 192.168.1.100), with each octet (group of eight bits) ranging from 0 to 255.

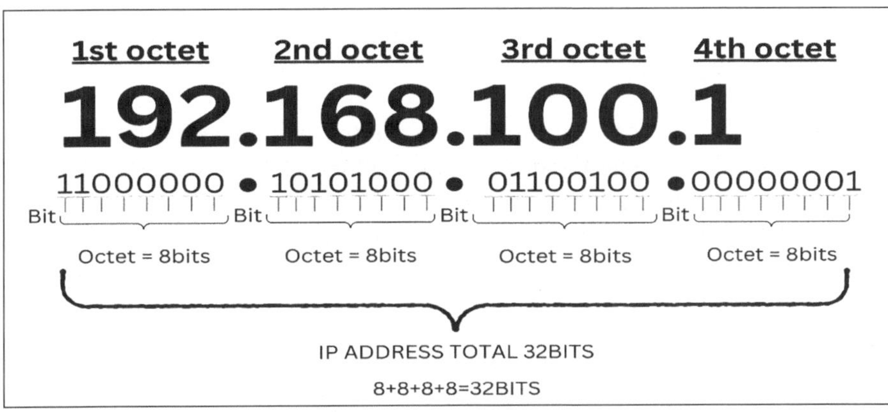

Figure 3.3: *Octet mapping*

Figure 3.3 explains how octet maps to IP addresses. Let us understand it better:

How Octets Map to IP Addresses

Let us understand this with the help of an example. Consider the above image; it shows an IP address:

192.168.1.100

Each section, separated by a dot, represents an octet of the IP address.

- **Octet 1**: 192 (decimal)
- **Octet 2**: 168 (decimal)
- **Octet 3**: 1 (decimal)
- **Octet 4**: 100 (decimal)

The word 'bit' refers to the binary representation of each octet. An octet comprises 8 bits, and each bit can be either 0 or 1.

Each decimal value of an octet can be converted to its corresponding 8-bit binary representation.

So, in the aforementioned example,

- **Octet 1 (192):** In binary, this translates to 11000000 (eight bits).
- **Octet 2 (168):** This translates to 10101000 (eight bits) in binary.
- **Octet 3 (1)**: In binary, this translates to 00000001 (eight bits).
- **Octet 4 (100):** In binary, this translates to 01100100 (eight bits).

Combining all the binary octets, we get the complete binary representation of the IP address 192.168.1.100:

11000000.10101000.00000001.01100100

IPv4 versus IPv6

IPv4 is the original and most commonly used edition. It uses 32 bits (or 4 octets) represented in dotted decimal format, such as 192.168.1.100. However, the number of unique IP addresses that can be allocated is limited to approximately 4.3 billion due to the restriction of having only 32 bits. Due to the limited address space, subnet masking is now essential for efficiently managing and regulating IPv4 addresses in larger networks.

IPv6 is the successor to IPv4, designed to address the limitations of the previous IP version. It employs 128 bits (16 octets), shown in eight groups of hexadecimal digits separated by colons, such as 2001:0db8:85a3:0000:0000:8a2e:0370:7334. To avoid running out of IP addresses, it offers more distinct addresses (approximately 3.4 x 1038).

Despite their differences, IPv4 and IPv6 maintain a crucial similarity; they serve the core function of uniquely identifying devices for internet communication. They achieve this through a hierarchical addressing structure, allowing efficient data packet routing. This continuity in functionality ensures a smooth transition from IPv4 to IPv6.

Subnetting: Carving Up the Network Strategically

Think of subnetting as dividing that small city into smaller, more manageable neighborhoods. We call these smaller neighborhoods subnets. Subnetting offers several advantages:

- **Security**: We can isolate network segments, restricting access between departments or guest networks. Imagine each building having its own security gate.

  What is a network segment?

  A network segment is a logical subdivision of a larger network. Imagine dividing a small city into separate blocks. Each block (segment) can have its own security controls, restricting access between them. This isolation helps prevent unauthorized access to sensitive data on other network parts.

- **Efficiency**: Subnetting helps reduce network congestion by controlling broadcast traffic within subnets. There is less overall "yelling in the hallways" for devices.

  What is network congestion?

  Network congestion happens when excessive traffic attempts to flow through a network simultaneously, similar to a busy street. This can slow down communication for everyone. Subnetting reduces broadcast traffic by limiting it to specific blocks, each with its public address system.

  What is broadcast traffic?

  In a network without subnets, broadcast traffic is similar to an announcement to all residents about a planned power outage. A single message is sent to every building (device) on the entire network, flooding the city.

- **Scalability**: As your network expands, you can easily incorporate new devices or subnets, like adding new buildings to a complex.

Subnetting Achieved Through a Subnet Mask

A subnet mask is a 32-bit number that defines the network and host portions of an IP address. It is like a blueprint for dividing the address space. Standard subnet masks include 255.255.255.0 (the default for Class C networks) or 255.255.0.0 (for Class A networks).

By manipulating the subnet mask, you can create subnets with varying numbers of usable devices. It is like adjusting the room layout in each building to accommodate different resident needs.

Mastering IP addressing and subnetting empowers you to:

- Design secure and efficient network layouts.
- Troubleshoot network connectivity issues more effectively.
- Optimize network performance for different workloads.

Building Secure, Scalable, and High-Performance Networks with AWS

AWS provides two key tools for protecting your resources: Security Groups and Network Access Control Lists (NACLs).

Security groups enforce stricter access controls for specific resources, whereas NACLs set a basic security framework for your subnet by defining the overall access level for all resources within it. Though they control inbound and outbound traffic, they are distinct in functional and application areas.

By understanding the strengths of security groups and NACLs, you can create a robust security configuration for your cloud environment.

Table 3.1 outlines the key differences between security groups and NACLs, helping you choose the right tool:

Feature	**Security Groups**	**NACLs**
Scope	Instance level	Subnet level
Defense Layer	First layer (inbound) or second layer (outbound)	First layer (inbound) or second layer (outbound)
Traffic Control	Inbound and outbound traffic to/from instances	Inbound and outbound traffic to/from a subnet
Rule Types	Allow only	Allow and deny
Stateful Inspection	No (return traffic needs explicit rule)	Yes (return traffic automatically allowed for allowed inbound)
Default Rule	Deny all inbound traffic	Deny all inbound traffic (and outbound by default)
Association	Attached to network interfaces	Attached to subnets
Multiple Instances	One security group can be associated with multiple instances	One NACL applies to all instances in a subnet
Additional Layer	Can be used alone for basic security	Additional layer of defense for NACLs

Table 3.1: *Security groups versus* NACLs

Unparalleled Breadth and Depth of Services

Imagine an architect has a vast toolbox at their disposal. This toolbox contains every conceivable tool needed to construct a building. AWS offers a wide range of networking and content delivery services.

- With the help of these services, you can build secure, scalable, and high-performance applications.

- AWS provides fundamental building blocks, such as virtual private clouds (VPCs). These VPCs establish logically isolated network segments within the AWS cloud.
- They act as your private network domain within the broader AWS infrastructure.
- Security groups function as virtual firewalls, meticulously controlling the flow of inbound and outbound traffic to your resources.

Fortifying Security at Every Layer

Security is paramount in today's digital landscape. AWS networking incorporates a multi-layered security approach to safeguard your data and applications.

- AWS provides various security services, such as AWS Shield and AWS Identity and Access Management (IAM).
- AWS Shield helps to reduce the impact of denial-of-service (DDoS) attacks.
- AWS IAM enforces granular access controls.
- With AWS's vigilant monitoring and comprehensive security features, you can be assured that your data remains confidential, integral, and available.

Unwavering Network Availability

Mission-critical applications require constant network uptime. AWS maintains a high level of availability through its diverse Geographical Regions and Availability Zones (AZs).

- AWS ensures outstanding network availability by utilizing widely distributed regions and Availability Zones (AZs).
- Regions are distinct geographical locations where AWS infrastructure resides.
- Many AZs and separate data centers within each region offer built-in redundancy.
- Should an outage occur in one AZ, your application can fail over to another, ensuring minimal disruption.

Delivering Consistent High-Performance

Low latency and high throughput are crucial for a responsive and efficient network.

- The AWS network is carefully designed to deliver high data transfer speeds with minimal delays.
- By taking advantage of this high-performance network infrastructure, you can provide your users with a significantly faster and more responsive experience.

Reaching a Global Audience

In today's interconnected world, delivering content and applications to a global audience is crucial. AWS boasts the most extensive global infrastructure footprint of any cloud provider.

- AWS boasts the most extensive global infrastructure footprint of any cloud provider.
- This expansive network of edge locations strategically placed worldwide ensures your content is geographically closer to your end users.

This rewrite breaks down the long sentences and focuses on the active verbs describing what AWS offers and how it benefits you.

Understanding a VPC

VPC stands for Virtual Private Cloud. It is your secure network inside the giant AWS cloud.

Building Your VPC

Figure 3.4 demonstrates an AWS Virtual Private Cloud (VPC) setup:

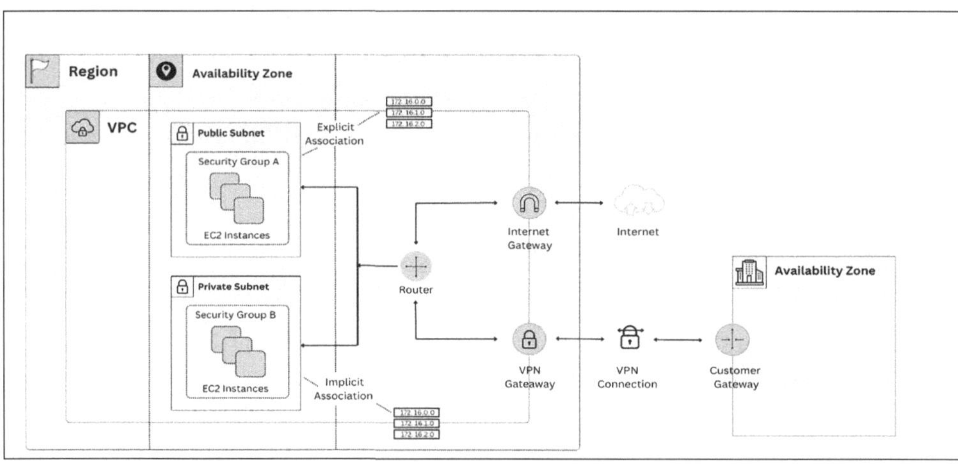

Figure 3.4: *Build your* VPC

Plan

- Choose IP ranges for your VPC and subnets.
- Pick Availability Zones (AZs) for your resources.
- Decide how your VPC will connect to the internet.

- **Create:** Go to the VPC console and click "Create VPC." Define the name, IP range, and (optional) IPv6 support.
- **Secure**: Security groups act like firewalls, controlling traffic to your resources. Route tables direct traffic within your VPC and to the internet (if needed).

Additional Security (Optional)

- **Network ACLs**: Add extra security filters at the subnet level.
- **Flow Logs**: Track network traffic for troubleshooting.
- **Traffic Mirroring**: Copy network traffic for monitoring.

Setting Up a VPC

Here is how you can set up your VPC:

Planning Your VPC Blueprint

- Choose CIDR blocks for both your VPC and subnets.
- Plan for future growth to avoid running out of IP addresses.
- Spread your resources across multiple AZs for redundancy.

Creating Your VPC

1. Log in to your AWS account and navigate to the VPC service.
2. Click **"`Create VPC`"** to begin building your private network.
3. Give your VPC a name and select the chosen CIDR block.
4. Optionally enable IPv6 support for future-proofing.

Securing Your VPC

- Define rules for security groups to allow only authorized communication.
- Configure routes to the internet gateway (if needed) and between subnets.

Optional Advanced Security Measures

- Add an extra layer of security by filtering traffic at the subnet level with Network Access Control Lists (ACLs).
- Track network traffic for troubleshooting purposes with Flow Logs.
- Copy network traffic to a monitoring tool for real-time analysis with Traffic Mirroring.

Step-by-Step Task Checklist

If you do not have an AWS account, create a free account by following the steps.

1. Verify that you have the necessary permissions to work with VPCs.
2. Plan your CIDR blocks for the VPC and subnets, avoiding conflicts with your existing network.
3. Choose AZs based on your needs.
4. Decide how your VPC will connect to the internet and configure subnets accordingly.
5. Follow the AWS Management Console steps to create your VPC using the chosen parameters.
6. Deploy your application resources using services such as EC2 Auto Scaling, EC2 Fleet, or Amazon ECS for production environments, or launch a single EC2 instance for development testing.

Public Subnet versus Private Subnet

The public and private subnets belong to the Virtual Private Cloud (VPC), a gated community that provides a secure and isolated network environment for cloud resources. Resources placed in a public subnet have direct access to the Internet, allowing them to be accessed from anywhere on the public web. These are usually used for resources such as web servers, application load balancers, or any service that needs to be reached by users over the Internet.

Public subnets can be easily scaled up or down to accommodate changing traffic demands, allowing you to increase resources readily during peak usage times. However, security measures must be prioritized to mitigate the potential risks associated with direct internet access.

On the other hand, resources placed on a private subnet do not have direct access to the internet. They are shielded from the public web by a firewall within the VPC. They are ideal for deploying resources that don't require direct internet exposure. These resources include backend systems, internal servers, and databases. Private subnets provide increased security for sensitive data and granular control over internet access for different resources.

Table 3.2 provides a comparison between public subnet and private subnet:

Feature	Public Subnet	Private Subnet
Route to Internet	Yes (via Internet Gateway)	No

Instance Type	Web servers, application servers	Database servers, backend servers
Security Groups	More open to allow inbound traffic	More restrictive, outbound traffic only (usually)
IP Address	Public IP address assigned	Private IP address assigned
Accessibility	Accessible from the internet	Not directly accessible from the internet
Use Cases	Hosting websites, applications	Secure databases, backend services

Table 3.2: *Public subnet versus private subnet*

VPC Best Practices and Enhancements: Optimize Performance, Security, and Manageability

Virtual Private Cloud (VPC) is the cornerstone of secure and isolated cloud environments for deploying applications and services. By implementing best practices and leveraging advanced features, you can significantly enhance the performance, security, and manageability of your VPCs. This guide explores essential VPC enhancements to empower you to build robust and efficient cloud networks.

Understanding VPC Endpoints

You create secure, private connections directly to AWS services within the AWS network using VPC endpoints. This eliminates the need for internet gateways, NAT devices, VPN connections, or Direct Connect. Traffic stays off the public internet for enhanced security, and you benefit from lower latency and higher bandwidth for improved performance.

Types of Endpoints

Interface Endpoints: Leverage Elastic Network Interfaces (ENIs) to connect to services powered by AWS PrivateLink. This ensures traffic remains solely within the AWS network for enhanced security.

Gateway Endpoints: Create a dedicated gateway to access specific services (currently S3 and DynamoDB) directly from your VPC, bypassing the internet for improved security and performance.

Best Practices for VPC Endpoints

Apply granular security: Implement restrictive security groups to interface endpoints to meticulously control access to connected AWS services.

Enforce fine-grained access control: Utilize endpoint policies to define granular access controls, specifying which resources within your VPC cannot access AWS services through the endpoint.

Design for high availability: Deploy multiple endpoints throughout different Availability Zones (AZs) to guarantee redundancy and fault tolerance. If one endpoint is temporarily unavailable, another endpoint in a different AZ effortlessly takes over.

Peering Between VPCs

Using VPC peering, establish secure connections between two VPCs within the same AWS region or across different regions. This facilitates resource sharing across accounts or between your VPC and a service provider VPC. You enable low-latency, high-bandwidth connectivity while maintaining isolation between VPCs.

Best Practices for VPC Peering

- **Plan CIDR blocks meticulously:** Carefully plan CIDR blocks for your VPCs to avoid conflicts. Ensure non-overlapping CIDR blocks to prevent IP address issues when peering VPCs.
- **Manage route tables**: Update route tables in both peered VPCs to direct traffic appropriately. Configure routes that point to the peered VPC's address space through the peering connection.
- **Enable DNS resolution**: Allow DNS resolution for resources in peered VPCs. This enables instances in one VPC to seamlessly access resources in the peered VPC using hostnames or private IPs.
- **Continuously monitor**: Regularly monitor peering connections to ensure optimal performance and identify any security concerns. Utilize CloudWatch metrics to track traffic flow, latency, and potential errors.

VPC Flow Logs Explained

VPC Flow Logs capture detailed information about IP traffic flowing to and from network interfaces within your VPC. You gain valuable data for network monitoring, troubleshooting, security analysis, and capacity planning.

Best Practices for VPC Flow Logs

- **Select a log destination**: Based on your needs, choose an appropriate destination for storing flow logs. Consider storing them in S3 for long-term archival and analysis or in CloudWatch Logs for near-real-time monitoring and filtering.

- **Set granular logging**: Based on your use case, select the appropriate logging granularity (all traffic, traffic at the VPC or subnet level, or traffic for specific network interfaces). More granular logging provides more detailed insights but also requires more storage space.
- **Integrate for deeper analysis**: Integrate VPC flow logs with AWS analytics services such as Amazon Athena or Amazon Elasticsearch Service to perform in-depth analysis and visualization of network traffic patterns and security events.

Comparison Between VPC Peering, Direct Connect, and Transit Gateway

Table 3.3 compares VPC Peering, Direct Connect, and Transit Gateway, focusing on connectivity, regions, hybrid options, scaling, security, performance, complexity, and use cases:

Feature	VPC Peering	Direct Connect	Transit Gateway
Connectivity Model	VPC to VPC (One-to-One)	VPC to On-premises Network	VPC to VPC (Hub-and-Spoke)
Supported Regions	Same or Different	Not Applicable	Same or Different
Hybrid Connectivity	No	Yes	Yes
Scalability	Limited (complex with many VPCs)	Limited (one connection per VPC)	High (centralized management)
Security	Requires careful route table management	Private, dedicated connection	Centralized security policies
Performance	Low latency, high bandwidth	Dedicated, predictable performance	Optimized routing for multi-VPC communication
Complexity	Simple setup and management	Moderate complexity	More complex setup and management
Use Cases	Sharing resources between VPCs	Connecting to on-premises network	Centralized VPC connectivity at scale

Table 3.3: *Comparison Between VPC Peering, Direct Connect, and Transit Gateway*

Comparison Between Gateway VPC Endpoints and Interface VPC Endpoints

Table 3.4 provides a *comparison between* VPC *Endpoints and Interface Endpoints:*

Feature	Gateway VPC Endpoint	Interface VPC Endpoint
Purpose	Connects your VPC resources to supported AWS services	Connects your VPC resources to services powered by AWS Private Link
Traffic Routing	Traffic never leaves the AWS network	Traffic routed through an ENI within your VPC
Service Access	Supports various AWS services and VPC endpoint services	Primarily supports AWS services and some partner services
Connectivity	Regional (within the same region as your VPC)	Regional (within the same region as your VPC)
Security	Requires route table configuration	Requires security group configuration
Components	VPC endpoint and, optionally security groups	Interface endpoint (collection of ENIs) and security groups
Management	Managed by AWS	Managed by AWS (ENI creation) but user-controlled security groups
Cost	May incur charges for data processing and endpoints	May incur charges for data processing and ENIs

Table 3.4*: Comparison between VPC Endpoints and Interface Endpoints*

Site-to-Site VPN

A Site-to-Site VPN is a virtual private network connecting your on-premises or another cloud network to the AWS VPC. This provides secure communication between your on-premises network and your AWS resources.

Key Features:

- **Secure Connection:** It supports IPsec, which is used to encrypt data that is transferred across the connection.
- **Managed VPN:** The AWS VPN Gateway is configured on your side of the VPC, and an on-premises router or firewall connects to it.
- **Routing Options:** Traffic flow between these two separate networks can be controlled with static routes or dynamic routing using BGP.
- **High Availability:** Support for multiple VPN connections and tunnels enhances its reliability.

Use Cases: These are primarily used to extend on-premises networks, secure data transfers, and hybrid cloud environments into the cloud.

Configuration Overview:

1. Create a VGW in AWS.
2. Now, create a customer gateway that represents the on-premises appliance.

3. Establish the VPN Connection between VGW and CGW.
4. Update Routing Tables to route traffic through the VPN connection.

Client VPN

AWS Client VPN provides secure access to your AWS resources from remote clients over the Internet. This managed VPN service allows users to connect to a VPC from their devices, thus providing security for access to your AWS resources.

Key Features:

- **Secure Remote Access:** SSL/TLS is used to secure the connection between clients and the VPC.
- **Managed VPN Service:** AWS manages all infrastructure for the VPN, such as scaling and high availability.
- **Integration with AWS Directory Service:** It supports authentication of users via AWS Directory Service or any other SAML-based Identity Provider.
- **Access Control:** Security groups and network ACLs allow for fine-grained control over network access.

Use Cases: This should be used when secure access to AWS resources or applications must be provided to remote employees or systems.

Configuration Overview:

1. Create a Client VPN Endpoint in AWS.
2. Configure Authentication and authorization settings.
3. Establish a network association to connect the VPN to your VPC and subnets. Share the client configuration with users to connect to the VPN.

Elastic Load Balancers: A Deep Dive

Load balancers are hardware or software devices that distribute incoming traffic across multiple network servers (backend servers). They act as a traffic director, ensuring no single server gets overloaded while others remain idle. This improves overall application performance, scalability, and fault tolerance.

How Load Balancers Work

- **Client Requests**: A client (example, web browser) sends a request to the load balancer.
- **Traffic Distribution**: The load balancer uses a specific algorithm (example, round robin, least connections) to select a healthy backend server.

- **Forwarding Request**: The load balancer forwards the client's request to the chosen server.
- **Server Response**: The backend server processes the request and responds to the load balancer.
- **Client Response**: The load balancer relays the server's response to the client.

Benefits of Load Balancers

- **Improved Performance**: By distributing traffic, load balancers prevent bottlenecks and ensure faster client response times.
- **Increased Scalability**: You can easily add or remove backend servers to handle fluctuating traffic volumes.
- **Enhanced Availability**: If a server fails, the load balancer automatically redirects traffic to healthy servers, maintaining application uptime.
- **Health Monitoring**: Load balancers continuously monitor the health of backend servers and remove unhealthy ones from the pool.

Elastic Load Balancing

Elastic Load Balancing (ELB) is a cornerstone service within the AWS infrastructure. It acts as a traffic director for your applications, efficiently distributing incoming network traffic across multiple backend targets. This ensures high availability, fault tolerance, and scalability.

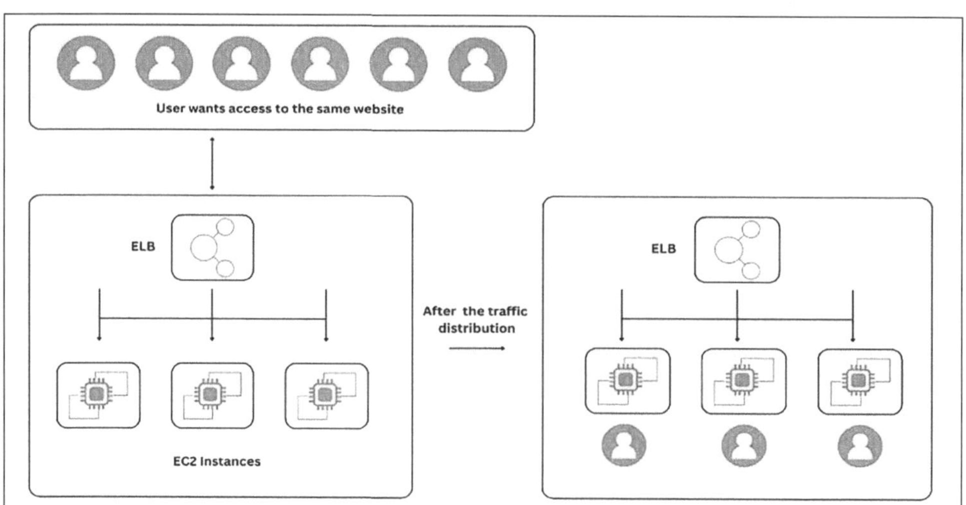

Figure 3.5: *Elastic Load Balancing*

Figure 3.5 explains Elastic Load Balancing. Let us look at its technical breakdown:

ELB Supports Diverse Targets: It can route traffic to various backend resources, including:

- **Amazon EC2 Instances**: These are the workhorses of AWS compute, ideal for traditional web applications.
- **Containers**: These are lightweight and portable environments for modern microservices architectures.
- **IP Addresses**: ELB can integrate with on-premises infrastructure or other cloud resources.

ELB Offers Distribution Strategies: It provides different algorithms to distribute traffic based on your needs:

- **Round Robin**: This is the most basic approach. ELB sends traffic to each healthy target in turn.
- **Weighted Targeting**: You can assign weights to targets based on capacity, ensuring that critical workloads receive more traffic.
- **Most minor Requests**: ELB routes traffic to the target with the currently lowest connection count for optimal distribution.
- **Priority Targeting**: Define a priority order for targets. This ensures mission-critical instances receive traffic first.
- **ELB Continuously Monitors Target Health**: It uses customizable health checks to monitor the health of your backend targets. These checks can be configured to ping specific URLs or ports or leverage application-specific metrics to identify unhealthy targets. ELB only routes traffic to healthy instances, ensuring a seamless user experience.
- **ELB Scales Automatically**: It scales its capacity to adapt to fluctuating traffic patterns, eliminating the need for additional load balancers and simplifying management manually.
- **ELB Leverages Availability Zones**: It can distribute traffic across multiple Availability Zones (AZs) within a region. This redundancy enhances fault tolerance. If an AZ becomes unavailable, traffic seamlessly reroutes to healthy targets in other AZs, maintaining application uptime.

Benefits of Using ELB

- **ELB Delivers High Availability**: By distributing traffic and isolating failures, ELB ensures your application remains accessible even if individual targets experience issues.
- **ELB Enables Scalability**: It automatically handles increased traffic demands, preventing performance bottlenecks and ensuring a smooth user experience.

- **ELB Enhances Fault Tolerance**: Traffic automatically reroutes to healthy targets in case of backend failures, minimizing downtime.
- **ELB Optimizes Costs**: It helps optimize resource utilization by efficiently distributing traffic and reducing the number of required EC2 instances.
- ELB Simplifies Management by automating traffic distribution and health checks, freeing you to focus on application development and maintenance.

Types of Load Balancers

Distributing traffic effectively across your resources is crucial for optimal performance and scalability in the AWS cloud.

Table 3.5 outlines the different types of Load Balancers to help you pick the best fit for your needs:

Feature	Application Load Balancer (ALB)	Network Load Balancer (NLB)	Gateway Load Balancer (GLB)	Classic Load Balancer (CLB)
OSI Layer	Layer 7	Layer 4	Layer 3	Layer 4 & 7
Path-Based Routing	Yes	No	No	No
Host-Based Routing	Yes	No	No	No
TLS Offloading	Yes	Yes	No	Yes
Web Sockets	Yes	No	No	No
Target Types	EC2, IP, Lambda, Containers	EC2, IP, Containers	Virtual Appliances	EC2 only
Health Checks	Detailed, application-level	Basic, transport-level	Monitors appliance health	Basic
Performance	High for HTTP/HTTPS	High for TCP/UDP, low latency	High for virtual appliance management	Basic
Static IP	No	Yes	No	No
Use Case	Advanced routing for HTTP/HTTPS	High performance for TCP/UDP	Managing and scaling virtual appliances	Basic load balancing for simple use cases

Table 3.5: *Types of load balancers*

Key features explained:

- **Path-based routing:** Directs traffic based on the specific path (URL) requested within an application.
- **Host-based routing:** Routes traffic to different applications based on the hostname in the URL.
- **TLS offloading:** Handles the encryption and decryption of TLS/SSL traffic, improving performance by offloading the workload from the application server.

Key Features and Routing Policy Options

- **Domain Registration and Management**: Simplify registering new domains or transferring existing ones directly within Route 53.
- **DNS Health Checks**: Route 53 actively monitors the health of your resources using configurable health checks. This ensures traffic is directed only to healthy endpoints, maximizing application uptime and user experience.
- **Flexible Routing Policies**: Route 53 empowers you to tailor traffic routing strategies based on specific requirements. Here is a breakdown of the available routing policy types:
    - **Simple Routing**: Use simple routing for single resources that fulfill a specific function within your domain (example, a web server, for example.com).
    - **Failover Routing**: Configure Route 53 for active/passive failover scenarios to ensure redundancy and uninterrupted service in case of primary resource failure.
    - **Geolocation Routing**: Route traffic based on your user's geographic location to deliver a more localized user experience and potentially reduce latency.
    - **Geo Proximity Routing:** Refine traffic routing based on user and resource locations. This allows you to optimize traffic flow and shift traffic away from overloaded resources.
    - **Latency Routing**: Distribute traffic across multiple AWS Regions by directing users to the region offering the lowest latency for an improved user experience.
    - **IP-based Routing**: Enable granular control over traffic flow by routing traffic based on the user's IP address origin.
    - **Multivalue Answer Routing**: Route users to a selection of up to eight healthy resources chosen at random. This enhances load balancing and redundancy.

- **Weighted Routing**: Distribute traffic amongst multiple resources according to predefined weightings. This allows you to prioritize specific resources based on capacity or performance.

Domain Name System

The Domain Name System (DNS) is a critical component of the Internet's infrastructure. It translates human-friendly domain names, such as www.example.com, into IP addresses that computers use to identify each other on the network. DNS is akin to a phone book for the Internet, enabling users to access websites using easy-to-remember names instead of numeric addresses.

DNS Fundamentals

At its core, DNS operates through a distributed database that uses a hierarchical structure. The primary elements of DNS include:

- **Domain Names**: Hierarchical names that identify network resources.
- **DNS Records**: Entries in the DNS database that provide information about a domain.
- **Name Servers**: Servers that store DNS records and respond to queries.
- **Resolvers**: Client-side services that query DNS servers to resolve domain names.

The Process of DNS Resolution

1. **User initiates request**: You enter a domain name (example, "google.com") in the address bar of your web browser.
2. **Resolver Queries Local Cache**: The resolver of your device initially searches its local cache for the IP address linked to the domain name. If it is located, the procedure concludes promptly.
3. **Querying Root Nameservers**: If the IP address is not cached, the resolver will send the query to a root nameserver. Root nameservers serve as the initial point of the DNS hierarchy by supplying the locations of top-level domain (TLD) nameservers such as ".com" and ".org."
4. **Adhering to the Hierarchy**: The resolver subsequently contacts the appropriate TLD nameserver depending on the domain's extension (such as ".com" for "google.com"). This server provides the location of the authoritative nameserver for that particular domain.
5. **Reaching the Authoritative Nameserver**: The resolver ultimately requests

information from the authoritative nameserver, which contains the true IP address for the domain name.

6. **Response and Connection**: The authoritative nameserver provides the IP address to the resolver, which stores it in its cache for later use. Your device then uses the IP address to connect with the desired website or service.

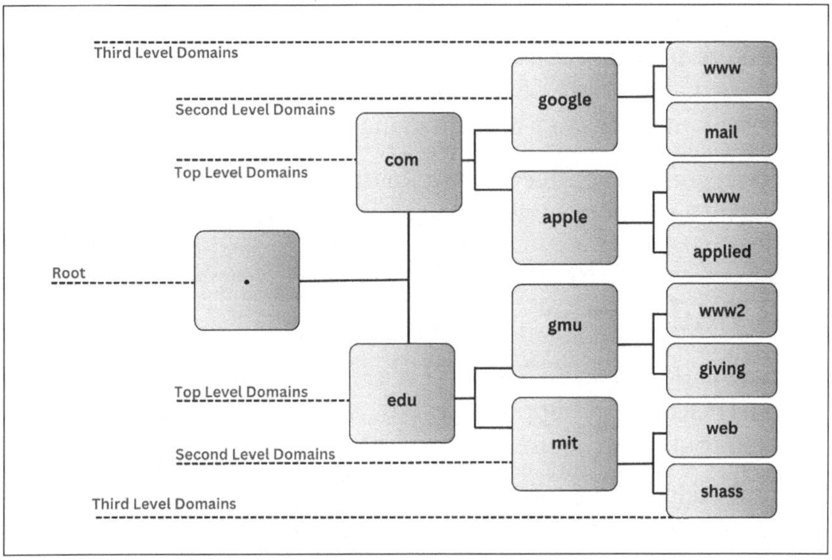

***Figure 3.6**: The hierarchy of Domain Name System*

Figure 3.6 depicts the hierarchical structure of the Domain Name System (DNS). At the very top is the root domain, represented by a single dot (.). Under the root domain are top-level domains (TLDs) such as .com, .org, and .edu. These TLDs categorize websites based on their purpose or origin.

Next comes second-level domains (SLDs), which are specific names chosen by the domain owner. In the image, "Google" and "Apple" are shown as SLDs. Finally, there can be third-level domains, which are subdomains of the SLD.

DNS Record Types

DNS records are various data entries associated with domain names, each serving a unique purpose. The most common types include:

- **A Record**: Maps a domain name to an IPv4 address.
- **AAAA Record**: Maps a domain name to an IPv6 address.
- **CNAME Record**: Canonical Name record that alias one domain name to another.
- **MX Record**: Mail Exchange record specifying mail servers for a domain.

- **TXT Record**: Text records store arbitrary text data, often used for verification purposes.
- **NS Record**: Nameserver records that delegate a domain to a set of DNS servers.

Amazon Route 53: Deep Dive

Amazon Route 53 is a highly available and scalable Domain Name System (DNS) web service designed to provide robust and reliable routing of end users to your internet applications. It can handle high volumes of DNS queries while offering a comprehensive suite of features to enhance your domain management capabilities.

This enhanced response dives deeper into Route 53's functionalities, providing a more tactical, technical, and informative explanation of hosted zones, health checks, and routing policies.

Route 53 Endpoints

High-Level Information Amazon Route 53 is a highly available, scalable domain name system (DNS) web service. It supports several endpoint types and services to resolve DNS queries and route the required traffic to the AWS resources.

- **Inbound Endpoints:** Route DNS queries from on-premises networks into your VPC. It allows systems on-premises to resolve private DNS names inside your VPC. This is very useful in hybrid cloud setups.
- **Outbound Endpoints:** This feature enables routing DNS queries that originated from your VPC to on-premises or external DNS resolvers.

Hosted Zones

Concept: Hosted zones act as virtual containers within Route 53, storing all DNS records (example, A records, CNAMEs, MX records) for a specific domain (example, example.com) and its subdomains. Think of them as virtual folders organizing your DNS entries.

Types

- **Public Hosted Zones**: Manage DNS records that are publicly resolvable on the Internet. These records point users to your website, email servers, and other internet-facing resources.
- **Private Hosted Zones**: Manage DNS records for domains within your Amazon VPC. These records are not publicly accessible and can be used for internal applications and resources requiring resolution within your VPC.

Example: You have a public website (example.com) and an internal application within your VPC. You'd create two hosted zones:

For example, a public-hosted zone has records pointing to your website servers.

A private hosted zone with records directing traffic within your VPC to the internal application.

Technical Considerations

- **DNS Record Types**: Route 53 supports various record types to map domain names to different resources (example, A records for IP addresses, CNAMEs for aliases, and MX records for mail servers). Understanding these record types is crucial for proper DNS configuration.
- **DNS Delegation**: You can delegate subdomains to other Route 53 hosted zones or external DNS providers, providing granular control over DNS management.

Health Checks

- **Purpose**: Health checks are ping mechanisms used by Route 53 to monitor the health of your resources, typically web servers, applications, or other endpoints. They perform periodic checks (configurable intervals such as HTTP GET requests) and report the resource's health status (healthy/unhealthy) to Route 53.
- **Supported Protocols:** Route 53 offers health checks for various protocols:
  - **HTTP/HTTPS**: Checks website/application availability by sending GET requests and verifying successful responses.
  - **TCP**: Checks for open ports on your servers, indicating basic reachability.

Integration with CloudWatch Alarms: You can leverage CloudWatch alarms to trigger health checks. This allows monitoring complex metrics such as CPU utilization or application errors and initiating failover based on alarm state changes.

Benefits

- **Automated Failover**: When a health check fails, Route 53 can automatically route traffic to healthy backup resources, ensuring service continuity and minimizing downtime.
- **Improved Reliability**: Health checks proactively identify potential issues with your resources, allowing for timely intervention before they impact the user experience.

Technical Considerations

- **Health Check Configuration**: Define the protocol, port, path (for HTTP/HTTPS), and desired frequency for the checks.

- **Thresholds and Timeouts**: Set appropriate thresholds for failed checks before marking a resource unhealthy and timeouts for waiting for responses.

Routing Policies: Directing Traffic with Intelligence

Route 53 provides a robust set of routing policies to control how DNS queries are answered and traffic is directed:

- **Simple Routing**: The most basic policy directs all traffic to a single resource record. This is ideal for simple setups with a single web server.
- **Failover Routing**: Implements high availability by directing traffic to a primary resource. If the primary becomes unhealthy (based on health check failures), traffic automatically fails over to a secondary resource. This ensures service continuity even if one resource becomes unavailable.
- **Geolocation Routing**: Routes traffic based on the user's geographic location. This benefits global applications by directing users to the nearest resource for optimal performance. Configuration involves defining geographic regions and associating them with specific resource records.
- **Latency-Based Routing**: Routes traffic to the resource with the lowest latency for the user's location. This optimizes user experience by minimizing delays. Requires integration with Amazon Route 53 Latency endpoints.
- **Weighted Routing:** Distributes traffic across multiple healthy resources based on pre-defined weights. This allows for load balancing in various web servers or applications.
- **Multivalue Answer Routing**: Returns multiple healthy resource records for a single domain name query. Clients (for example, web browsers) can choose the optimal record based on latency or performance.
- **Combining Policies for Complex Scenarios**: Route 53 allows combining these policies to create sophisticated routing configurations. For example, you could implement failover routing with weighted routing as a secondary option, ensuring high availability and load balancing.

Content Delivery: Amazon CloudFront

Amazon CloudFront is a content delivery network (CDN) service that delivers web content, including static and dynamic files, to users with low latency and high transfer speeds. It leverages a global network of edge locations to cache content closer to end users, improving load times and reducing bandwidth costs.

When to Leverage Amazon CloudFront

Amazon CloudFront is a powerful tool for delivering content faster and more efficiently. It is best suited for:

- **Speeding up static content delivery:** CloudFront caches static assets such as images, JavaScript files, and CSS at its global edge locations, significantly reducing the distance data travels and improving website loading times.
- **Streaming video on demand or live video:** CloudFront supports popular streaming formats, such as MPEG DASH and HLS, ensuring smooth playback for viewers worldwide.
- **Boosting website performance:** By offloading static content, CloudFront reduces the load on your origin server, leading to better website performance and scalability.
- **Enhancing security:** CloudFront offers features such as origin access control, WAF integration, and HTTPS support, strengthening your content and user protection.
- **Cutting costs:** By caching frequently accessed content, CloudFront can significantly reduce data transfer costs compared to serving directly from your origin server.

Overall, CloudFront is valuable for improving your web and media content delivery's performance, security, and cost-effectiveness.

CloudFront Distribution Types

- **Web Distributions**: Target static and dynamic web content delivery. They support HTTP, HTTPS, and HTTP/2 protocols and allow you to customize caching behaviors for various file types (HTML, CSS, JavaScript, and images).
- **Streaming Distributions**: These are ideal for delivering live or on-demand media streams. They support protocols such as RTMP (deprecated), HTTP Live Streaming (HLS), and Smooth Streaming. These distributions offer features such as connection switching to ensure uninterrupted playback.
- **Choose the right type**: Before selecting a distribution type, consider the content type (web assets versus media streams), access patterns (static versus dynamic updates), and desired functionalities.

Deep Dive into Request Routing and Caching

Origin: Identify the source of your content, such as an S3 bucket, an EC2 instance, or a custom HTTP server.

Edge Locations:

CloudFront maintains a geographically distributed server network that caches content closer to end users.

Cache Behavior:

Define how CloudFront caches objects based on file type, origin request settings, and time-to-live (TTL) values. To optimize performance and cost, you can customize caching behavior for different content types.

Request Flow:

1. A user requests content from a CloudFront distribution URL.
2. CloudFront routes the request to the closest edge location.
3. If the requested object is cached at the edge location with a valid TTL.
4. CloudFront serves the object directly from the edge location, reducing latency and origin server load.

If the object is not cached or the TTL has expired:

1. CloudFront fetches the object from the origin server.
2. Based on the cache behavior configuration, CloudFront might cache the object at the edge location for future requests.
3. CloudFront delivers the object to the user.

Advanced Caching Features:

- **Origin Shield**: Offload some security tasks (such as SSL/TLS termination) from your origin server, improving its performance.
- **Lambda@Edge** lets you run custom code at the edge location to modify requests or responses before delivery. It enables dynamic content manipulation or security checks closer to users.

Securing CloudFront Distributions:

- **HTTPS with Custom SSL/TLS Certificates**: Configure HTTPS on your distribution and use custom certificates for enhanced trust and encryption. Consider using AWS Certificate Manager for certificate management.
- **Origin Access Identity (OAI):** Restrict direct access to your origin (example, S3 bucket) and allow access only through CloudFront using a secure identity.
- **Restricting Access with Signed URLs and Cookies**: Implement temporary access to specific content by generating signed URLs or cookies that expire after a set time.
- **Web Application Firewalls (WAFs):** Integrate CloudFront with AWS WAF to filter malicious traffic and protect against common web attacks.
- **Security Policies (Security Groups):** Use security groups to control inbound

and outbound traffic to your origin servers, further restricting unauthorized access.

Designing Cost-Optimized Network Architectures:

- **Implement Granular Cache-Control:** Configure cache behavior for different content types with varying access patterns. Set longer TTLs for static assets and shorter TTLs for frequently updated content.
- **Design Custom Error Pages**: Create custom error pages (example, 404 Not Found) to be served from CloudFront, reducing the origin server load for these requests.
- **Leverage Pay-Per-Request Pricing**: Take advantage of CloudFront's pay-per-request pricing model by optimizing content delivery and minimizing unnecessary data transfer.
- **Choose the Right CloudFront Pricing Class**: Select the appropriate pricing class based on your expected usage patterns. Consider using the lower-cost "Use Class Pricing" class for predictable traffic patterns and the "On-Demand Pricing" class for bursty workloads.

Additional Cost Optimization Strategies:

- **Use Amazon Route 53 Geolocation Routing**: Route users to the closest CloudFront edge location based on their geographic location to minimize latency and data transfer costs.
- **Configure CloudFront Origin Failover**: Set up failover to a secondary origin if the primary origin becomes unavailable, ensuring high availability and minimizing downtime.

By demystifying the critical role of Domain Name System (DNS) and content delivery networks (CDNs) in modern web applications, we have established a strong foundation for optimizing performance and reliability. Amazon Route 53 and CloudFront exemplify powerful tools that provide granular control over DNS resolution and content delivery, ensuring efficient, secure, and cost-effective experiences for your users. This control translates to features like:

- **Highly available DNS**: Route 53 offers geographically distributed DNS servers, ensuring fast and reliable routing of user requests to your application's origin, regardless of their location.
- **Traffic management**: Leverage Route 53's traffic routing policies (example, weighted routing, latency-based routing) to distribute user traffic across multiple resources or applications based on specific criteria.
- **Global content delivery**: CloudFront's network of edge locations worldwide caches your static content (example, images, videos, JavaScript) closer to users, minimizing latency and improving load times.

- **Security features**: Route 53 and CloudFront offer robust security options, including support for Secure Sockets Layer/Transport Layer Security (SSL/TLS) encryption and access control mechanisms.

AWS Global Accelerator

AWS Global Accelerator is a service that augments the availability and performance of your applications by operating at the edge, using AWS's global network infrastructure. In this section, an overview of its key features and benefits is shared.

The key features of Global Accelerator are:

- **Global Network Optimization:** With AWS Global Accelerator, user traffic will be routed to the most available endpoint. It takes into consideration health, geography, and routing policies. This reduces latency and improves application performance due to traffic routing via AWS's high-speed, low-latency global network.
- **Static IP Addresses:** It provides two static IP addresses to provide a fixed entry point into your application. This gives a single point of management for IP addresses and makes it easier to reach an application if the underlying infrastructure changes.
- **Health Checks and Failover:** The AWS Global Accelerator continuously checks the health of your application endpoints. When one becomes unhealthy, it quickly shifts the traffic to other healthy endpoints, improving the application's in-service availability.
- **Traffic Dials:** You can set up traffic dials to control the traffic percentages directed to specific endpoints. This is useful during gradual deployment or while you are testing.
- **Integrates with Other AWS Services:** Global Accelerator supports traffic acceleration to various AWS resources, including Amazon EC2, Elastic Load Balancing, and Amazon S3.

Some benefits of using Global Accelerator are:

- **Improved Performance:** Since it deploys the AWS global network, Global Accelerator reduces latency and increases your application's response time performance.
- **High Availability:** Self-failover and health checking ensure your application is always up, even when some endpoints go down.
- **Easy Management:** Static IP addresses with simple configurations make network management easier, and DNS configuration is much simpler.

- **Scalability:** It supports large traffic volumes and scales as your application grows.
- **Improved Security**: Integration with AWS Shield and AWS WAF for protection against DDoS attacks and other security threats.

Some of the applications of Global Accelerator include :

- **Web Applications:** Improved performance and availability for global web applications.
- **Gaming:** Delivering a better gaming experience through lower latency and higher responsiveness.
- **Financial services:** It assures high availability and low latency for financial transactions and services.
- **Media and entertainment:** Low latency and reduced buffering provide high-quality streaming experiences across media and entertainment applications.

AWS Global Accelerator helps in improving performance, availability, and management of applications globally.

Conclusion

By grasping the basics of networking in AWS, which encompasses the OSI model, essential protocols, and fundamental concepts such as IP addresses and subnetting, you have established the foundation for building secure and expandable cloud environments.

With a thorough understanding of VPCs, subnets, security groups, and gateway options, you can securely manage and separate your cloud resources. Moreover, utilizing advanced functionalities such as VPC peering, Direct Connect, and Transit Gateway enables smooth communication between various VPCs and on-premises networks.

In addition, knowing about DNS and load balancing services such as Route 53 and CloudFront helps to ensure that your applications can be easily accessed and are always available to your users. You can ensure your network architecture is efficient and budget-friendly by implementing cost optimization techniques.

The next chapter explores cloud storage on AWS. You will examine different storage choices, such as S3 and EBS, each with distinct features and purposes. You will also be educated on strategies for managing the data lifecycle and utilizing these services to store and control your data in the cloud efficiently.

Multiple Choice Questions

1. At which OSI model layer are the connections between applications established, managed, and terminated?
    a. Assertion about the Data Link Layer
    b. Assertion about the Transport Layer
    c. Assertion about the Session Layer
    d. Assertion about the Application Layer
2. How many layers can be found in the OSI model?
    a. 5
    b. 6
    c. 7
    d. 8
3. Which protocol operates at the Transport layer of the OSI model?
    a. IP
    b. TCP
    c. DNS
    d. HTTP
4. Which of the following is a faster data transmission but less reliable connectionless protocol?
    a. TCP
    b. UDP
    c. HTTP
    d. FTP
5. Which AWS load balancer is ideal for working with HTTP/HTTPS traffic?
    a. Application Load Balancer (ALB)
    b. Network Load Balancer (NLB)
    c. Classic Load Balancer (CLB)
    d. Gateway Load Balancer (GWLB)

6. Which AWS service is for DNS management?
    a. CloudFront
    b. Route 53
    c. Elastic Beanstalk
    d. Lambda
7. What kind of routing method in Route 53 can route the traffic from the nearest region of the user accessing the application?
    a. Weighted Routing
    b. Geolocation Routing
    c. Latency-Based Routing
    d. Failover Routing
8. What Route 53 feature enables high availability by individually routing users to any healthy endpoint?
    a. Route 53 Resolver
    b. Health Checks
    c. DNSSEC
    d. Traffic Flow
9. What is the primary role of Amazon CloudFront?
    a. Database services management
    b. DNS management
    c. Low latency content delivery
    d. Serverless function running
10. How does CloudFront enhance the performance of the content delivery?
    a. By caching content at the edge locations all around the world
    b. By storing data on Amazon S3
    c. By auto-encrypting all the content
    d. By processing all requests with EC2 instances

Answers

1. c
2. c
3. b
4. b
5. a
6. b
7. c
8. b
9. c
10. b

References

- https://docs.aws.amazon.com/vpc/latest/userguide/VPC_Security.html
- https://docs.aws.amazon.com/vpc/latest/userguide/VPC_Subnets.html#VPC_Sizing
- https://docs.aws.amazon.com/vpc/latest/userguide/VPC_Scenario3.html
- https://www.geeksforgeeks.org/open-systems-interconnection-model-osi/
- https://docs.aws.amazon.com/Route53/latest/DeveloperGuide/routing-policy.html
- https://cloudacademy.com/course/introduction-to-amazon-web-services-aws/aws-networking-1/
- https://cloudacademy.com/course/networking-fundamentals-of-aws-for-cloud-practitioner/architectural-essentials-1/
- https://www.geeksforgeeks.org/aws-cloudfront/
- https://medium.com/multi-cloud-networking-netdevops/aws-vpc-demystified-best-practices-for-effective-design-d68a0cb22388
- https://k21academy.com/amazon-web-services/aws-elastic-load-balancing-overview-and-types/
- https://aws.amazon.com/compare/the-difference-between-the-difference-between-application-network-and-gateway-load-balancing/

Chapter 4
Cloud Storage

Introduction

An architect is entrusted with creating a spectacular building. They ensure that every aspect is carefully planned, from the foundation's solidity to the facade's fine features. However, their blueprint remains just an idea without the crucial element–the building materials. Data is the architect's blueprint in the digital age, and cloud storage is the primary material used in construction.

Our digital creations, including websites, programs, and even personal files, need a safe and dependable place to live, just as a skyscraper cannot exist without steel, concrete, and glass. This is where cloud storage comes in. It provides the foundation for all our digital endeavors, offering a vast and scalable repository to house our ever-growing data.

This chapter explores the exciting realm of cloud storage offered by AWS. We will look at all possibilities, including affordable object storage for large datasets and high-performance block storage for mission-critical applications. We will provide the information you need to select the best storage option for your requirements, guaranteeing that your digital works of art have a safe and dependable place in the cloud. Therefore, knowing cloud storage is essential to developing reliable and scalable solutions in the always-changing digital ecosystem, regardless of experience level with cloud architecture.

Structure

In this chapter, we will cover the following topics:

- Block Storage
  - Amazon Elastic Block Store (EBS)
- File Storage
  - Amazon Elastic File System (EFS)
  - Amazon FSx

- Object Storage
    - Amazon Simple Storage Service (S3)
- Storage Gateways
- Snowball
- Snowcone
- Snowmobile
- AWS Backup
- Cost Optimization Techniques

The Three Types of Cloud Storage: A Comprehensive Introduction

Imagine a bustling digital kingdom where data reigns supreme. To keep this kingdom organized and accessible, we rely on robust storage solutions. Just as a magnificent kingdom requires a strong foundation, efficient cloud storage is the bedrock for all our digital endeavors.

In this realm, three primary storage options emerge as the "Three Pillars of Cloud Storage": block, file, and object storage. Each serves a distinct purpose and offers unique advantages for specific data needs. Understanding these pillars is the key to building a secure and scalable foundation for your cloud applications.

Block Storage: The Bedrock of Performance

Block storage acts as the virtualized equivalent of a traditional hard drive. Data is stored in uniformly sized blocks, offering persistent and high-performance storage ideal for mission-critical applications such as databases and virtual machines. Think of it as the solid foundation upon which virtual machines are built, providing them with the raw storage space they need to function flawlessly.

File Storage: Collaboration Made Easy

File storage is similar to your desktop computer's well-known file system architecture. Its advantage over your desktop system is that it can be easily made available over the network, allowing file sharing on multiple computers or servers. The ability to create folders, subfolders, and files makes collaboration and organization simple. A shared file system is ideal for collaboration and shared applications since it allows several users to view and edit data. Envision a centralized digital filing cabinet open to all team members, promoting smooth project collaboration.

Object Storage: The King of Scalability and Cost-Effectiveness

Object storage excels when handling enormous volumes of unstructured data, such as backups, logs, and media files. In contrast to the organized blocks seen in block storage, each piece of data in object storage is treated as a distinct object with a unique identity. This adaptable strategy offers remarkable scalability and financial effectiveness. Imagine a huge, constantly growing warehouse where every information item is appropriately tagged and easily accessible, guaranteeing effective storage for your rapidly expanding digital library.

Storage Option	Use Cases	Data Format	Performance	Cost	Limitations
Block Storage (example, AWS EBS)	Databases, transactional applications, virtual machines	Structured data in blocks of equal size	High performance for frequent data access	Higher cost per GB	High cost per GB, complex management
File Storage (example, AWS EFS)	File sharing, collaboration, and applications requiring a traditional file system interface	Semi-structured data in a hierarchical file system	Lower performance than block storage	Varies depending on access frequency	Higher cost than object storage, complexity for scaling
Object Storage (example, AWS S3)	Backups, archives, media files, big data lakes	Unstructured data	Lower performance than block storage	Lower cost per GB, ideal for large data sets	Limited file system access, potential retrieval fees

Table 4.1: *Comparison Chart of the Three Primary Cloud Storage Solutions*

Choosing the Right Pillar

The optimal storage solution depends on your specific needs. Block storage excels in high-performance scenarios, file storage fosters collaboration, and object storage reigns supreme in scalability and cost-effectiveness for unstructured data. By understanding the strengths of each pillar, you can make informed decisions about where to store your valuable digital assets, ensuring optimal performance, collaboration, and cost management within your cloud kingdom.

This chapter delves deeper into each storage type, exploring its functionalities, use cases, and best practices. We will equip you with the knowledge to choose the proper storage solution for your cloud applications, ensuring your digital creations have a secure and reliable home in the cloud. So, whether you are a seasoned architect or a budding cloud enthusiast, this journey will empower you to build robust and scalable storage solutions for a thriving digital future!

Block Storage Deep Dive: Amazon EBS

Selecting an appropriate storage solution is critical to guaranteeing optimal performance and security in the constantly changing world of cloud storage, where data is king. Let us introduce you to the Amazon Elastic Block Store (EBS), the dominant force in persistent block storage in the extensive AWS ecosystem. This part explores the complex features of EBS, enabling you to decide on the best way to store your important data.

Imagine your high-performance cloud applications as vital outposts within the kingdom. Just as these outposts, like bustling marketplaces or strategic fortresses, demand dependable resources to thrive, similarly, your applications rely on robust storage solutions to function flawlessly. Your virtual machines rely on EBS as a solid foundation, giving them the high-performance, long-lasting storage capacity required to run as efficiently as possible. By starting this in-depth exploration, you will thoroughly grasp EBS's capabilities, limitations, and best practices. With this newfound understanding, you can choose the best storage option for your particular requirements, ensuring that your mission-critical apps run without a hitch and protecting your priceless data inside the haven of the AWS cloud.

Beyond the Instance: EBS versus Instance Store

Amazon Elastic Block Store (EBS) volumes offer a robust solution for persistent storage within the AWS cloud. This means your data remains secure and accessible even when you stop, reboot, or terminate your EC2 instances. EBS acts as a reliable repository for your valuable information, independent of the virtual machine it is attached to. This allows you to access your data from any compatible instance within the AWS environment, fostering flexibility and uninterrupted workflows. Within cloud storage solutions, two primary options emerge: EBS volumes and instance stores. EBS volumes, as discussed above, provide persistent storage, ensuring data security and accessibility beyond the lifespan of an individual EC2 instance.

On the other hand, instance stores function as temporary disks directly attached to EC2 instances. Similar to a notepad specific to a single meeting, data stored on instance stores disappears upon instance termination. This impermanence makes them suitable for temporary data or specific use cases where immediate availability outweighs long-term storage needs. Unlike the ephemeral storage offered by instance stores, EBS volumes provide persistent storage independent of the instance lifecycle. This ensures data security and accessibility even when you stop, reboot, or terminate your EC2 instances. Imagine the instance store as a notepad specific to a single meeting; its contents disappear once the meeting ends. In contrast, EBS acts like a secure external hard drive; preserving your data after the meeting allows you to access it from any compatible instance.

Feature	**Elastic Block Store (EBS)**	**Instance Store**
Persistence	Persistent	Ephemeral
Data Retention	Data remains after instance stop/reboot/termination	Data is lost after instance stop/hibernation/termination
Use Case	Ideal for critical data, applications requiring persistent storage	Suitable for temporary data, workloads requiring low latency
Analogy	External hard drive	Notepad specific to a meeting
Accessibility	Accessible from any compatible EC2 instance	Accessible only from the instance it is attached to

***Table 4.2**: Comparison between Elastic Block Store (EBS) and Instance Store*

A Spectrum of Options: EBS Volume Types

EBS offers diverse volume types, each catering to specific performance and cost requirements. It is essential to comprehend these choices to choose the best storage option for your applications. The main actors are broken down as follows:

- **General Purpose (GP2):** An economical and balanced solution with minimal input/output per second needs that works well for a variety of workloads, such as databases and development environments.
- **IOPS Provisioned (PIOPS):** PIOPS volumes allow you to reserve a specific amount of IOPS, ensuring steady response times for applications such as real-time analytics and high-performance databases. Applications requiring reliable and constant performance are the ones for which they are intended. Imagine a highway with designated lanes for high-priority traffic; PIOPS volumes provide dedicated IOPS lanes for your applications, guaranteeing smooth operation.
- **Magnetic (HDD):** Cost-optimized for storing large datasets that require infrequent access, such as backups and archives. Imagine a large, cost-effective warehouse where rarely-accessed data is kept.
- **Solid State Drives (SSD):** Perfect for high-performance databases, real-time apps, boot volumes, and applications requiring low latency and fast throughput.

Imagine working with your apps in a data center where lightning-fast access and high-speed processing guarantee optimal performance.

Finding the Perfect Fit: Use Cases and Capabilities

The optimal EBS volume type hinges on your specific needs. Here is a glimpse into common use cases for each type:

- **GP2:** Ideal for development and test environments, web servers with moderate traffic, and relational databases with predictable workloads.
- **PIOPS:** Excellent use case for mission-critical applications that require consistent performance, such as high-performance computing (HPC), real-time analytics platforms, and production databases.
- **Magnetic (HDD):** Ideal where cost-effectiveness is critical, such as for data backups, archives, and rarely accessed log files.
- **SSD:** Perfect for high-performance databases, virtual desktops, boot volumes, and real-time applications where quick data access and minimal latency are essential.

Recognizing Your Limits: Best Practices and Consideration

While EBS offers exceptional flexibility, understanding its limitations empowers you to optimize performance and cost-effectiveness:

- **IOPS Constraints:** Provisioned IOPS volumes are allocated the maximum IOPS capacity. Thoroughly consider the IOPS requirements for your workload to avoid overprovisioning and unnecessary spending.
- **Volume Size Limitations:** EBS volumes have a maximum size depending on the kind of volume. Plan your storage needs accordingly to avoid fragmentation and potential performance bottlenecks.
- **Monitoring and Scaling:** Utilize CloudWatch to monitor volume performance and identify potential bottlenecks. You can scale provisioned IOPS volumes up or down dynamically to match your workload's evolving needs.

Snapshots: Preserving the Present for a Safe Tomorrow

Imagine having a way to rewind time for your EBS volume. Snapshots act as that rewind button, creating a copy of your data at a specific moment. This lets you restore your volume to a previous healthy state if something goes wrong, such as an accidental deletion or file corruption. Think of it as a digital safety net, similar to how a photograph captures a specific moment.

Starting Small, Scaling Smart: Optimization Strategies

This section offers strategies to optimize your cloud storage costs. To scale efficiently, it is recommended that you start with the right volume size and use CloudWatch for performance monitoring.

- **Right-size Your Volumes:** Begin with a volume size that adequately accommodates your initial needs. EBS allows for volume expansion, so avoid over-provisioning upfront.
- **Leverage Performance Monitoring:** Utilize CloudWatch to identify potential performance issues proactively. This allows you to optimize instance types, adjust IOPS provisioning, or implement vertical scaling (adding more CPU or memory to your instance) as needed.
- **Embrace Snapshots:** Create snapshots regularly for disaster recovery purposes. However, lifecycle management policies should be implemented to automate snapshot deletion and avoid unnecessary storage costs for obsolete backups.

Beyond the Basics: Advanced Considerations

Upgrading EBS volumes involves creating a larger volume and migrating your data using tools like AWS Data Migration Service. This process can introduce downtime, especially for mission-critical applications. To minimize disruption, consider these strategies:

- **EBS Snapshots for Volume Upgrades:** Leverage EBS snapshots as an upgrade staging ground. Create a snapshot of your current volume, then expand the new volume's size. Restore the snapshot data to the newly expanded volume. This approach minimizes downtime as the application can continue running from the original volume while the data transfer occurs in the background. Once the migration is complete, you can switch the instance to the upgraded volume with minimal interruption.
- **Elastic Volume Replication for High Availability:** For mission-critical applications requiring maximum uptime, explore Elastic Volume Replication. This service creates an exact copy of your EBS volume in another Availability Zone, enabling automatic failover in case of a zone outage. Upgrades can then be performed on the replicated volume without impacting the primary production instance.

Cost Optimization: A Balancing Act

While EBS offers robust features, cost management remains a crucial consideration. Here are some strategies to keep your EBS bill in check:

- **Utilize the Right Volume Type:** Select the most cost-effective EBS volume type that meets your performance requirements. Opt for magnetic volumes for cold storage and reserve higher-performance options such as provisioned IOPS or SSDs for mission-critical workloads.
- **Automate Lifecycle Management:** Implement automated lifecycle management policies for EBS snapshots. Retain backups based on compliance or recovery needs for a designated period, and then automatically delete older snapshots to avoid unnecessary storage charges.
- **Stop versus Terminate:** When instances are not in use, consider stopping them instead of terminating them. Stopped instances retain their EBS volumes, allowing you to incur minimal charges while preserving your data for future usage.

By being well-informed about these intricate details of EBS, you can choose the best block storage for your cloud apps. This gives you the flexibility to fully utilize its scalability, performance, and security, guaranteeing that your data is safe, readily available, and tailored to your changing cloud requirements.

Demystifying File Storage in AWS: EFS versus FSx

Imagine working on projects as a team and easily sharing and accessing files from a single digital filing cabinet. This dream becomes a reality with the power of file storage on AWS. Unlike the structured blocks of block storage, file storage offers a more intuitive and user-friendly approach to data organization.

This section serves as a roadmap as you explore the world of AWS file storage options. We will examine the internal mechanisms of Amazon Elastic File System (EFS) and Amazon FSx, the two main choices. Knowing their distinct advantages and features, you can choose the best fit for your file-based data requirements in the AWS cloud. With this increased understanding, team cooperation will be streamlined, and you'll be able to handle and access your data more effectively. So grab a seat, because we are about to embark on a voyage to discover AWS file storage's full potential!

Beyond the Blocks: A Familiar Structure

Unlike block storage, which handles data like Lego bricks, file storage provides a recognizable file system structure. Consider files, folders, and subfolders like you would on a home computer. This intuitive organization makes sharing, accessing, and managing your data easy, making it perfect for collaborative environments and applications that rely on files.

EFS versus FSx: Choosing Your Champion

While both EFS and FSx cater to file storage within AWS, they have distinct personalities:

- **Amazon EFS:** The "scale-up superhero." EFS is ideal for applications that need a shared file system accessible by multiple EC2 instances. It automatically scales storage as data grows, making it a cost-effective choice for web apps, content repositories, and development environments with fluctuating storage demands.
- **Amazon FSx:** The "performance powerhouse." FSx offers a broader range of file system options, catering to specific performance needs. It provides pre-configured file systems compatible with popular protocols such as Windows File Server (SMB) and Network File System (NFS), allowing smooth integration with your existing setups. FSx shines for applications demanding high performance, strict access controls, or compatibility with specific file system protocols.

Picking the Perfect Tool

Selecting between EFS and FSx boils down to your specific requirements. Here are some key factors to consider:

- **Scalability:** If you need a file system that grows with you, EFS is your champion.
- **Performance:** FSx offers optimized performance options when lightning-fast speeds are required.
- **Compatibility:** If your application relies on a specific file system protocol, FSx provides pre-configured options for seamless integration.
- **Cost:** EFS is generally more cost-effective for basic needs, while FSx offers additional features at a slightly higher price point.

Safeguarding Your Data

Both EFS and FSx offer built-in protection for your valuable data:

- **EFS Backups:** Use AWS Backup to plan and automate EFS file system backups. This guarantees that you can restore individual files or entire file systems in case of data corruption or inadvertent deletion.
- **FSx Snapshots and Backups:** FSx offers built-in snapshot functionality depending on the file system type. Additionally, some FSx options integrate with AWS Backup for comprehensive data protection strategies.

Knowing the subtle differences between EFS and FSx will enable you to make well-informed judgments regarding file storage in your AWS environment. Your cloud apps will have a strong foundation, streamlined collaboration, and effective data management.

Conquering the Content Cavern: Mastering Object Storage with Amazon S3

Imagine an enormous cave filled to the brim with ancient and modern riches. This cave is a metaphor for the digital age's ever-expanding data space. Social media posts, financial records, scientific discoveries, and more contribute to this ever-growing collection. But unlike a traditional library with its meticulously categorized shelves, this cavern holds a vast, unstructured sea of information.

Here is where Amazon S3, the Simple Storage Service, emerges as your spelunker's guide. Unlike block storage, which functions like a well-organized vault ideal for precious artifacts requiring immediate access or file storage, akin to a filing cabinet facilitating collaboration on specific documents, S3 offers a different approach. It acts as a colossal warehouse, perfectly suited for storing and managing this massive, unstructured data in a scalable and cost-effective manner.

This section serves as your map to navigate the depths of the S3 cavern. By exploring its functionalities, you will be able to master object storage, adeptly managing and accessing your digital treasures within the vast expanse of the AWS cloud.

A Spectrum of Storage Options: Unveiling S3 Storage Classes

Think of S3 as your digital warehouse. It offers a spectrum of storage options tailored to your specific data needs. Here is a breakdown of the key players in this storage vault:

- **S3 Standard:** The "go-to" option for frequently accessed data, such as website content, application logs, or regularly downloaded backups. Think of it as the well-lit area of your warehouse where you can quickly and easily get what you need.
- **S3 Standard-Infrequent Access (S3 Standard-IA):** Perfect for data that is not in constant use but still needs occasional retrieval. Think of it as a section with slightly lower lighting (and access fees), but the items are still readily available when needed.
- **S3 Glacier Instant Retrieval:** This system provides safe storage for information that must be retrieved in hours or minutes. Imagine a temperature-regulated space where your seldom-used stuff is methodically arranged to guarantee prompt retrieval when needed.

- **S3 Glacier Flexible Retrieval:** The most budget-friendly option for data, with retrieval times ranging from hours to days. This acts like a remote storage facility for rarely accessed information, but retrieval might take longer than Instant Retrieval.
- **S3 Glacier Deep Archive:** The ultimate choice for long-term archival needs, like historical data. It boasts the lowest storage costs but retrieval times can range from 12 to 48 hours. It is a secure vault for information you would not need immediately, offering the most economical storage solution.

Automating Efficiency: S3 Lifecycle Management

But managing a vast warehouse can be overwhelming! That is where S3 Lifecycle Management comes in. This feature automates the movement of your data between storage classes based on your defined rules. For example, you can set a rule to automatically move any object in the "Standard" class to "S3 Standard-IA" after 30 days of inactivity. This helps you optimize storage costs for data that is infrequently accessed.

Safeguarding Your Data: S3 Replication and Versioning

Peace of mind is paramount, especially when it comes to your data. Here are two functionalities that ensure your data's safety:

- **S3 Replication:** You can create copies of your S3 buckets in different zones or regions. This ensures your data remains readily available from the replicated bucket, even if an outage occurs in one area.
- **S3 Versioning:** S3 also protects your data history. With S3 Versioning enabled, every version of an object you upload is saved. This allows you to roll back to a previous version if an accidental deletion or modification occurs. Imagine having a complete history of your files, similar to a version control system developers use!

Optimizing Performance: S3 Transfer Acceleration

Transferring massive datasets can feel like a chore. S3 Transfer Acceleration utilizes a global network to optimize and speed up data transfers. This significantly reduces upload times, especially for large files or transfers from faraway locations.

Serving Up Simplicity: S3 Static Website Hosting

Did you know S3 can even host websites? You can host basic websites straight from S3 by installing static website hosting on an S3 bucket. This provides a scalable and affordable website option without the need for intricate server-side coding.

You will become an expert in the data storage industry by using S3's storage classes, replication, versioning, transfer acceleration, and static website hosting features. You will be ready to use the constantly growing AWS cloud environment to manage, protect, and access your data efficiently.

Venturing Beyond the Cavern: Unveiling Additional Storage Solutions in the AWS Cloud

Although S3 is undoubtedly the industry leader in object storage on the AWS platform, its capabilities are not isolated. The AWS cloud offers a wide range of storage options, each painstakingly designed to meet particular needs for data storage. This section explores three more choices that work in unison with your S3 plan, taking you outside the realm of S3. Gaining knowledge of these supplementary services will enable you to design a comprehensive data storage architecture that meets the particular requirements of your constantly changing digital environment. The following three alternatives can be easily incorporated into your S3 strategy:

Storage Gateway: Your Hybrid Cloud Bridge

Imagine you have a data center brimming with valuable information, yet you also crave the scalability and flexibility of the AWS cloud. Storage Gateway is your hybrid cloud bridge, seamlessly connecting your on-premises storage to S3. This allows you to leverage the power of cloud storage for specific datasets while keeping sensitive information or frequently accessed data locally.

Storage Gateway comes in various flavors, each tailored to different use cases:

- **Storage Gateway for File Cache:** Ideal for caching frequently accessed S3 data locally, improving performance for on-premises applications.
- **Storage Gateway for Tape Archive:** Bridges the gap between on-premises tape libraries and S3 Glacier, offering a cost-effective solution for long-term archival needs.
- **Storage Gateway for Volume Gateway:** Enables low-latency access to S3

volumes from on-premises applications, treating cloud storage like locally attached disks.

Snowball: Edge Computing for Massive Data Transfers

Data transport restrictions can be a hindrance when working with enormous datasets. Snowball is your high-speed data transfer appliance, delivered directly to your location. All you have to do is put your data onto the Snowball device, send it back to AWS securely, and it transfers to S3 without any problems. With this ideal approach, large datasets can be sent from far-off places or surroundings with little bandwidth.

Snowmobile: Exabyte-Scale Data Migration

Snowmobile emerges as your champion for truly massive data migrations (think exabytes). Imagine a colossal mobile data truck designed for secure and rapid data transfer to AWS. Snowmobile offers a faster and more cost-effective alternative to traditional methods for migrating petabytes of data to the AWS cloud.

Snowcone: Micro-Sized Data Transfer on the Edge

Snowcone is the most recent addition to the AWS Snow family. It caters to edge computing environments with limited space and data transfer requirements. This compact, portable device simplifies secure data collection and transfer from edge locations to S3. It is ideal for scenarios where traditional data transfer methods are impractical due to size or resource constraints.

By understanding these additional storage options, you can craft a comprehensive data storage strategy that leverages each service's strengths. This empowers you to seamlessly integrate on-premises storage with the cloud, tackle massive data transfers, and securely collect and migrate data from edge environments, all within the robust and scalable AWS ecosystem.

Fortifying Your Data: Unveiling AWS Backup and Cross-Storage Protection

The digital world thrives on the constant creation and manipulation of data. But safeguarding this valuable information is paramount. This is where AWS Backup comes into play like a shining knight. This managed service helps you centralize and streamline the backup procedure for your AWS storage infrastructure, protecting your data from outside threats.

The All-Encompassing Shield: Backup Coverage Across Storage Options

One of the key strengths of AWS Backup lies in its versatility. It transcends the limitations of siloed solutions, offering comprehensive backup coverage for a variety of storage services within the AWS cloud:

Block Storage Shield: Protecting Amazon EBS

AWS Backup protects the information on your volumes in the Amazon Elastic Block Store (EBS). You can manually start on-demand backups and schedule automated snapshots to be taken at predetermined intervals. This guarantees a quickly available recovery point in the event of hardware failure, inadvertent data erasure, or other unanticipated events.

File Storage Security: Guarding Amazon EFS

AWS Backup provides another layer of protection for your data on Amazon Elastic File System (EFS). Thanks to automated Backups, your EFS file system's additions and alterations are recorded and safely stored. This allows you to restore your file system to a certain point if needed.

Object Storage Security: Safeguarding Your S3 Treasure Trove

Consider your S3 buckets to be your object storage strategy's gold mine. AWS Backup provides an essential line of defense to guarantee the security of these priceless assets. With AWS Backup, you can create point-in-time backups of your S3 buckets so that you can restore your data to a particular version in an emergency. This covers data corruption recovery from ransomware attacks, inadvertent deletions, and other incidents. You can feel secure knowing that your S3 assets are protected and recoverable with AWS Backup, even in the face of possible threats.

Beyond Individual Services: Cross-Storage Backup Strategies

While protecting individual storage services is crucial, a comprehensive data protection strategy goes beyond isolated solutions. AWS Backup empowers you to create cross-storage backup policies, safeguarding your data across different storage services within your AWS environment. This holistic approach offers several advantages:

- **Streamlined Management**

  AWS Backup streamlines your data protection procedures by handling backups from several storage providers under one roof. Instead of juggling several tools for each service, you can configure access limits, retention policies, and backup schedules from a single console.

- **Enhanced Disaster Recovery**

  A strong basis for disaster recovery is offered by cross-storage backups. You can rapidly and effectively restore your data and apps by using backups kept in a separate storage provider or region in the case of a service outage or regional disruption.

- **Improved Compliance**

  Many industries have strict data protection regulations. By implementing cross-storage backups, you can demonstrate a commitment to data security and compliance with relevant regulations.

With its comprehensive coverage across various storage services and its ability to facilitate cross-storage backup strategies, AWS Backup empowers you to construct a unified fortress for your data within the AWS cloud. This centralized approach streamlines management, bolsters disaster recovery capabilities, and enhances compliance, ensuring your valuable information remains protected and readily recoverable in an ever-changing digital landscape.

Unlocking Cost-Effective Data Storage on AWS: Understanding Best Practices

With the ever-growing amount of data businesses generate, efficient storage solutions are critical for data analysis, app development, backups, and regulations. Cloud storage can be expensive, but luckily, Amazon Web Services (AWS) offers a variety of features and storage options. Understanding your data and selecting the right AWS service and storage tier can significantly reduce storage costs without sacrificing security, scalability, or performance. This ensures your data remains secure and accessible while saving you money. This manual covers essential recommended practices for using the AWS storage landscape and making informed decisions for cost-effective data storage on AWS. Here is a breakdown of key practices to consider:

Selecting the Right AWS Storage Service

It is important to pick the right AWS service for your cloud storage needs. Use EBS for frequent data access, S3 for massive backups, and EFS for user-friendly file sharing.

- **Amazon Elastic Block Store (EBS):** This storage solution is perfect for applications (such as virtual machines and databases) that need frequent access to high-performance data. Although it is more expensive per gigabyte, it provides good IOPS and throughput.
- **Amazon Simple Storage Service (S3):** Highly suitable for storing enormous amounts of unstructured data, including media files, backups, and archives. S3 provides unparalleled scalability and cost for these kinds of use scenarios. It offers various storage classes with varying costs and access speeds.
- **Amazon Elastic File System (EFS):** Ideal for file sharing and collaboration, offering a recognizable file system interface. However, despite being more user-friendly, EFS is more expensive than S3 for data that is not regularly accessed.

Optimizing Storage Costs Within AWS Services

Let us look at key strategies for optimizing storage costs within AWS services:

- **Right-size EBS Volumes:** Analyze workload requirements and provision the appropriate EBS volume size to avoid over-provisioning storage.
- **Utilize EBS General Purpose (GP3) Volumes:** Consider migrating from magnetic (GP2) to SSD-based (GP3) volumes for improved performance and potentially lower costs due to their higher IOPS and throughput compared to GP2 volumes.
- **Choose the Right S3 Storage Class:** AWS S3 offers a variety of storage classes, each with varying costs and access patterns:
    - **S3 Standard**: Ideal for frequently accessed data.
    - **S3 Intelligent-Tiering**: Preserves speed for commonly requested data while optimizing costs by automatically relocating data between access levels based on usage.
    - **S3 Glacier and S3 Glacier Deep Archive**: Extremely affordable solutions for long-term archival needs, with retrieval times varying from hours to days.
- **Put S3 Lifecycle Rules into Practice:** Transfer data across S3 storage classes automatically, following preset retention policies and access patterns. This ensures cost-effective data storage.
- **Enable EFS Infrequent Access with Lifecycle Management:** This feature automatically migrates infrequently accessed data to a significantly lower storage tier within EFS, reducing costs while maintaining accessibility.

Advanced Cost Optimization Techniques on AWS

Some advanced cost optimization techniques in AWS include:

- **AWS Cost Explorer:** Use this tool to learn more about your storage consumption habits and spot areas where you might save money.
- **Reserved Instances (RIs) on Amazon for EBS:** Buying EBS RIs can provide significant savings over on-demand pricing for predictable workloads.
- **Data Transfer Optimization:** To reduce network transfer costs, consider utilizing AWS Snowball or AWS Snowmobile data transfer services for large-scale migrations.
- **Storage Gateway:** By locally caching frequently requested data, AWS Storage Gateway can help you seamlessly combine on-premises storage with cloud storage and lower egress costs.

Remember: Cost optimization is an ongoing process. Regularly monitor your storage usage with AWS CloudWatch and leverage cost management tools such as AWS Cost Explorer to identify opportunities for further optimization and cost reduction.

Conclusion

This chapter examines Amazon Web Services (AWS) wide range of cloud storage options. It delves into block, file, and object storage–the three main types of storage–and explains their uses and features. Block storage (example, Amazon EBS) acts like a well-organized vault, ideal for frequently accessed data requiring high performance, such as virtual machine disks. File storage solutions (example, EFS, FSx) act as a digital filing cabinet, facilitating document collaboration. While object storage (example, Amazon S3) relates to a huge warehouse aptly suited to store and manage massive amounts of unstructured data, such as backups, archives, and video files. It offers various storage classes with varying costs and access speeds.

Focusing on S3, the chapter delves into its functionalities, such as lifecycle management for automated cost optimization and versioning for data protection. It also explores additional features like S3 Transfer Acceleration for faster data transfers and static website hosting for simple website deployment directly from S3 buckets.

The chapter ventures beyond S3 to discuss other storage solutions that complement your AWS cloud storage strategy. These are: Storage Gateway–a hybrid cloud bridge seamlessly connecting on-premises storage to S3 and the AWS Snow Family (Snowball, Snowmobile, Snowcone)–facilitates high-speed data transfer appliances for large datasets or edge computing environments.

Data protection is paramount, and the chapter explores AWS Backup, a service that centralizes backups for various AWS storage options such as EBS, EFS, and S3. It also highlights the benefits of cross-storage backup strategies for enhanced disaster recovery and compliance.

Finally, the chapter emphasizes cost-effective storage practices. It provides a breakdown of key considerations for choosing the right AWS storage service and optimizing storage costs within those services. This includes selecting the appropriate storage class for your data access needs and leveraging lifecycle management rules for automatic data movement based on usage patterns.

By understanding the diverse storage options and best practices outlined in this chapter, you'll be well-equipped to design a comprehensive and cost-effective cloud storage strategy for your needs within the AWS ecosystem.

The next chapter, titled *Deep Dive into AWS Compute* ventures, into the realm of EC2 and containerization. It also explains the potential of serverless computing using AWS Lambda and serverless offerings such as API Gateway, SAM, and DynamoDB for constructing scalable serverless applications.

Multiple Choice Questions

1. Which storage types will you use to store unstructured data, such as images, videos, and backups?
    a. Block Storage
    b. File Storage
    c. Object Storage
    d. Tape Storage
2. Which of the following is typically scaled for object storage regarding a service by AWS?
    a. Amazon S3
    b. Amazon EBS
    c. Amazon EFS
    d. AWS Backup
3. For what is typically Amazon Elastic Block Store used?
    a. Simple website hosting
    b. Running relational databases and applications requiring low-latency access to data

   c. Storing large volumes of data that are infrequently accessed

   d. Archiving logs and backups

4. Which Amazon EBS feature below provides data redundancy within a single availability zone?

   a. Multi-AZ replication

   b. Snapshots

   c. Configuration in RAID 0

   d. EBS-optimized instances

5. Which AWS services provide managed file storage that can be mounted on multiple EC2 instances simultaneously?

   a. Amazon S3

   b. Amazon EBS

   c. Amazon EFS

   d. AWS Backup

6. Which type of file systems does Amazon FSx support?

   a. Window File System and Lustre

   b. Ext4 and NTFS

   c. HDFS and FAT32

   d. Btrfs and ZFS

7. What is the maximum size of an object that can be uploaded in a single upload to S3?

   a. 1 GB

   b. 5 TB

   c. 50 GB

   d. 5 GB

8. Which Amazon S3 feature reduces the storage fees by automatically moving data to a lower-cost storage class as a predefined period passes?

   a. Versioning

   b. Lifecycle Policies

   c. Bucket Policies

   d. Server-Side Encryption

9. Which of the following is the primary purpose of the AWS Storage Gateway service?

   a. To manage cloud-based databases

   b. To provide a cloud storage gateway for on-premises environments

   c. To deliver content globally with low latency

   d. Create VPCs and manage network connections

10. Which AWS Service will you use to physically carry large volumes of data into AWS when the Bandwidth is limited?

    a. AWS Direct Connect

    b. AWS Snowball

    c. Amazon S3 Transfer Acceleration

    d. Amazon CloudFront

Answers

1. c
2. a
3. b
4. b
5. c
6. a
7. d
8. b
9. b
10. b

References

- https://aws.amazon.com/products/storage/
- https://aws.amazon.com/ebs/
- https://aws.amazon.com/cloudwatch/
- https://aws.amazon.com/dms/
- https://docs.aws.amazon.com/ebs/latest/userguide/ebs-volumes.html
- https://aws.amazon.com/efs/
- https://aws.amazon.com/fsx/
- https://aws.amazon.com/backup/
- https://aws.amazon.com/s3/
- https://docs.aws.amazon.com/AmazonS3/latest/userguide/Welcome.html
- https://docs.aws.amazon.com/amazonglacier/latest/dev/introduction.html
- https://docs.aws.amazon.com/storagegateway/
- https://aws.amazon.com/snowball/
- https://aws.amazon.com/snowcone/
- https://docs.aws.amazon.com/cost-management/latest/userguide/what-is-costmanagement.html
- https://docs.aws.amazon.com/AWSEC2/latest/UserGuide/ec2-reserved-instances.html
- https://docs.aws.amazon.com/AmazonCloudWatch/latest/monitoring/cloudwatch_architecture.html

Chapter 5
Deep-Dive into AWS Compute

Introduction

Imagine you are an architect building a magnificent structure. EC2 serves as the groundwork, offering essential components for your project. This section explores further, revealing the wide range of accessible tools.

After that, we will explore beyond EC2 and the thrilling realm of containerization. We will examine the benefits of utilizing containers and how Docker and Amazon ECS can be utilized to create and oversee containerized applications.

Finally, we will tap into the potential of serverless computing using AWS Lambda. Uncover how this groundbreaking method removes the need for server administration, allowing you to dedicate all your attention to your application's logic. We will also investigate additional serverless offerings such as API Gateway, SAM, and DynamoDB, which offer a comprehensive set of tools for constructing contemporary, scalable serverless applications.

This extensive understanding enables you to choose the ideal 'compute solution' for every architectural obstacle, guaranteeing that your cloud environment is optimized and customized to your specific requirements.

Structure

In this chapter, we will cover the following topics:

- AWS EC2 and Beyond
- Containers on AWS
- AWS Serverless Services
- Reservations and Savings Plans

AWS EC2 and Beyond

Let us explore how to launch virtual computers (EC2 instances) in the cloud, choose the right ones for your tasks, and manage them efficiently.

Introduction to AWS EC2

Imagine renting a computer instead of buying one. That is the job of AWS Elastic Compute Cloud (EC2). It allows you to do things in the cloud, providing flexibility for computing needs.

Defining EC2

Amazon Web Services (AWS) offers a web service called Elastic Compute Cloud (EC2) that provides on-demand virtual servers in the cloud. Consider leasing computing power instead of purchasing and maintaining your physical servers. EC2 lets you rent virtual servers, called instances, with various processing power, memory, storage, and operating system configurations. You can launch only a single instance or scale up to thousands to manage bursts in traffic or heavy workloads.

Benefits of Using EC2

EC2 gives you the exact computing power you need, whenever you need it. It is like having a helpful genie in the cloud environment. Let us look at the benefits of using EC2, one by one:

- **On-demand**: You can create and terminate virtual servers as and when needed, providing flexibility and cost-effectiveness.
- **Scalability**: This enables you to easily modify your computing resources' capacity to align with your applications' evolving needs. With EC2, you can adjust your computational capacity according to changes in your requirements.
- **Range of choices**: An extensive selection of virtual server setups allows you to choose the instance type that best meets your processing, memory, storage, and other needs.
- **Operating system options**: Your EC2 instances can be installed with Windows, Linux, and macOS. With EC2, you can concentrate on deploying and overseeing your applications without purchasing hardware, managing datacenters, or allocating bandwidth.
- **Cost efficiency**: You are charged based on the resources you utilize. In contrast to traditional physical servers, which necessitate initial capital and continuous

upkeep, EC2 enables you to pay hourly. This removes the responsibility of overseeing unutilized server capacity and yielding substantial cost savings.

- **Variability:** EC2 offers a wide range of virtual server setups, allowing you to select the instance type that best meets your application's processing, memory, and storage needs.

Key Concepts (Instances, AMIs, Instance Types, and Security Groups)

In the world of EC2, efficiency and security are paramount. This section provides information about the four key concepts that will help you manage your cloud resources effectively.

- **AMIs:** Amazon Machine Images (AMIs) consist of pre-configured operating systems, applications, and software packages, eliminating the necessity of manually setting up each instance. AWS offers a wide range of pre-built AMIs to meet different requirements, or you can create custom AMIs with your specific software configurations.
- **Instances:** EC2 instances are virtual counterparts to physical servers. They are the workhouses that run your applications and workloads in the cloud. Each instance has its own CPU, memory, storage, and networking capabilities. This flexibility allows you to avoid dealing with physical servers, saving you time and money.
- **Instance Types:** Not all virtual servers are created equal. EC2 offers various instance types, each optimized for specific tasks. If you need raw processing power for complex calculations, choose a compute-optimized instance. If you are running memory-intensive databases, a memory-optimized instance is your friend. If you have massive datasets to store, look for storage-optimized instances. This variety ensures you have the correct virtual server for the job, maximizing performance and cost-efficiency.
- **Security Groups:** Security groups function as virtual firewalls, protecting your EC2 instances by managing incoming and outgoing traffic. Consider them like bouncers at a club, permitting only authorized traffic to enter and exit your instances. Configuring security groups with specific rules will enable you to restrict unauthorized access and maintain a robust security posture for your entire EC2 environment.

Launching and Managing EC2 Instances

This section elevates you from an EC2 user to a strategic cloud architect. We will delve into the tactical aspects of launching, configuring, and safeguarding your EC2 instances, ensuring optimal performance, cost-efficiency, and robust security.

Instance Type Families

Instance-type families classify virtual machines in cloud computing according to their capabilities. Choosing the best family for your workload enhances efficiency and reduces expenses. Let us examine typical families and when they are best suited for use.

- **General Purpose: Your Everyday Cloud VM:** Consider general-purpose VMs as reliable sedans of the cloud. They offer a balanced mix of processing power, memory, and storage, making them perfect for daily tasks. They are budget-friendly, too, perfect for web servers, development environments, basic applications, and anything that does not require top-of-the-line specs. Examples include AWS M/T/A and Alibaba Cloud g6/g7/g8a series.
    - **T4g, T3, T3a, T2**: Burstable performance instances are great for applications that use a moderate CPU level but occasionally spike.
    - **M6g, M5, M5a, M4**: General-purpose instance types can be used when a good balance of CPU, memory, and network is needed.
- **Compute Optimized: Geared for Speed:** Look no further than compute-optimized instances when you need a cloud VM built for acceleration. These are the cloud's muscle cars, designed to handle demanding CPU tasks easily. They are ideal for scientific computing, simulations, video editing, high-traffic web servers, and any workload that needs serious processing power. Consider a compute-optimized instance such as the AWS C/R or Alibaba Cloud c6r/c8y series for complex calculations, large data batch processing, or high-resolution video rendering.
    - **C6g, C5, C5a, C4**: These instances are well-suited for compute-heavy workloads, such as batch processing, high-performance web servers, and scientific modeling.
- **Memory Optimized: Keeping Everything at Your Fingertips:** If your applications rely heavily on memory, memory-optimized VMs would be the ideal choice. These cloud-based SUVs are packed with RAM, run in-memory databases, perform real-time analytics, handle large application caches, and tackle complex data simulations. If your workload involves keeping a lot of data readily available in memory, consider an AWS R/X1 or Alibaba Cloud r8y series instance.
    - **R6g, R5, R5a, R4**: Suitable for memory-intensive workloads such as databases and in-memory caching.
    - **X2gd, X1e, X1**: For larger memory sizes for in-memory databases and analytics.
    - **z1d:** Provide high single-threaded performance and large memory

- **Storage Optimized: A Haven for Your Data:** While dealing with massive amounts of data, storage-optimized VMs are your data center workhorses. These offer massive storage capacity, often with faster access speeds. They' are ideal for data-intensive tasks such as log processing, big data analytics, data warehousing, media streaming, or content repositories. If you focus on storing and processing large datasets, AWS D/I/Sd or Alibaba Cloud g7se (storage-enhanced general purpose) could be your perfect fit.
  - **I3, I3en**: High I/O instances suitable for databases and storage solutions.
  - **D3, D2**: Dense storage instances for data warehousing and Hadoop clusters.
- **Accelerated Computing: The Powerhouse with a GPU:** Accelerated computing VMs are the ultimate powerhouses of the cloud. Consider them high-performance sports cars, packing GPUs or other specialized hardware for workloads that require intense graphical processing. They are best suited for machine learning, deep learning, video processing, scientific computing with heavy graphics, or simulations. If your project involves complex calculations or manipulation of large visual datasets, consider an AWS P/G or Alibaba Cloud E/F series instance.
  - **P4, P3, P2**: Corresponding instances with powerful GPUs for machine learning, AI, and computational class workloads.
  - **Inf1:** These instances are optimized for deep learning inference.

Choosing the Right Instance Type

Selecting the right instance type is like picking the ideal car for a road trip. There are better choices than a fuel-efficient sedan for hauling a trailer across mountains. Choosing the right instance type is important for cost-effectiveness and appreciable application performance.

Here is how to make an informed decision:

- **Match Your Workload's DNA**: Identify your application's resource demands. If it craves raw processing power for complex calculations, go for a compute-optimized powerhouse. A memory-optimized instance is your best friend. Storage-optimized instances offer the necessary muscle for data-intensive workloads with frequent storage access.
- **Benchmarking for Peak Performance:** Each instance type boasts unique specs–CPU clock speed, memory capacity, and network throughput. Evaluate these against your application's performance benchmarks. If you need lightning-fast processing for real-time simulations or high memory capacity for intricate data analysis, choose an instance that aligns with your application's performance requirements.
- **Cost Optimization:** Striking a balance between cost and performance is

critical. Explore pricing models: On-Demand Instances for short-term bursts, Reserved Instances for predictable workloads (think running a web server 24/7), and Spot Instances for flexible, non-critical tasks that can tolerate interruptions. Consider cost-saving strategies such as purchasing Reserved Instances for predictable workloads or leveraging Spot Instances for test environments.

- **Scaling for Growth:** Building for the Future: Think beyond today's needs. If your application experience a surge in traffic in the future, choose an instance type with built-in scalability, or design your architecture to leverage auto-scaling features that automatically adjust resources based on demands.

By following these steps, you can ensure your application runs smoothly with the help of EC2.

Launching and Configuring Your Instance

Launching an EC2 instance is like building a custom computer in the cloud. Here is a step-by-step guide:

1. Select an Amazon Machine Image (AMI) for your instance's operating system and software foundation. You can choose from pre-built AMIs offered by AWS, community-developed AMIs, or custom AMIs you create from existing cases.

2. Next, you define the specific settings for your instance. Choose the instance type you selected earlier, configure network settings for secure access, define storage options (think hard drive size and speed), and set up security groups to control inbound and outbound traffic.

3. Create or choose an existing key pair to secure SSH access to your instance. Think of this as the digital key that unlocks your virtual server. Store the private key securely and restrict access to prevent unauthorized logins.

4. Review your configuration settings before initiating the launch process. Once launched, you will receive the public IP address or DNS name to access your instance remotely using SSH or RDP.

Managing and Monitoring Your Instances: Keeping Your Cloud Running Smoothly

Similar to how a car needs routine upkeep, monitoring and managing your EC2 instances for the best performance, availability, and security is important. These are the necessary guidelines to adhere to:

- **Turn into a Performance Investigator**: Use Amazon CloudWatch to oversee your instance's health, resource usage, and metrics. Establish automated notifications to detect and resolve problems such as elevated CPU usage or insufficient memory levels before they affect your application's efficiency.

- **Configuration consistency**: The most important thing is maintaining consistent configurations across instances by using tools such as AWS Systems Manager or third-party solutions for automation and standardization. This guarantees uniformity, adherence, and protection throughout all your EC2 instances in operation.
- **Disaster Recovery**: Develop a strategy to safeguard your vital data and programs from unforeseen occurrences. Amazon EBS snapshots, Amazon S3 backups, and other third-party backup options regularly create backups to guarantee data integrity during interruptions.
- **Fixing Weaknesses**: Consistently install security patches and software updates on your systems to reduce vulnerabilities and improve security. Use AWS Systems Manager Patch Manager or external tools to automate patch deployment and guarantee that your instances are constantly updated with the newest security patches.

Methods to Log into an EC2 Machine

There are a few methods for logging in to an EC2 instance; the choice depends on the operating system and security preferences of the owner.

- **Secure Shell (SSH) Access:** The most common method for Linux/Unix-based EC2 instances to gain access is through SSH.
    - **Using an SSH Client:** Any user can connect to an instance using an SSH client, such as OpenSSH or PuTTY, via a key pair.
    - **Session Manager:** The AWS Systems Manager Session Manager grants access to an instance without a bastion host or SSH key. This provides secure access through the use of IAM policies along with the AWS CLI, or Management Console.
- **EC2 Instance Connect:** EC2 Instance Connect allows secure connections to your instances using a one-time-use SSH key managed by AWS. It is also fully integrated with the AWS Management Console, allowing easy access to cases without spending much time managing SSH keys.
- **Remote Desktop Protocol (RDP):** RDP is the standard protocol for remote desktop access for Windows-based EC2 instances.
    - **Using Remote Desktop Connection:** You can also use the Remote Desktop Connection on a Windows, Mac OS, or Linux computer. You will need your administrator password, which you can get through the AWS Management Console, the .rdp file, or your instance's public DNS.

Security Best Practices for EC2

Security is the cornerstone of any robust cloud infrastructure, and EC2 is no exception. Here is a battle plan to secure your EC2 instances and keep your data safe from invaders:

- **Principle of Least Privilege:** This means not allowing everyone access to a master key. IAM roles, security groups, and network ACLs can help you manage access to your EC2 instances by determining who and what can access them. Implement the "least privilege" principle by giving users and resources only the necessary permissions to operate. This reduces the risk of harm in the event of of unauthorized entry.
- **Encryption**: Encrypt valuable information stored on EC2 instances when not in use (on storage drives) and during data transfers (moving across networks). The AWS Key Management Service (KMS) functions as a secure vault for the storage and management of encryption keys. It can be used to encrypt Amazon EBS volumes (storage) and Amazon S3 buckets (object storage). Secure network communication with robust SSL/TLS protocols.
- **Monitor and Analyze:** Constant vigilance is critical. Implement logging and auditing mechanisms to monitor user activity, system events, and API calls within your EC2 environment. Enable AWS CloudTrail to serve as your digital logkeeper, recording API activity. Integrate it with Amazon CloudWatch Logs for real-time monitoring and analysis. Think of CloudWatch Logs as your war room, allowing you to identify and address suspicious activity.
- **Secure Network Configuration:** Security groups and network ACLs are your digital firewalls, controlling traffic flow to and from your EC2 instances. Imagine them as fortified walls with restricted gates. Only allow authorized traffic through by configuring security groups and network ACLs accordingly. Consider using bastion hosts, which act as secure entry points into your network, or leverage Virtual Private Networks (VPNs) and AWS Direct Connect for secure remote access. These measures minimize the exposure of your instances to external threats.
- **Patch Up the Weaknesses:** Update your EC2 instances with the latest security patches and software updates to address vulnerabilities before attackers exploit them. Automate the tedious task of patch management using AWS Systems Manager Patch Manager or trusted third-party solutions. These automated processes are your loyal scouts, constantly checking for weaknesses and repairing them before they become critical.

With these security best practices, you can significantly improve the security posture of your EC2 environment. This multi-tiered approach will make it much more difficult for unauthorized access, data breaches, and security incidents to penetrate your cloud fortress.

Beyond EC2: Introduction to Other AWS Compute Services

While Amazon EC2 is a fundamental computing service in AWS, the cloud platform offers additional computing services tailored to specific use cases and architectural requirements. Understanding these services enables users to leverage the full potential of AWS for their computing needs. Here is an overview of some critical AWS compute services beyond EC2:

AWS Lambda: The Serverless Revolution

Imagine code execution without worrying about servers! AWS Lambda offers a serverless computing paradigm. Developers write code (functions) that trigger in response to events such as HTTP requests, data changes, or schedules. Key benefits include:

- **Event-Driven Magic:** Lambda functions react instantly to events, scaling automatically based on demand. This eliminates idle servers and optimizes resource usage.
- **Pay-Per-Use Efficiency:** You only have to pay for the execution time and resources your functions use, making it ideal for unpredictable workloads.
- **Scalability and Flexibility:** Developers can focus on writing quality code without getting overwhelmed by server provisioning and management tasks.

Amazon ECS: Container Orchestration Made Easy

Amazon Elastic Container Service (ECS) simplifies managing containerized applications at scale. Think of it as a conductor for your container orchestra. Key features include:

- **Seamless Deployment and Orchestration:** ECS automates Docker container deployment, scaling, and scheduling across EC2 instances or AWS Fargate (a serverless container engine). This streamlines container management and ensures smooth application operation.
- **Power of Integration:** ECS integrates seamlessly with other AWS services such as Amazon ECR (container registry), CloudWatch (monitoring), and IAM (identity management). This holistic approach simplifies container management, monitoring, and security.
- **Customization at Your Fingertips:** ECS offers granular control over container environments, networking, and scaling. You define the rules, and ECS implements them, ensuring optimal performance for your application needs.

Amazon EKS: Managed Kubernetes for the Win

For individuals who are already involved in the Kubernetes community, Amazon Elastic Kubernetes Service (EKS) offers a fully managed service. EKS handles deploying, managing, and scaling containerized applications using Kubernetes. Key features include:

- **Handling the Kubernetes Control Plane:** EKS takes away the responsibility of overseeing the Kubernetes control plane (API servers, etcd clusters, and more). This decreases operational overhead and guarantees the high availability of your Kubernetes environment.
- **The Power of AWS Integration:** EKS integrates with core AWS services such as EC2, EBS (storage), and VPC (networking). This allows you to leverage the reliability and performance of AWS infrastructure for your Kubernetes clusters.
- **Compatibility You Can Count On:** EKS supports standard Kubernetes APIs and tooling, enabling smooth migration of existing Kubernetes workloads to AWS. You can continue using familiar tools while benefiting from managed AWS infrastructure.

ECS Versus EKS

This table compares Amazon ECS and EKS, both used for managing containerized applications. ECS offers a simpler, AWS-focused experience, and EKS offers the flexibility of Kubernetes with additional configuration. Choose ECS for ease of use and tight AWS integration or EKS for portability and advanced Kubernetes features.

Feature	Amazon ECS	Amazon EKS
Service Model	AWS-managed container orchestration service	AWS-managed Kubernetes service
Underlying Technology	Proprietary AWS technology	Open-source Kubernetes
Deployment Complexity	Easier to set up and use	Requires more configuration and Kubernetes expertise
Vendor Lock-in	Yes (AWS platform)	No (portable across Kubernetes environments)
Networking	More limited control over networking	Offers granular control over networking with Kubernetes capabilities
Integrations	Deep integration with other AWS services	Integrates with various tools and services through Kubernetes ecosystem

Scalability	Highly scalable with Fargate or EC2 instances	Highly scalable with horizontal pod autoscaling
Security	Integrates with AWS security features	Leverages Kubernetes security features and requires additional configuration
Use cases	It is ideal for those starting with containers or preferring deep AWS integration	Suitable for experienced users who need the portability and flexibility of Kubernetes

***Table 5.1**: ECS Versus EKS*

Table 5.1 compares ECS with EKS to help you choose the right service to manage containerized applications.

Scaling and Automating Your Infrastructure with EC2

The constant changes in cloud computing pose a unique challenge, ensuring steady performance and uninterrupted business operations during varying needs. Fixed infrastructure frequently faces challenges in accommodating these changes, resulting in congestion and service interruptions. This is when autoscaling becomes essential for modern cloud orchestration.

Autoscaling enables applications to adjust their resource allocation in real-time according to their requirements. This results in increased scalability, efficiency, and cost-effectiveness. Imagine a website experiencing a sudden traffic surge because of a successful marketing campaign. By implementing autoscaling, the system automatically adds resources as needed to manage higher demand and maintain a seamless user experience. Conversely, when there is low traffic, autoscaling can scale down resource allocation, thus cutting unnecessary expenses. This guarantees optimal application performance and prevents unnecessary resource expenses, leading to significant cost savings over time.

By adopting autoscaling, companies can effectively function in the ever-changing cloud environment, upholding consistent performance, maximizing resource usage, and operating cost-efficiently. Scaling and automating infrastructure management are essential in modern cloud computing, enabling organizations to adjust to changing demands, optimize resource utilization, and enhance operational efficiency. We will also look at vertical scaling and horizontal scaling. These are the methods to adjust your resources manually. Let us consider a bakery. In this context, vertical scaling is like buying more ovens for the existing bakery, and horizontal scaling is like renting another bakery next door.

Let us look at how to leverage EC2 for optimal resource utilization and efficiency:

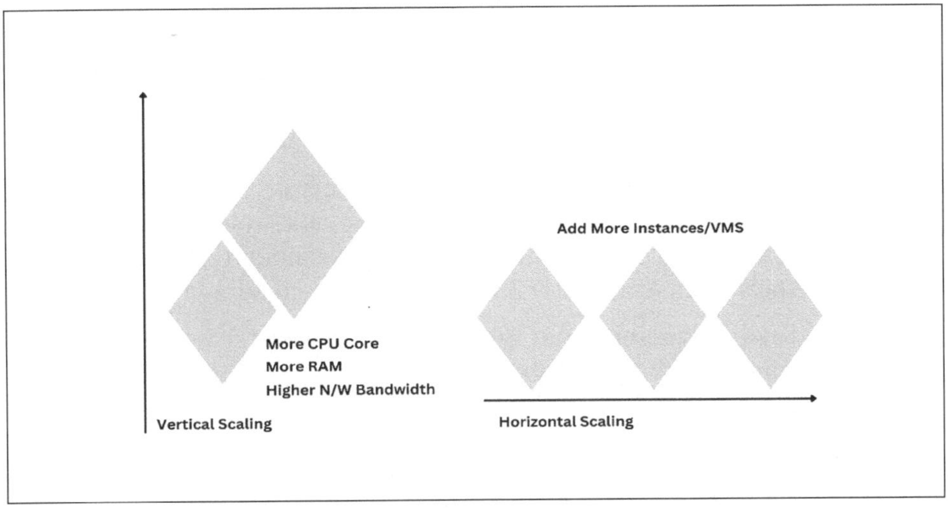

Figure 5.1: *Vertical scaling Versus Horizontal scaling*

Figure 5.1 compares vertical scaling with horizontal scaling.

Vertical scaling upgrades a single machine's hardware (CPU, RAM, and storage) for increased performance. It is simpler to implement and manage initially, but limited by hardware capabilities. It does not handle workload distribution well. As your requirements increase, adding resources becomes difficult. However, it is cost-effective for short-term needs or when adding resources to existing infrastructure. It is best-suited for development and testing environments, databases with occasional surges in activity, and stand-alone web servers for start-ups.

On the other hand, horizontal scaling utilizes multiple machines (VMs) to distribute workloads and increase capacity. It is more versatile and can easily adjust to changing requirements, making it more adaptable and scalable. Additionally, it can be more economical in the long run, especially for handling unpredictable workloads. However, establishing and managing a cluster of servers demands more expertise and configuration than a single server. It is ideal for large e-commerce platforms, real-time collaboration tools, and cloud gaming platforms.

The best approach depends on your specific needs:

- Vertical scaling is a good option for short-term needs, simple applications, and limited-budgets.
- Horizontal scaling is better suited for high-traffic websites, mission-critical applications, and long-term growth.

Auto Scaling Groups

Auto Scaling Groups automate the scaling of EC2 instances, ensuring your capacity adapts to demand fluctuations.

Key features include:

- **Dynamic Scaling:** Auto Scaling Groups automatically add or remove EC2 instances based on predefined policies. For ultimate control, these policies can be based on CPU utilization, network traffic, or custom metrics.
- **Built-in High Availability:** Auto Scaling Groups distribute instances across multiple Availability Zones for enhanced fault tolerance. Auto Scaling automatically replaces unhealthy instances to maintain desired capacity if an instance fails or an Availability Zone experiences an outage.
- **Elastic Load Balancing:** Auto Scaling Groups work seamlessly with Elastic Load Balancing (ELB) to distribute incoming traffic across multiple instances. This ensures optimal performance and fault tolerance for your EC2-based applications.

CloudWatch: The All-Seeing Eye for Monitoring and Scaling

CloudWatch is your central nervous system for monitoring and managing your AWS resources, including EC2 instances and Auto Scaling Groups. Key features include:

- **Metrics and Alarms:** CloudWatch collects and stores performance metrics for your EC2 instances. Based on these metrics, you can define custom alarms to trigger scaling actions or notify you of potential performance issues.
- **Log Analysis and Insights:** CloudWatch Logs provides centralized logging and analysis for your EC2 instances. By analyzing these logs, you can gain valuable insights into application behavior, troubleshoot issues, and proactively identify security threats.

Containers on AWS

Containers have significantly improved the ease of deploying and managing software. This section will discuss the functioning of containers and how Docker, a widely used tool for using containers, can be integrated with Amazon Web Services (AWS) to run your software.

Introduction to Containerization

Containerization revolutionizes application development and deployment. It packages your application, along with its runtime, libraries, and dependencies, into a self-contained entity called a container. Imagine it as a shipping container for your software—all necessary components are packed together, ready for deployment.

Containers

Containers provide a quicker, simpler, and more efficient way of running your software. Imagine a container as an independent enclosure for your software. This box contains everything your program needs to run, including its code, tools, and libraries. Due to its lightweight, it is easy to move around. It is compatible with almost any computer, such as different servers or even your laptop, in contrast to older virtual machines, such as big, clunky computers requiring more time and resources.

Benefits of Containerization

Here is a breakdown of the key benefits:

- **Portability:** Containers run consistently across any environment, from your laptop to the cloud. No more worrying about compatibility issues; your app runs the same way everywhere.
- **Isolation:** Containers keep your applications separate from each other and the underlying system, preventing conflicts and ensuring predictable behavior. Think of them as tiny apartments in a building; each app gets its own space without interfering with its neighbors.
- **Resource Efficiency:** Containers are lightweight because they share the host operating system. This translates to faster startups, lower memory usage, and efficient utilization of your cloud resources. Imagine tiny, fuel-efficient cars compared to gas-guzzling VMs.

Comparison to Virtual Machines

While both containers and virtual machines (VMs) isolate applications, they have distinct approaches:

- **Architecture:** VMs mimic entire computer systems, creating isolated environments with their operating systems. Containers share the host's OS, making them lighter and faster to start.
- **Resource Utilization:** VMs require more resources due to the overhead of running multiple operating systems. Containers share resources efficiently, making them ideal for scaling applications in the cloud.
- **Isolation Level:** VMs offer more robust isolation with separate kernels and runtime environments. Containers provide a lighter form of isolation using namespaces and control groups, but it is still effective for most use cases.

Using Docker on AWS

Docker is the go-to platform for containerization, offering tools for building, deploying, and managing containers. Here is how to leverage Docker on AWS:

Introduction to Docker

Docker is like a containerization workshop with two key components:

- **Docker Engine:** This is the workhorse that runs your containers. It manages their lifecycle, including image management, networking, and storage.
- **Docker Images:** These are blueprints for your containers, containing the application code, dependencies, and configuration. Think of them as recipes for building your containers.

Building and Running Docker Containers on EC2

Amazon EC2 provides the foundation for running Docker containers in the cloud. Here is how to get started:

1. **Install Docker Engine:** First things first, install Docker Engine on your EC2 instances. It's like setting up the workshop in your cloud environment.
2. **Grab the Blueprints (Pull Docker Images):** Use Docker Hub or a private registry to download the Docker images you need. These blueprints contain everything you need to build your containers.
3. **Run the Containers:** The docker run command launches containers based on the downloaded images. It's like using blueprints to build and run your applications in containers. To fine-tune your containers, you can customize settings such as ports, environment variables, and storage.

Managing Docker Images with Amazon Elastic Container Registry (ECR)

Amazon ECR simplifies managing Docker images in the cloud. Think of it as a secure warehouse for your container blueprints. Here is how to use it:

1. **Create a Repository:** Create a repository in Amazon ECR to store your images. This is like having designated shelves for different versions of your blueprints.
2. **Push Docker Images:** Use the docker push command to upload your Docker images from your local environment to the ECR repository or build a pipeline. Make sure you have the proper permissions to access the warehouse securely.
3. **Tag and Versioning:** Use meaningful tags to differentiate between different versions of your images. This is like adding labels to your blueprints to keep track of various builds and deployments.

Combining Docker with AWS services such as EC2 and ECR, gives you a powerful toolkit for building, deploying, and managing containerized applications at scale. This approach streamlines the development process, improves application portability, and allows for faster deployments in the cloud.

Amazon ECS: Orchestrating Containerized Applications

Let us dive into Amazon ECS and learn the tricks of the trade for running containerized applications on AWS. We will cover how to deploy them quickly, scale them up or down as needed, and keep things running smoothly, all with the help of ECS's built-in features and best practices.

Introduction to Amazon ECS

Here is what you need to know to deploy and manage your containerized applications on Amazon ECS like a pro:

- **Managed Orchestration:** Focus on building your app, not server headaches. ECS automates launching, scheduling, and managing your containers across servers or a serverless option (Fargate).
- **Integration with AWS Services:** ECS works excellently with other AWS services you already use, such as load balancing and monitoring. This makes your apps more reliable and easier to operate.
- **Task Definitions:** Create "task definitions" that specify how your app runs, including memory, CPU, network settings, and the Docker image it uses. Think of it as a recipe for launching your app on ECS.

Deploying Containerized Applications with ECS

Deploying applications on ECS involves several steps, including creating ECS clusters, defining task definitions, and configuring service deployments. Here's an overview of the deployment process:

1. **Create ECS Cluster:** To start, create an ECS cluster, essentially a group of servers or Fargate tasks where your app will run. You can do this easily from the AWS console or with code.

2. **Craft Your App Blueprint:** Define task definitions that tell ECS exactly how to run your app. This includes the Docker image, resource limits, and how it connects to networks and storage.

3. **Scale Up and Down Automatically:** Configure ECS services to manage your app. Services ensure the correct number of containers are running and automatically restart them if anything goes wrong.

Scaling and Managing Containerized Applications with ECS

ECS provides built-in mechanisms for scaling and managing containerized applications based on workload demand and performance metrics. Here are critical practices for scaling and managing ECS applications:

- **Scale to Meet Demand:** Do not worry about manually scaling your app. ECS Auto Scaling can adjust the number of containers running based on how busy your app is. This saves you money and keeps your app performing well.
- **Connect Your Services:** Use service discovery to allow different parts of your app (microservices) to talk to each other easily. AWS CloudMap or other options can help.
- **Deploy Updates Continuously:** Automate deploying new versions of your app with tools like AWS CodePipeline. This lets you deliver updates quickly and reliably.

With these steps, you can use Amazon ECS to deploy and manage your containerized applications efficiently with minimal effort. Focus on building great software and let ECS handle the infrastructure requirements.

Amazon EKS: Managed Kubernetes on AWS

Amazon Elastic Kubernetes Service (EKS) is a managed Kubernetes service that simplifies the deployment, management, and scaling of Kubernetes clusters on AWS. Let's delve into the fundamentals of Kubernetes and the benefits of using EKS for container orchestration:

Understanding Kubernetes

Kubernetes, also known as K8s, is a free tool for controlling containerized applications. Imagine having numerous small programs (containers) that form your larger application. Kubernetes assists in deploying containers automatically, adjusting their scale based on requirements, and maintaining their performance effectively. It conceals the base infrastructure and offers a platform-independent framework for scaling and managing containers. Horizontal Pod Autoscaler (HPA) and Cluster Autoscaler enable automatic scaling, enhancing resource usage and cost-effectiveness.

The benefits of using Amazon EKS are:

- **Control Plane Management**: This allows you to concentrate on your application rather than dealing with the technical aspects of Kubernetes. AWS manages the setup, updating, and upkeep of the control component's infrastructure for Kubernetes clusters, guaranteeing their security and uninterrupted operation.

- **Integration with AWS Services:** EKS seamlessly integrates with other AWS services to simplify load balancing, networking, and security. This improves the general security and compatibility of Kubernetes workloads.
- **Enterprise-level security**: EKS adheres to AWS security standards and offers security measures such as encryption for data at rest and in transit, RBAC using IAM roles, and network policies. It ensures that your containerized applications are secure and meet requirements.

Deploying and Managing Containerized Applications with EKS

Using Kubernetes and Amazon EKS, you can deploy and manage your containerized applications on AWS quickly and easily, helping you deliver software faster and more efficiently.

1. **Set up your cluster:** Create a Kubernetes cluster using AWS management tools. EKS provides the necessary infrastructure for Kubernetes clusters, including controller and worker nodes.
2. **Deploy workloads:** Define Kubernetes what your application needs using blueprints called manifests, such as Deployment, Service, and Ingress resources, to specify the desired state of containerized applications.
3. **Scale and manage workloads:** Use Kubernetes such as Horizontal Pod Autoscaler (HPA) and Deployment strategies features to scale your application and monitor its health automatically.

Here is how you can scale EKS Clusters with Cluster Autoscaler:

Cluster Autoscaler is a powerful tool for automatically scaling your EKS cluster based on real-time resource utilization. It ensures:

- **All pods have a place to run**: CA dynamically adds nodes to the cluster when pods are waiting to be scheduled due to insufficient resources on existing nodes.
- **No unnecessary nodes**: CA also removes nodes from the cluster when they are consistently underutilized for a significant amount of time, optimizing resource usage and cost.

Servers versus Virtual Machines versus Container

A server runs one operating system and multiple applications. A virtual machine acts like a separate computer with its operating system and programs. Likewise, containers isolate applications and their dependencies. Figure 5.2 explains their differences.

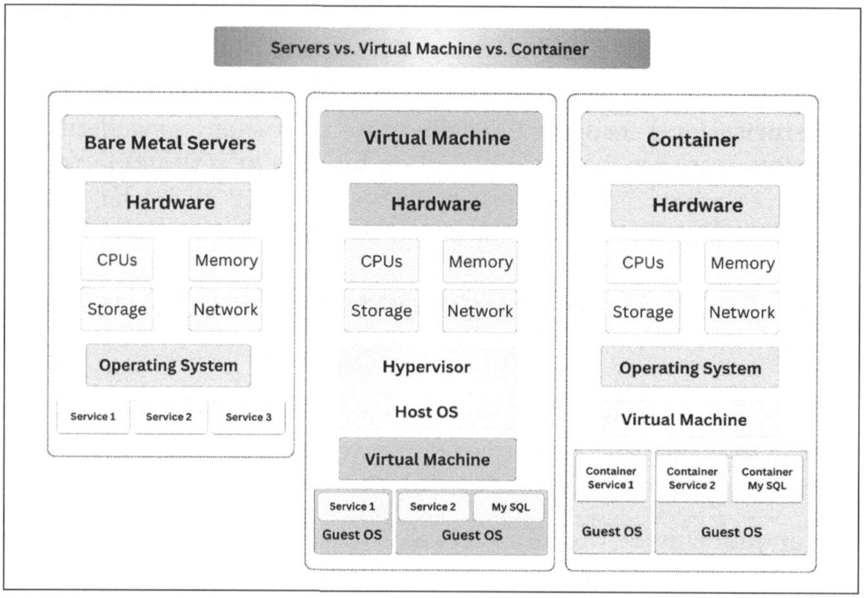

***Figure 5.2**: Servers versus Virtual Machines versus Containers*

AWS Serverless Services

Let us delve into the core service, AWS Lambda and supporting services such as API Gateway and DynamoDB, to help you build and deploy scalable, cost-effective applications on AWS without servers.

Introduction to Serverless Computing

Imagine a world where you write code without worrying about servers. That is the wonder of serverless computing! It is a development approach that operates on cloud technology, allowing you to pay solely for the resources consumed by your code, eradicating the need to handle servers, scaling, and infrastructure. Serverless computing is ideal for applications that experience sudden spikes in traffic or perform specialized functions, such as image processing or email delivery. Paying only for the resources your application utilizes, such as paying for the food you consume at your rented apartment, makes it a cost-efficient option.

Serverless Computing

Think of it like renting an apartment instead of buying a house. With serverless, you rent the computing power you need, on-demand, from a cloud provider like

AWS. Serverless Computing is a cloud computing model where the cloud provider dynamically manages the allocation of machine resources. In this model, developers can focus solely on writing code without worrying about provisioning, scaling, or managing servers. It allows developers to execute code in response to events without server management.

Benefits of Serverless Computing

Serverless computing offers a win-win for developers and businesses. Here is why:

- **Effortless scaling**: Serverless architectures automatically scale to handle varying workloads, ensuring that applications can seamlessly handle spikes in traffic without manual intervention.
- **Cost-Effectiveness**: With serverless computing, users only pay for the computing time consumed by their functions rather than for provisioned server capacity. This pay-per-execution model can result in significant cost savings, especially for sporadically used applications or those with unpredictable traffic patterns.

AWS Lambda: The Core Serverless Service

AWS Lambda is a computing service provided by Amazon Web Services (AWS) that allows you to run code without provisioning or managing servers. It enables developers to choose the language that best fits their application requirements.

AWS Lambda

AWS Lambda allows developers to upload their code as Lambda functions, which are then executed in response to specific events, such as changes to data in Amazon S3 buckets, updates to DynamoDB tables, or HTTP requests via Amazon API Gateway. Think of Lambda as a super-efficient execution environment for your code. You upload your code (functions), and Lambda takes care of the rest, running it in response to events such as user actions, API calls, or data changes.

Developing and Deploying Lambda Functions

Developing for Lambda is like writing regular code. You can use various programming languages and deploy your functions with a few clicks. It's that easy! Developers can write Lambda functions using their preferred programming language and dependencies, package them into ZIP files, and upload them to AWS Lambda using the AWS Management Console, AWS CLI, or SDKs. AWS Lambda automatically manages the execution environment, including provisioning and scaling resources as needed.

Triggering Lambda Functions

Various events, such as a new image uploaded to S3 storage or an API request, can trigger Lambda functions. This event-driven approach makes your code more responsive and efficient.

- **Events:** Lambda functions can be triggered by other AWS services, such as object creation in Amazon S3, messages in Amazon SQS, or changes to records in Amazon DynamoDB.
- **APIs:** Lambda functions can serve as backend logic for RESTful APIs created using Amazon API Gateway, allowing developers to build scalable, serverless web applications.
- **SQS:** Lambda functions can be triggered by messages sent to Amazon Simple Queue Service (SQS) queues, enabling asynchronous task processing and decoupling of components in distributed systems.

AWS Lambda simplifies building scalable and cost-effective applications by providing a fully managed serverless computing environment. Developers can focus on writing code and delivering value to their users, while AWS takes care of the underlying infrastructure and operational tasks.

Lambda Limitations

AWS Lambda, a serverless computing service, runs your code in response to events. Though it has many advantages, there are some limitations that should be known:

- **Execution Timeout:** The maximum execution timeout for a Lambda function is 15 minutes.
- **Memory:** It can assign memory to the Lambda functions from 128 MB to 10,240 MB.
- **Ephemeral Storage:** The /tmp directory contains 512 MB for temporary storage with each Lambda function.
- **Deployment Package Size:** The maximum size of a deployment package is 50 MB when directly uploaded and 250 MB when uploaded as a ZIP file on Amazon S3.
- **Environment Variables:** It can use 4 KB of environment variables.
- **Concurrency Limits:** The default concurrency limit on executions across all regional functions is 1,000.
- **Payload Size:** The maximum request and response payload size for synchronous invocation is 6 MB; for asynchronous invocation, it is 256 KB.
- **Language Support:** This is limited to supported programming languages such as Node.js, Python, Ruby, Java, Go, .NET, and a custom runtime.

Other AWS Serverless Services

Beyond Lambda, AWS offers a rich ecosystem of serverless services to empower your applications:

Amazon API Gateway (Creating APIs for Serverless Applications)

Imagine a single entry point for your serverless application. API Gateway lets you create and manage APIs that seamlessly connect to your Lambda functions, making them accessible worldwide. It allows users to easily interact with the different functions you have created without them needing to know the specific location of each one. Here is how it makes life easier:

- **Easy access:** API Gateway translates user requests (such as ringing the doorbell) into a format that your functions (the units) understand.
- **Find the suitable unit:** API Gateway determines which function (unit) is best suited to handle the user's request and directs them there.
- **Security:** API Gateway acts like a security guard, ensuring only authorized users can access your functions.
- **Scalability:** Just like a big apartment building can handle many tenants, API Gateway can manage a vast number of user requests at once.

Overall, API Gateway simplifies how users interact with your serverless application, making it efficient and secure.

AWS Serverless Application Model (SAM) for Easy Deployment

Building and deploying serverless applications can be streamlined with AWS SAM. It provides a template-based approach that simplifies packaging and deploying your serverless codebase.

SAM is a tool that makes deploying serverless applications on AWS a breeze. It lets you define your entire application infrastructure using a single template file written in YAML. This template specifies the code, configurations, and resources your application needs to run. Think of SAM as a magic wand for deployment. With SAM, you do not have to worry about manually setting up and configuring servers. SAM takes care of everything behind the scenes, allowing you to focus on what matters most that is building great applications. It is fast, efficient, and much easier for your developer life. So, ditch the deployment headaches and embrace the power of SAM!

DynamoDB (NoSQL Database for Serverless Applications)

DynamoDB can be used when you need a flexible database for your serverless app. DynamoDB is a NoSQL database that scales effortlessly and integrates seamlessly with other serverless services. It is a special kind of database, called a NoSQL database, that is ideal for serverless applications.

Here is what makes DynamoDB so useful for serverless applications:

- **Super-Fast:** It retrieves data in milliseconds, no matter how much data you have stored. Imagine finding a document in a filing cabinet instantly, even if the cabinet is overflowing.
- **Scales Up and Down:** If you need more storage or processing power, then DynamoDB automatically adjusts to your needs, so you only pay for what you use. It is like having a filing cabinet that magically expands when you need more space.
- **No Server Hassle:** Since it is serverless, you do not have to worry about managing servers or software. You can focus on building your application, and DynamoDB handles the behind-the-scenes work.

DynamoDB lets you store and access data quickly and efficiently without the headaches of managing your servers. In Chapter 6, *Deep Dive into AWS Databases*, we will explore DynamoDB in detail.

S3 (Object Storage for Serverless Applications)

Store and manage any amount of data, from images to log files, with S3, a highly scalable and cost-effective object storage service that integrates perfectly with serverless applications.

Think of it this way: you are building a serverless application, like a mobile app that lets users upload photos. With S3, you do not need to worry about setting up and maintaining your storage servers. Instead, you upload the user's photos to S3, and S3 takes care of everything behind the scenes. It scales up or down automatically based on how much storage you need, so you only pay for what you use.

That is the beauty of S3 for serverless applications: it provides a secure, reliable, and cost-effective way to store all your data without the burden of managing servers yourself. It is like having an infinite storage room in the cloud, always available for your serverless apps.

AWS AppSync

AppSync is a serverless service from AWS that acts as a layer between your application and your data sources. It used GraphQL, a query language, to request specific data from various sources.

Benefits of AppSync:

- GraphQL lets developers request the needed data, reducing the back-and-forth communication between the app and the servers.
- An AppSync API can query data from different sources, such as DynamoDB (a NoSQL database), RDS (a relational database), and custom APIs, and present it in a unified way to your application.
- AppSync supports subscriptions, which allows your app to receive real-time updates whenever the data in the backend changes to build dynamic and interactive features.
- AppSync offers authorization and built-in authentication features to control access to your data.

AWS Step Functions

AWS Step Functions is a serverless orchestration service that helps glue together different application parts. Step Functions let you define workflows for your application to complete a task.

Some key terms include:

- **State machine**: These define the order of any steps, any decision points, and handle errors.
- **States**: Each step in the workflow is called a state. The types of states are:
  - **Wait states:** These pause the workflow until a certain condition is met.
  - **Pass states**: These pass data between steps without processing.
  - **Task states**: These call upon AWS services or external APIs to perform actions.

Benefits of using Step Functions:

- Step Functions provide a drag-and-drop interface to design your workflows, which makes it easier to understand complex logic.
- They integrate with other AWS services, allowing you to trigger workflows based on events from those services.
- They can handle large-scale workflows with millions of tasks, automatically scaling with your needs.
- They automatically retry failed tasks and allow you to define fallback procedures for unexpected situations.

AWS Fargate

Fargate is a serverless compute engine running Docker containers in the AWS cloud. It is an on-demand service for containerized applications. You provide the container image and the resources needed (CPU, memory), and Fargate takes care of the rest.

Benefits of using Fargate:

- It allows you to focus on building and deploying your applications quickly by removing server management from the equation.
- It handles everything–provisioning, configuring, and scaling.
- The pay-per-use model ensures you only pay for the resources you use.
- It automatically scales your containers up or down based on traffic.
- It integrates with both ECS and EKS, allowing you to manage your containers.

Comparison between AWS Serverless Services

This table briefly overviews the other AWS Serverless services discussed in the aforementioned section. It highlights their core functionalities and gives you a roadmap for choosing the right service based on your needs. If you are working on tasks related to data storage, serverless development, data access, or workflow automation, AWS provides various tools to simplify your development process.

Service	Description	Use Case
API Gateway	Creates and manages APIs that act as a front-end for other AWS services.	Build APIs to access data or functionality from other AWS services.
SAM (Serverless Application Model)	Helps define, package, and deploy serverless applications on AWS.	Simplify development and deployment of serverless applications using templates.
DynamoDB	NoSQL database for key-value pairs.	Store data that requires fast access and flexible schema.
S3	Scalable object storage for various data types.	Store and retrieve data, from images and videos to documents and archives.
AppSync	GraphQL API service for real-time data queries.	Build data applications with real-time features, offline capabilities, and fine-grained authorization.
Step Functions	Orchestrates AWS services into serverless workflows.	Automate complex workflows that involve multiple AWS services.

Fargate	Provisions serverless containers for running code.	Run containerized applications without managing servers.

Table 5.2: *Comparison between other serverless services*

Table 5.2 provides an overview of the AWS Serverless services discussed.

ECS vs EKS vs Fargate

You have the following options when you deploy containerized applications on AWS: Amazon Elastic Container Service, Amazon Elastic Container Service for Kubernetes, and AWS Fargate. These services offer various degrees of control, customization, and operational overhead. *Table* 5.3 briefly compares ECS with EKS and Fargate

Feature/Aspect	Amazon ECS	Amazon EKS	AWS Fargate
Definition	Fully managed container orchestration service	Managed Kubernetes service	Serverless compute engine for containers
Control Plane	Managed by AWS	Managed Kubernetes control plane	Managed by AWS
Orchestration	ECS Task Definitions	Kubernetes	ECS or EKS
Compute Options	EC2 instances or Fargate	EC2 instances or Fargate	Fargate only
Ease of Use	Simpler, AWS-specific	More complex, Kubernetes-standard	Simplest, no infrastructure management
Scaling	Managed scaling with ECS Service Auto Scaling	Kubernetes native scaling	Automatic scaling by AWS
Cost	Pay for EC2 instances or Fargate vCPU/memory	Pay for EKS cluster + EC2 or Fargate resources	Pay per vCPU and memory
Integration	Deep integration with AWS services	Kubernetes ecosystem, including non-AWS services	Deep integration with AWS services
Customizability	Limited compared to Kubernetes	Highly customizable with Kubernetes	Less customizable, focuses on simplicity
Operational Overhead	Lower than managing Kubernetes	Requires Kubernetes knowledge	Minimal, as it abstracts the infrastructure

Use Cases	AWS-native workloads, simpler setups	Standardized Kubernetes workflows, multi-cloud	Serverless, event-driven, or unpredictable workloads
Security	IAM roles and policies, security groups	Kubernetes RBAC, Network Policies	IAM roles and policies, security groups
Learning Curve	Lower, AWS-specific	Steeper, standard Kubernetes concepts	Very low, no infrastructure to manage
Monitoring and Logging	CloudWatch integration	CloudWatch, Kubernetes-native tools	CloudWatch integration
Community and Ecosystem	AWS-specific	Large, active Kubernetes community	AWS-specific

Table 5.3: *ECS versus EKS versus Fargate*

Building Serverless Applications on AWS

Now that you have explored the building blocks, let us get into the implementation.

Designing Serverless Architectures

Crafting a robust serverless architecture is critical. Here, you will learn design patterns and best practices to build scalable, fault-tolerant, serverless applications.

Imagine you are building a new city. Instead of laying bricks and mortar for every building, you have prefabricated structures that can be quickly assembled for different purposes. That is the beauty of serverless architecture!

In serverless, you do not worry about managing servers or provisioning resources. Instead, you focus on your application's core functionality. It is like having a team of specialists pre-configure everything for you so you can concentrate on building the most incredible theme park in town (your application).

So, how do we design these serverless cities? Here is a step-by-step approach:

1. **Break it Down:** Like any good city planner, you first need a blueprint. This means dividing your application into smaller, independent functions. These functions are modular buildings, each with a specific purpose (like processing payments or handling user logins).
2. **Pick the Perfect Plot:** Different functions might have different needs. Some might need to handle a lot of traffic (think bustling marketplaces), while others

might be more background tasks (such as the sewage system). Serverless offers various services, such as cloud functions or event-driven triggers, that are the foundation for these functions. Choose the exemplary service based on the function's requirements.

3. **Get Connected:** Just like a city needs roads and bridges, your serverless functions need a way to communicate with each other and external systems. Here is where event queues and APIs come in. Imagine event queues as messengers carrying information between functions and APIs as the bridges connecting your serverless city to the rest of the world.
4. **Scaling for the Future:** Cities are designed to grow, and so should your serverless applications. The beauty of serverless is that it scales automatically. You do not have to worry about adding more servers or managing resources; the cloud provider handles that. It is like having a city that can magically expand its roads and utilities as more people move in.

By following these steps, you can design robust and scalable serverless architectures that focus on building excellent applications!

Best Practices for Building Serverless Applications

Building serverless applications comes with its own set of considerations. This section dives into best practices to ensure your serverless journey is smooth and successful.

- **Security First:**
    - Allow access to only what is needed.
    - Use Virtual Private Clouds (VPCs) to limit who can get close to your application.
    - Store sensitive data such as passwords securely, and never put them directly in your code.
- **Building for Reliability:**
    - Design your application to keep running smoothly, even if things go wrong.
    - Have backup plans in place to handle errors and failures gracefully.
- **Making it Speedy:**
    - Reduce those cold starts where your serverless function takes a while to wake up.
    - Store frequently used data so you can avoid grabbing it from scratch.
- **Keeping Costs Down:**
    - Refrain from paying for more memory or processing power than your functions need.

  - Avoid keeping functions constantly warmed up if they're not being used continually.
- **Monitoring and Optimization:**
  - Track how your serverless application is performing so you can identify areas for improvement.
  - Use monitoring tools to understand how your entire application, not just the serverless parts, works together.

By following these best practices, you can build secure, reliable, fast, and cost-effective serverless applications.

Monitoring and Debugging Serverless Applications

Keeping an eye on your serverless applications is crucial. Here are some practical monitoring and debugging tactics:

Monitoring:

- Track key metrics such as invocation counts, duration, and errors. This helps identify trends and potential bottlenecks. Think of these metrics as your fingerprints at the scene; they tell the story of what happened.
- Use clear and concise logging statements throughout your code. Include details such as timestamps, function names, and error messages. Detailed logs are your witness statements; they provide a chronological account of events.
- Set up alerts for critical events such as error spikes or unusually long execution times. This allows you to catch problems before they snowball into major issues. Imagine alerts as alarms that wake you up if there is a break-in!

Debugging:

- Use tools to simulate real-world scenarios and test your functions locally. This helps catch bugs before they reach production like a detective practicing before questioning a suspect.
- Utilize distributed tracing tools to visualize the data flow across your serverless application. This helps pinpoint precisely where an issue occurs, similar to following a trail of footprints to find the culprit.
- Use the debugging tools your cloud provider offers to step through your code line by line. This allows you to inspect variables and identify where things go wrong, just like a detective examining evidence at a crime scene.

By following these tactics, you can master monitoring and debugging your serverless applications. Remember, a little proactiveness goes a long way toward keeping your serverless world running smoothly!

Reservations and Savings Plans

AWS offers these commitment-based pricing models to help you manage cloud costs while aligning with your usage patterns and scalability requirements. Let us look at these in detail:

AWS Reserved Instances (RIs)

Reserved Instances are designed for customers who can commit to using a specific AWS instance type and region for one or three years. Customers commit to a specific instance type, operating system, and region for the reservation, allowing AWS to offer up to 72% in cost savings compared to On-Demand rates.

Types of Reserved Instances:

- **Standard RIs**: These provide the highest discounts (up to 72%) but give the least flexibility. They are fixed to a specific instance type and region.
- **Convertible RIs**: These offer slightly lower savings (up to 66%) but provide enough flexibility to change the instance family, operating system, and region during the term, allowing you to adapt to changing requirements.

Payment Options

RIs can be purchased with various payment options, including:

- **All Upfront**: Pay the entire cost at the beginning of the term, which provides the highest discount.
- **Partial Upfront**: Pay part of the cost upfront and the rest over the term.
- **No Upfront**: Pay as you go throughout the term.

Capacity Reservation

Standard RIs provide capacity reservation, guaranteeing the availability of the reserved capacity within the selected Availability Zone.

AWS Savings Plans

Savings Plans offer a more flexible pricing model than RIs, allowing you to save up to 66% off your AWS compute costs. Instead of committing to a specific instance type, Savings Plans require you to commit to a particular dollar amount per hour for compute usage, which applies across multiple AWS services.

Types of Savings Plans:

- **Compute Savings Plans**: These provide the most excellent flexibility and apply to various services, including Amazon EC2, AWS Fargate, and AWS Lambda, across any instance family, region, operating system, or tenancy. You can switch instances and regions without affecting your committed rate.

- **EC2 Instance Savings Plans**: These offer higher discounts (up to 72%) but are limited to a specific instance family in a single region. They automatically apply to any size within the chosen family and region but are less flexible than Compute Savings Plans.

Payment Options

Similar to RIs, Savings Plans can be paid for with all upfront, partial upfront, or no upfront payments, providing flexibility in managing your finances.

Automatic Application

Savings Plans automatically apply to the most cost-effective usage first, helping you maximize savings with minimal management. They do not require manual monitoring and adjustments.

Ideal Use Cases:

- **Compute Savings Plans**: These are ideal for customers with variable usage across multiple services and regions who need flexibility to adapt to changing requirements.
- **EC2 Instance Savings Plans**: These are best for customers with predictable workloads in a specific instance family and region who can take advantage of higher discounts due to their consistent usage patterns.

Comparison and Selection

While both RIs and Savings Plans offer substantial savings, the choice between them depends on your specific needs:

- **Flexibility**: Choose Savings Plans if you need flexibility in your instance types, regions, and services. They are handy for dynamic and evolving workloads.
- **Predictability and Savings**: Opt for Reserved Instances if you have a stable, predictable workload that can commit to specific instance configurations for extended periods. RIs provide higher savings for fixed, consistent usage.

Conclusion

This chapter equips you with the knowledge to leverage the power of cloud computing for your applications. It started with a deep dive into EC2, a core service for launching virtual machines, and how to choose the right instance type, configure security, and even scale your infrastructure as needed. The chapter explored containers, a more lightweight alternative to VMs, discovering the advantages of containerization and how to leverage Docker on AWS, including managing container images with a dedicated registry. It also introduced Amazon ECS, a service for orchestrating containerized applications, and the benefits of using a managed Kubernetes service such as Amazon EKS. Finally, the chapter unveiled serverless computing, a revolutionary approach that removes the burden of server management. You also gained valuable knowledge on designing serverless architectures, best practices for development, and even how to troubleshoot these applications. The chapter wrapped up with AWS reserved instances and savings plans.

The next chapter, *Deep Dive into AWS Databases*, explains databases' applications, classifications, and advantages, with a special focus on SQL and NoSQL databases. It also highlights the essential factors for effective data storage, retrieval, and administration.

Multiple Choice Questions

1. Which of the following is a key feature of AWS EC2?
    a. Serverless execution
    b. Elastic block storage
    c. VPC Peering
    d. Managed database services
2. Which of the following services gives a fully managed container orchestration service?
    a. Amazon ECS
    b. Amazon S3
    c. Amazon RDS
    d. AWS Lambda
3. AWS Lambda is an example of which kind of service?
    a. Container service
    b. Compute service
    c. Serverless service
    d. Database service

4. What is the primary benefit of using Reservations and Savings Plans on AWS?
    a. Improved security
    b. Less latency
    c. Cost reduction
    d. More scalability
5. Which of the following AWS services allows the customer to run Docker containers on a managed service?
    a. Amazon ECS
    b. AWS Lambda
    c. Amazon S3
    d. AWS Fargate
6. Which of the following AWS services is a fully managed service for running and managing Docker containers?
    a. Amazon EC2
    b. AWS Lambda
    c. AWS Fargate
    d. Amazon RDS
7. Which of the following AWS services will automatically scale compute capacity based on incoming traffic to your application?
    a. Amazon EC2 Auto Scaling
    b. AWS Elastic Beanstalk
    c. Amazon S3
    d. Amazon VPC
8. What is one of the major advantages of using AWS Savings Plans?
    a. Improved security
    b. Discounts on compute usage
    c. Increased scalability
    d. Faster deployment through automation

9. Which of the following AWS services is designed for running event-driven code without provisioning or managing servers?
    a. AWS Lambda
    b. Amazon ECS
    c. Amazon EC2
    d. AWS Fargate
10. Which of the following is a key benefit of using Reserved Instances in AWS?
    a. Reduced latency
    b. Lower cost compared to On-Demand Instances
    c. Increased security
    d. Better integration with on-premises resources

Answers

1. b
2. a
3. c
4. c
5. d
6. c
7. a
8. b
9. a
10. b

References

- https://aws.amazon.com/ec2/ec2-get-started/
- https://www.geeksforgeeks.org/what-is-elastic-compute-cloud-ec2/
- https://www.digitalocean.com/community/tutorials/transitioning-from-amazon-ec2-to-digitalocean-s-control-panel
- https://docs.aws.amazon.com/ec2/

- https://aws.amazon.com/lambda/
- https://aws.amazon.com/ecs/
- https://aws.amazon.com/cloudwatch/
- https://a4937.medium.com/serverless-jenkins-on-aws-ecs-with-fargate-and-ecr-using-terraform-771e638d6abb
- https://docs.aws.amazon.com/AmazonECS/latest/developerguide/AWS_Fargate.html
- https://docs.aws.amazon.com/step-functions/
- https://docs.aws.amazon.com/appsync/
- https://aws.amazon.com/s3/
- https://aws.amazon.com/serverless/sam/
- https://aws.amazon.com/eks/
- https://redhat.com/en/topics/containers
- https://docs.aws.amazon.com/autoscaling/
- https://docs.docker.com/

CHAPTER 6
Deep Dive Into AWS Databases

Introduction

As an architect, one can be fascinated by the precise planning and structured design that goes into creating magnificent buildings. This same fascination can be found in designing robust and scalable database systems within software development. Just like in architecture, the foundation is critical. In database design, authorizing a solid foundation is essential.

A structured database system ensures software applications' reliability, efficiency, and growth potential, just as a sturdy base is essential for a building's stability.

In a major project to design the data infrastructure for a rapidly growing e-commerce platform, the client required a system to handle millions of transactions daily, maintain high availability, and provide swift data retrieval for a seamless user experience. Choosing the right type of database was paramount to the project's success.

Picture this: a thriving online marketplace is gearing up for a growth phase. Its existing data framework is facing challenges in keeping up with the demands. Millions of daily transactions, seamless user experiences, and constant uptime are critical for their success. To achieve this, they need a database that can handle the heat.

Analyzing diverse use cases reveals that different database types serve distinct functions.

Examining various use cases demonstrates that different kinds of databases fulfill specific purposes. SQL databases suit transactional activities such as order placements, inventory management, and user identification because of their ACID qualities (Atomicity, Consistency, Isolation, Durability). These properties guarantee dependability and maintain data integrity. However, when managing substantial amounts of unorganized data such as user reviews, product suggestions, and browsing history, a NoSQL database can be more appropriate because of its schema-less nature and ability to scale horizontally.

Databases are important in contemporary applications, serving as the foundation for effective data storage, retrieval, and administration. This chapter examines the many applications, classifications, and advantages of databases, specifically focusing on SQL and NoSQL databases and comparing them while highlighting the essential factors that software engineering necessitates. Let us begin our expedition to promote knowledge.

Structure

In this chapter, we will cover the following topics:

- Introduction to Databases
- Deep Dive into RDS
- Introduction to Aurora
- Strategies for Cost-Effective Database Design
- Optimizing Database Performance
- Overview of NoSQL Databases and Available Services on AWS
- Deep Dive into DynamoDB
- Other AWS NoSQL Databases
- Big Data and Analytics on AWS
- Additional AWS Services for Data Management and Analytics
- Introduction to Caches

Introduction to Databases

Databases are pivotal in today's applications, serving as the foundation for handling, organizing, and storing data.

This segment delves into scenarios, categories, and advantages of databases, highlighting the contrast between SQL and NoSQL databases. It resembles an architect's transition from designing buildings to establishing data systems

Use Cases, Types, and Benefits

Databases are used in diverse scenarios, each with specific needs and a particular choice of database type. To choose the correct tool for the task or job, you need to be able to differentiate between them by categories and use cases.

Online Analytical Processing (OLAP) Versus Online Transaction Processing (OLTP)

In the following table, we will cover the different types of processing database types.

OLAP	OLTP
Consists of historical data from various Databases	Consists of only operational current data
It is used for data mining and is subject-oriented	It is used for business tasks and is application-oriented
Tables are not normalized	Tables are normalized
Queries are relatively slower	Queries are relatively faster
It is not often updated	It is often updated for data integrity
Only read and rare write operations	Both read and write operations

Table 6.1: *OLAP versus OLTP*

Table 6.1 contrasts Online Analytical Processing with Online Transaction Processing.

The ACID Properties

ACID, short for Atomicity, Consistency, Isolation, and Durability, comprises aspects that influence database transactions. These elements ensure the correctness and consistency of data in situations where multiple users are making changes to the data simultaneously.

- **Atomicity (A):** This characteristic ensures that a transaction is considered inseparable. Every operation inside the transaction must either succeed, resulting in the changes being committed to the database, or fail, leaving the database unchanged. This is accomplished using methods such as redo/undo logging, guaranteeing no incomplete modifications occur.
- **Consistency (C):** This guarantees that a transaction successfully transitions the database from a valid state to another valid one. The transaction adheres to all specified constraints, referential integrity rules, and data validation tests, ensuring no incorrect or contradictory data is added to the database.
- **Isolation (I):** Isolation ensures that concurrent transactions are completed in a way that makes it seem like they were done sequentially, even if they occur concurrently. This helps prevent data races and inconsistencies when multiple transactions try to edit the same data simultaneously. Isolation methods, such as locking, guarantee that only one transaction may access data at a time throughout its execution.
- **Durability (D):** Durability guarantees that if a transaction is successfully committed, the modifications made to the database will be permanently preserved. The modifications remain intact regardless of a system failure after the commit. The transaction logs are typically written to a stable storage medium, such as a disc, before committing the transaction.

The ACID features synergistically contribute to establishing a resilient framework for reliably and predictably handling database transactions. Database systems that follow these principles provide data dependability and consistency, even in situations involving high concurrency and possible system failures.

Imagine you are managing a bank account with your friend. ACID properties ensure everything runs smoothly, even if you both try to edit the balance simultaneously.

- **Atomicity (A):** All or nothing. Think of a bank deposit. Either the entire amount goes in, or nothing changes. It is like both of you writing down the deposit amount together or not at all. No half-deposits!
- **Consistency (C):** It is like having the bank verify your current balance before allowing a withdrawal, ensuring you have enough funds and the new balance makes sense.
- **Isolation (I):** Imagine using separate ATM booths to check and withdraw money. You do not see each other's transactions, which appear to happen independently.
- **Durability (D):** Changes are permanent, even in emergencies. The change is saved permanently once a transaction is committed (such as a successful withdrawal). Even if the power goes out, the bank has backups to record your updated balance securely.

The BASE Properties

BASE (Basically Available, Soft State, Eventual Consistency) is a design philosophy for data systems that prioritizes availability over absolute consistency. To elaborate,

- **Basically Available**: The system is almost always running, even during failures.
- **Soft State**: Data state can change over time without user interaction.
- **Eventual Consistency**: Data will eventually have consistency across all replicas, but not immediately.

Two Pillars of Database Systems: SQL and NoSQL

Relational databases almost all use SQL, but it's not a requirement, and some less well-known relational databases do not use SQL or don't implement all of the standards. Non-relational databases are typically grouped as NoSQL, but so many different types of databases and data stores fall under this umbrella that this is not a uniform category. Relational databases, such as MySQL, store data in tables. Depending on your needs, you can consider options such as column-oriented databases for massive data analysis or document-oriented databases such as MongoDB for storing flexible, JSON-like data. There are even graph databases that excel at modeling relationships between data points and key-value stores that prioritize fast retrieval of specific data items.

Choosing Your Database Champion: SQL versus NoSQL

In the data storage arena, developers have two main allies: relational databases (SQL) and non-relational databases (NoSQL). Each offers distinct strengths and caters to specific data requirements. Selecting the right database is crucial, as it is the foundation for your application.

The Structured Kingdom: SQL Databases

Structured Query Language (SQL) databases, commonly called databases, hold a position in managing structured data. They systematically arrange data into tables composed of rows and columns, creating connections between data elements. This feature makes them particularly well-suited for situations where data relationships are crucial, such as in software or systems used for inventory control.

Advantages of SQL Databases:

- **Reliable Transactions**: SQL boasts ACID compliance, ensuring data integrity through properties such as Atomicity (transactions are all-or-nothing), Consistency (data remains consistent), Isolation (transactions don't interfere with each other), and Durability (committed transactions are permanent).
- **Structured Data Mastery**: SQL excels at managing data with predefined schemas. This structured approach makes it perfect for complex queries and applications that require a rigid data model, such as financial transactions or customer records.
- **Data Integrity**: Maintains strong data integrity through constraints, foreign keys, and normalization.

Common Use Cases of SQL Databases:

- Financial applications require precise transaction handling.
- Enterprise applications with intricate querying needs.
- Applications where data consistency and accuracy are paramount.

Examples of SQL Databases:

- MySQL
- PostgreSQL
- Oracle Database
- Microsoft SQL Server

The Power of NoSQL Databases

NoSQL databases diverge from SQL's framework. Some are proficient at managing a range of data formats, such as semi-structured data. NoSQL provides adaptability in designing schemas and horizontal scalability, making it well-suited for ever-changing data settings.

Benefits of NoSQL Databases:

- **Schema Flexibility:** Allows dynamic schema design and easy modifications, perfect for evolving data models.
- **Horizontal Scalability**: Handles massive datasets by scaling out across multiple servers.
- **Performance:** Tailored for reading and writing tasks.
- **Diverse Data Models:** Compatible with data structures such as documents, key-value pairs, column families and graphs.

Common Use Cases of NoSQL Databases:

- Social media applications storing diverse user-generated content.
- Real-time analytics and big data applications.
- Content management systems require flexible and scalable storage.

Examples of NoSQL Databases:

- MongoDB (Document Store)
- Cassandra (Wide Column Store)
- Redis (Key-Value Store)
- Neo4j (Graph Database)

SQL versus NoSQL: A Real-World Example

Let us consider an e-commerce platform to illustrate the distinction between SQL and NoSQL databases.

SQL for E-commerce:

- **Product Catalog**: A table stores product details such as ID, name, description, price, and stock.
- **Customer Information**: A table stores customer details such as ID, name, email, and address.
- **Order Management:** Separate tables manage orders, order items, and payments, ensuring transaction integrity and accurate reporting.

NoSQL for E-commerce:

- **User Reviews**: Stores user-generated reviews with various formats and ratings in a flexible schema.
- **Session Data**: Captures user sessions and interactions for personalized recommendations in real-time.
- **Product Recommendations**: Utilizes graph databases to analyze user behavior and recommend products.

Choosing Wisely: SQL versus NoSQL

Understanding your data and application requirements is key to choosing between SQL and NoSQL. By recognizing these strengths, developers can make informed decisions and build robust and scalable database systems.

Common Use Cases of SQL Databases:

- Financial applications require precise transaction handling.
- Enterprise applications with intricate querying needs.
- Applications where data consistency and accuracy are paramount.

Examples of SQL Databases:

- MySQL
- PostgreSQL
- Oracle Database
- Microsoft SQL Server

SQL versus NoSQL Comparison:

Feature	SQL Databases	NoSQL Databases
Data Model	Relational (tables)	Document, Key-Value, Column-Family, Graph
Schema	Fixed schema	Generally variable schema
Scalability	Often requires vertical scaling (scaling up)	Usually supports horizontal scaling (scaling out)
Transactions	ACID-compliant	BASE-compliant (Basically Available, Soft state, Eventual consistency)
Query Language	Usually supports Structured Query Language (SQL)	Varies by database (example, MongoDB uses JSON-based queries)
Use Cases	Structured data, complex queries, transactional systems	Unstructured data, big data, real-time analytics

Table 6.2: *Comparison between SQL and NoSQL databases*

Table 6.2 provides a brief comparison between SQL and NoSQL databases

When developers grasp the variances between SQL and NoSQL databases, they can confidently select the database type for their applications, considering their unique requirements and limitations.

Like architects strategize the groundwork and framework of their endeavors, contemporary developers must thoughtfully choose and configure their database setups to guarantee top-notch efficiency, scalability, and dependability.

Introduction to RDS: Manage Your Relational Databases in the Cloud

This section provides information about the key features, benefits, and best practices for using Amazon RDS, and how it empowers you to harness the full potential of your relational databases.

Eliminating the Burden of Complex Database Management

Amazon's Relational Database Service (RDS) is a cloud-based offering from AWS designed to simplify database management. With RDS, developers can focus on building applications without navigating the intricacies of configuring, operating, and scaling databases.

What RDS can do for you:

- RDS handles tasks like setting up hardware, configuring databases, updating software, and backing up data automatically, allowing you to focus on higher-level tasks.
- If you get caught up in database management, you can dedicate time to developing exceptional applications.

RDS: Your High-Performance Database on Autopilot

Like equipping your car for a smooth ride, Amazon RDS provides the features you need for a high-performing database experience. Let us explore these features and how they benefit you:

Amazon RDS: Supported Database Engines- Find Your Perfect Match

Amazon RDS offers a diverse range of popular relational database engines tailored to fit your specific requirements:

Amazon Aurora:

- Built specifically for the cloud, ensuring high performance and scalability.
- Fully compatible with MySQL and PostgreSQL syntax.
- Provides up to five times the throughput of MySQL and three times that of PostgreSQL.
- It guarantees high availability with automatic replication across multiple availability zones.
- Continuously backs up data to Amazon S3, enhancing durability.

MySQL:

- A popular relational database engine that is commonly utilized.
- Suitable for web applications and small-to-sized systems.
- Known for its user-friendliness and cost efficiency.
- AWS RDS, for MySQL, provides a managed service.

MariaDB:

- An open-source relational database and a community-developed fork of MySQL.
- Highly compatible with MySQL, offering additional features.
- Designed for enhanced performance, scalability, and security.
- AWS RDS provides a managed service for MariaDB deployments.

PostgreSQL:

- A popular open-source database is known for its flexibility and adherence to industry standards.
- It can handle various data formats and advanced search queries, making it ideal for use in various settings, from basic websites to complex scientific calculations.
- AWS RDS provides a managed solution for PostgreSQL databases.

Oracle Database:

- A widely used enterprise database solution celebrated for its robustness.
- Delivers strong performance, scalability, and reliability.
- Ideal for demanding enterprise applications.
- AWS RDS supports various Oracle editions (Standard, and Enterprise) to meet specific needs.

SQL Server:

- A relational database developed by Microsoft, renowned for its Windows integration.
- Offers enterprise-grade features for security and manageability.
- Ideal for software designed to work within the Microsoft ecosystem.
- AWS RDS offers a service for hosting SQL Server in a cloud environment.

Instance Type Options: Balancing Performance and Cost

Like choosing the right car size for a trip, instance types in RDS cater to different performance and budget requirements. Here is a breakdown:

- **General Purpose (T3, T4g):** Cost-effective option for small to medium workloads, offering a balance of compute, memory, and network resources.

  Think of it as a reliable sedan, perfect for everyday use.
- **Memory Optimized (R5, R6g, X1, X2):** Designed for high-performance databases with large memory needs (real-time analytics, caching, large-scale database applications).

  Imagine a high-performance sports car, ideal for speed and handling massive data.
- **Compute Optimized (C5):** Ideal for applications requiring high CPU power (high-performance web servers, scientific modeling, batch processing).

  Think of it as a powerful off-road vehicle, built for demanding tasks.
- **Storage Optimized (I3):** Perfect for databases requiring intensive I/O operations (transactional databases, NoSQL databases, data warehousing).

  Imagine a heavy-duty truck, built for handling large volumes of data efficiently.

Multi-AZ Deployments: Ensuring High Availability

Imagine your car has a spare tire– that is what Multi-AZ deployments are for RDS! They provide high availability and data protection:

- **Automatic Replication**: Your database is automatically replicated across multiple Availability Zones (AZs) for redundancy.
- **Synchronous Standby**: A duplicate of your database (standby replica) is maintained in a different AZ, ready to take over if needed.
- **Minimized Downtime**: RDS automatically switches to the standby replica during an outage, minimizing your application's downtime.

Think of it as peace of mind, knowing your database is always protected.

DB Parameter and Option Groups: Fine-Tuning Performance

Imagine customizing your car's engine for optimal performance. DB Parameter and Option Groups offer similar control for your RDS database:

- **DB Parameter Groups**: These groups allow you to adjust engine configuration values (memory allocation, query optimization) to optimize performance for specific workloads.
- **DB Option Groups**: Activate and configure additional features to extend the functionality of your DB instance. Examples include Oracle Advanced Security and SQL Server Transparent Data Encryption (TDE).

With these groups, you can fine-tune your database for maximum efficiency.

RDS Backups: Safeguarding Your Data

Just like backing up important documents, RDS Backups ensure your data is always protected:

- **Automated Backups**: RDS automatically takes daily backups of your database and transaction logs, storing them in Amazon S3 for up to 35 days. This allows you to restore your database to any point within the retention period.
- **Manual Snapshots**: Create user-initiated backups that can be retained indefinitely. Useful for creating backups before major changes or maintenance activities.

Think of it as a safety net for your valuable data.

RDS Read Replicas: Scaling for Read-Heavy Workloads

Imagine having a team to handle customer inquiries. Read Replicas are similar for RDS.

- **Boost Performance**: Distribute read traffic across multiple replicas, freeing up your primary database for essential tasks.
- **Scale with Ease**: Create up to 5 read replicas to handle growing user demands.
- **Maintain Availability**: Promote replicas to primary in case of an outage for seamless application continuity.

Think of it as a customer service team for your database– handle inquiries efficiently while the main staff tackles complex tasks!

Let RDS Handle the Heavy Lifting; You Focus on What Matters Most!

By leveraging RDS, developers can focus on building applications without getting bogged down in database management complexities. The comprehensive features and flexibility RDS offers ensure that database performance, availability, and scalability meet the demands of modern applications.

Deep Dive into RDS

In this section, we will explore RDS Security and RDS Instances.

RDS Security

In Relational Database Service (RDS), it is easy to configure and protect your data to ensure it is secure and compliant with company policies and legal requirements. This section delves into the essential security considerations for RDS.

- **Protecting Your Data in the Cloud**

  Securing your databases is paramount when managing them in the cloud. Thankfully, Amazon Relational Database Service (RDS) offers a robust suite of features and best practices to safeguard the security and compliance of your database instances. **Controlling Access with Precision: Access Control Mechanisms**

  These tools meticulously control access to your database instances, restricting connection attempts to authorized users and applications.

- **Encryption: Safeguarding Data at Rest and In Transit**

  This layered approach encrypts your data at rest (stored data) and in transit (data being transmitted), adding an extra shield for sensitive information.

- **Network Isolation: Securing Your Databases with VPC**

  Amazon Virtual Private Cloud (VPC) empowers you to establish a logically isolated network for your AWS resources, including RDS instances. This isolation significantly reduces the attack surface, minimizing the potential for unauthorized database access.

- **Maintaining a Watchful Eye: Monitoring and Auditing**

  Proactively monitoring your RDS instances for suspicious activity and meticulously auditing access logs are crucial for robust security. By implementing these practices, you can effectively identify and address potential threats, safeguarding your valuable database information.

The Security Powerhouse: Security Groups and VPC

Security Groups and VPC are two fundamental pillars of securing your RDS instances within the AWS environment. Let us explore each in detail:

- **Security Groups: Virtual Firewalls for Granular Control**

  Security Groups function as virtual firewalls, meticulously controlling inbound and outbound traffic to your RDS instances. You can define granular rules specifying authorized IP addresses, CIDR blocks, and permitted ports and protocols. For instance, you can restrict access to your trusted application servers or corporate network on the standard MySQL port (3306). This granular control ensures that only authorized entities can interact with your databases.

- **VPC: Creating a Secure Network Enclave**

  Amazon VPC allows you to create a logically isolated network within the AWS cloud, providing a dedicated space to launch your AWS resources, including RDS instances. Configuring your VPC correctly is essential for optimal security. Here are key considerations:

  - Network isolation
  - Subnet segmentation
  - Security group configuration
  - NACLs (Network Access Control Lists)

Working with RDS Instances

Amazon Relational Database Service (RDS) simplifies managing your database in the cloud by offering pre-configured database instances that are ready to use. This section empowers you to leverage RDS instances effectively, covering essential tasks from launching your first instance to connecting and managing your database.

Launching an Instance

You can launch an RDS instance through the AWS Management Console. Here is a simplified breakdown:

1. Choose a Database Engine (example, Aurora, MySQL, MariaDB, PostgreSQL).
2. Specify Details (Engine Version, Instance Class, Storage Type, Allocated Storage).
3. Configure Settings (VPC, Subnet, Public Access, Security Groups, Authentication).
4. Launch the Instance.

Connecting to an RDS Instance

Use a database client that supports your chosen engine. Database clients are like specialized tools to access and manage information stored on servers, similar to software for a giant warehouse. They let you connect, query, manage the structure, and visualize data. The steps typically involve:

1. Retrieving Endpoint Information (address and port) from the RDS dashboard.
2. Configuring Security Groups to allow inbound traffic from your client machine's IP address.
3. Using a Database Client to connect with the endpoint, port, database name, username, and password.

Common database clients include MySQL Workbench, pgAdmin, SSMS, Navicat (commercial), and command-line tools (MySQL, psql).

Creating and Recovering from Snapshots

Snapshots are backups of your RDS instances at a specific point in time. Snapshots generally cover the changes over a period of time (hence, they can be created and applied relatively quickly). In contrast, backups are usually an entire dataset (often take a long time to create or apply). A good data strategy involves both full backups and snapshots.

- **Creating a Snapshot:** Navigate to the RDS dashboard, select your instance, and choose **`"Take a snapshot."`**
- **Recovering from a Snapshot:** Select the snapshot you want to restore from the **`"Snapshots"`** section and choose **`"Restore snapshot"`** to create a new instance from the snapshot.

Monitoring RDS Instances

Monitoring is crucial for performance, availability, and reliability. Here are some AWS services for monitoring RDS:

- **Amazon CloudWatch:** Monitors CPU utilization, read/write IOPS, disk space, and network throughput. You can set up alarms and view logs.
- **RDS Performance Insights:** Provides a dashboard for visualizing database load and identifying bottlenecks.
- **AWS CloudTrail:** Logs API calls to RDS, providing visibility into changes and actions performed.

Chapter 8, AWS Management and Services, covers monitoring tools such as CloudWatch and CloudTrail in detail.

Migrating to AWS RDS

Migrating a database to AWS RDS involves several steps:

1. **Planning:** Assess your current database environment, choose the appropriate RDS engine and instance type, and evaluate network requirements, security configurations, and backup strategies.
2. **Schema Conversion:** Use the AWS Schema Conversion Tool (SCT) to convert your database schema to a format compatible with your chosen RDS engine.
3. **Data Migration:** Use the AWS Database Migration Service (DMS) to migrate data from your source database to RDS.
4. **Testing:** Thoroughly test the migrated RDS instance to ensure data integrity and application compatibility.
5. **Cutover:** Plan the cutover to minimize downtime. This typically involves synchronizing final changes, switching DNS settings, and directing application traffic to the RDS instance.

Introduction to Aurora

Let us look at the integration of Aurora with multiple AWS services for securing your applications.

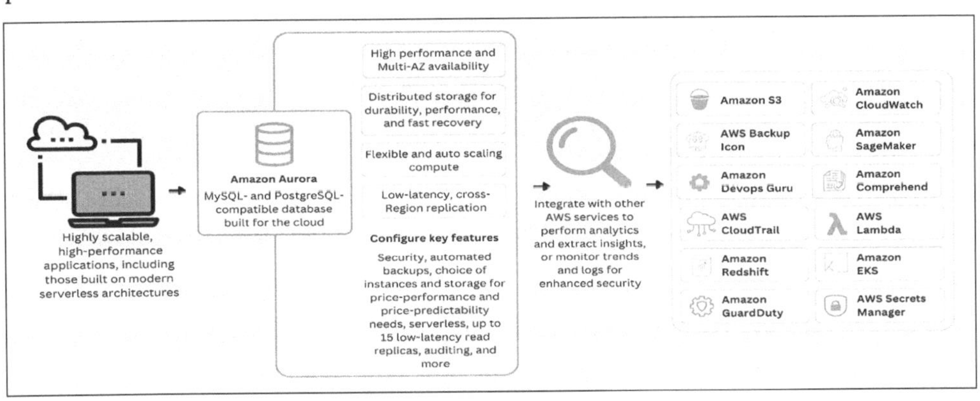

Figure 6.1: *Amazon Aurora*

Figure 6.1 depicts how Amazon Aurora integrates with various AWS services to support highly scalable, high-performance applications with enhanced security and analytics capabilities.

Aurora Overview

This managed database service is offered by Amazon Web Services (AWS). It is a relational database (such as MySQL or PostgreSQL) built for high performance, scalability, and reliability. It is a popular choice for businesses that need a robust database solution for their applications.

Benefits of using Aurora include:

- **Scalability**: You can easily scale storage and compute resources up or down to meet your application's needs.
- **Performance**: Aurora delivers high availability and fast read/write performance for your database workloads.
- **Cost-effective**: You only pay for the resources you use.
- **Security**: Aurora benefits from the robust security features of the AWS platform.

Amazon Aurora goes beyond your typical database, offering a compelling blend of high performance, availability, scalability, and cost-effectiveness. Let us delve into two key features that elevate Aurora.

Aurora Global Databases: Reach Beyond Your Region

Imagine geographically dispersed users accessing your database with minimal lag. Aurora Global Databases makes this a reality. Here is how:

- **Low-Latency Global Reads:** Reduce read latency for users worldwide by offloading traffic to read-only replicas (Aurora Replicas) strategically placed across different AWS regions. Applications automatically connect to the nearest replica, ensuring a smooth user experience.
- **Disaster Recovery with a Global Safety Net:** Unforeseen regional outages become less disruptive. Aurora automatically replicates your primary database cluster to secondary clusters in other regions. If a disaster strikes, one of these replicas can be quickly promoted to become the primary cluster, minimizing downtime and data loss.

Aurora Serverless: Auto-Scaling for a Dynamic World

Managing database capacity can be a constant battle. Aurora Serverless introduces a welcome change:

- **Effortless Auto-Scaling:** Say goodbye to manual scaling! Aurora Serverless automatically adjusts database capacity based on your application's workload, scaling up during peak times and down during lulls. This optimizes resource utilization and keeps costs in check.
- **Pay-Per-Use Efficiency:** Only pay for what you use! This pricing model is ideal for applications with unpredictable or variable workloads. You are billed by the

second for the database capacity consumed by your application, eliminating unnecessary expenses.

- **Instantaneous Scalability:** Sudden traffic spikes would not bring your application down. Aurora Serverless scales from zero to full capacity in seconds, ensuring smooth operation even during unexpected bursts.
- **Pause and Resume for Cost-Consciousness:** Minimize costs during periods of inactivity. With Aurora Serverless, you can pause database capacity, meaning you only pay for storage while the application is not in use. When you need it again, simply resume and get back to business.
- **The Power of Choice:** Aurora offers standard and serverless configurations, allowing you to choose the option that best suits your needs.
- **Combined Benefits:** By leveraging Aurora Global Databases and Aurora Serverless, you can build highly available, scalable, and cost-effective database solutions on AWS. Reach a global audience with low-latency reads, ensure disaster recovery with automatic failover, and enjoy the benefits of auto-scaling and pay-per-use pricing with Aurora Serverless.

Strategies for Cost-Effective Database Design

Keeping your database costs under control is crucial. Here is how you can do it effectively:

- **Right-size your instances:** Choose an instance type with the processing power and storage capacity that matches your application's needs. Do not overpay for resources you do not use.
- **Reserved instances:** For predictable workloads, consider purchasing reserved instances for significant cost savings compared to on-demand pricing.
- **Serverless options:** Explore serverless database options such as Aurora Serverless, eliminating the need to manage and provision database servers yourself.
- **Optimize storage:** Select the storage type that best suits your needs. General Purpose SSD offers a balance, while Provisioned IOPS SSD is ideal for performance-critical workloads. Magnetic disks provide cost-effective storage for infrequently accessed data.
- **Data compression:** Utilize data compression techniques to reduce storage size and costs while improving performance by minimizing disk I/O.
- **Offload read operations:** Implement read replicas or caching to handle read-heavy workloads, reducing the load on your primary database instance.

- **Archive historical data:** Move infrequently accessed data to lower-cost storage solutions such as Amazon S3 or Glacier, freeing up space in your primary database.
- **Monitor and optimize queries:** Regularly analyze and optimize database queries to improve efficiency and reduce resource consumption.
- **Automate tasks:** Leverage automation tools for routine tasks such as backups and patching, reducing operational overhead and costs.
- **Cost allocation tags:** Tag your database resources with appropriate cost allocation tags to track and allocate costs accurately.

Optimizing Database Performance

A well-performing database translates to a smooth user experience. Here are some strategies to keep your database running fast:

- **Indexing:** Properly index tables (create access points for specific data) based on how you typically query them. This speeds up data retrieval significantly.
- **Query optimization:** Analyze and optimize your database queries to minimize resource utilization and improve response times.
- **Data partitioning:** Consider partitioning for large datasets to distribute data across multiple storage devices, improving query performance. This is similar to dividing a large project into smaller, manageable chunks.
- **Caching:** Utilize caching mechanisms such as Redis or Memcached to store frequently accessed data, reducing the load on your database which is similar to having quick access to commonly used reference books.
- **Normalization and denormalization:** When designing your database schema, balance normalization (for data integrity) and denormalization (for performance). Normalization is like organizing your files neatly to avoid duplicates, while denormalization might involve some redundancy for quicker access (just like storing copies of original documents).
- **Optimized storage:** Choose the appropriate storage type based on your workload requirements. Solid-state drives (SSDs) offer superior performance for high-traffic applications.
- **Connection pooling:** Implement connection pooling to reduce overhead associated with establishing and closing database connections.
- **Load balancing:** Distribute database read and write operations across multiple instances using load balancers to improve scalability and availability.
- **Performance monitoring:** Continuously monitor your database performance using monitoring tools to proactively identify and address performance issues. Set up alerts for abnormal behavior or performance degradation.

- **Scaling strategies:** To maintain optimal performance under varying loads, implement vertical scaling (increasing instance size) or horizontal scaling (adding more instances) based on workload demands.
- **Sharding:** Sharding works by splitting a large database into smaller, self-contained units called shards and distributing them across multiple servers. This allows for parallel query processing and improved performance for massive datasets, especially when queries only require a specific shard of data.

Overview of NoSQL Databases and Available Services on AWS

NoSQL databases are a good option for handling large amounts of unstructured or semi-structured data. Here is an overview of popular NoSQL services offered by AWS:

- **Amazon DynamoDB:** A fully managed NoSQL database offering seamless scalability and low-latency response times, ideal for high-traffic applications.
- **Amazon DocumentDB (with MongoDB compatibility):** This managed service offers the scalability and flexibility of MongoDB with the reliability, performance, and security of Amazon Aurora.
- **Amazon Neptune:** A fully managed graph database service optimized for storing and querying highly connected data, such as social networks and recommendation engines.
- **Amazon Keyspaces (for Apache Cassandra):** This managed service provides Apache Cassandra's scalability, availability, and durability without the operational overhead.
- **Amazon ElastiCache:** A fully managed in-memory caching service that improves application performance by caching frequently accessed data.
- **Amazon Timestream:** A fully managed time-series database service designed for ingesting, storing, and querying time-series data, such as IoT sensor data and application logs. Next, we will deep dive into DynamoDB.

Amazon DynamoDB is a fully managed NoSQL database service provided by Amazon Web Services (AWS). It is designed to provide fast and predictable performance with seamless scalability. This deep dive thoroughly explores DynamoDB, covering its introduction, advanced techniques, and best practices based on credible sources.

Introduction to DynamoDB

Amazon DynamoDB is a key-value and document database that delivers single-digit millisecond latency at any scale. Key features of DynamoDB include:

- **Fully Managed:** DynamoDB is a fully managed service, eliminating the need for database administration tasks such as hardware provisioning, setup, configuration, patching, or scaling.

- **Scalable Performance:** DynamoDB provides seamless scalability, allowing users to handle traffic without manual intervention. It automatically scales resources to accommodate changing workload demands.
- **High Availability:** DynamoDB offers built-in high availability with data replication across multiple Availability Zones within a region, ensuring durability and fault tolerance.
- **Flexible Data Model:** DynamoDB supports key-value and document data models, making it suitable for various use cases, including web applications, gaming, IoT, and mobile applications.
- **Pay-Per-Use Pricing:** DynamoDB follows a pay-per-use pricing model, where users only pay for the resources consumed (example, provisioned throughput, storage). There are no upfront costs or long-term commitments.

Advanced Techniques with DynamoDB

Advanced techniques for DynamoDB include:

- **Partitioning and Sharding:** DynamoDB partitions data across multiple storage nodes to ensure scalability and performance. Understanding partitioning and sharding strategies is crucial for optimizing performance and evenly distributing workloads.
- **Data Modeling:** Designing an efficient data model is essential for maximizing DynamoDB's performance and minimizing costs. Techniques such as hierarchical data modeling, indexing, and attribute projection can improve query performance and reduce read/write costs.
- **Transactions:** DynamoDB supports transactional operations that allow users to perform multiple write operations within a single transactional request. Understanding transactional capabilities and implementing atomic operations is critical for maintaining data consistency.
- **Global Secondary Indexes (GSI):** GSIs enable efficient data querying based on non-primary key attributes. Effectively utilizing GSIs can improve query flexibility and reduce the need for full table scans.
- **DynamoDB Accelerator (DAX):** Amazon DynamoDB Accelerator (DAX) is an in-memory caching service that can improve read performance and reduce latency for frequently accessed data. Integrating DAX with DynamoDB can enhance application performance and scalability.

Best Practices for DynamoDB

Best practices for DynamoDB include:

- **Provisioning Throughput:** Provide appropriate read and write capacity units (RCUs and WCUs) based on expected workload and access patterns. Utilize DynamoDB Auto Scaling to adjust throughput capacity automatically based on demand.
- **Data Modeling:** Design efficient data models that optimize for query patterns, minimize hot partitions, and avoid unnecessary data duplication. Use composite primary keys, sparse indexes, and sort keys to organize data effectively.
- **Indexing Strategies:** Utilize Global Secondary Indexes (GSI) and Local Secondary Indexes (LSI) to support diverse query patterns and access paths. Evaluate indexing strategies based on query frequency, selectivity, and projected throughput.
- **Batch Operations:** Use batch operations (example, BatchGetItem, BatchWriteItem) to efficiently retrieve or modify multiple items in a single request, reducing the number of API calls and improving throughput efficiency.
- **Error Handling and Retries:** Implement robust and retry logic to handle transient errors, throttling, and provisioned throughput exceptions. Use exponential backoff and jitter strategies to manage retries and prevent request throttling.
- **Monitoring and Optimization:** Monitor DynamoDB performance metrics, including consumed capacity, throttled requests, and provisioned throughput utilization. Use Amazon CloudWatch alarms and Amazon CloudWatch Contributor Insights to proactively detect and troubleshoot performance issues.
- **Cost Optimization:** Optimize DynamoDB costs by right-sizing provisioned throughput, leveraging on-demand capacity mode for sporadic workloads, and optimizing data storage use. Utilize cost allocation tags and AWS Cost Explorer to effectively track and analyze DynamoDB costs.
- **Security and Access Control:** Implement fine-grained access control using AWS Identity and Access Management (IAM), AWS Key Management Service (KMS) for encryption, and Amazon VPC endpoints for secure communication. Follow AWS security best practices to protect sensitive data and prevent unauthorized access.

By following these best practices and implementing advanced techniques, organizations can maximize DynamoDB's benefits, attain optimal performance, and minimize costs while ensuring scalability, availability, and reliability.

Other AWS NoSQL Databases

In addition to DynamoDB, Amazon Web Services (AWS) offers several other NoSQL databases customized to specific use cases and requirements. These databases provide different data models and features for various data management needs. However, when choosing a NoSQL database, it is important to consider the trade-offs inherent in distributed systems. This is where the CAP theorem comes in.

The CAP theorem is a fundamental concept that applies to all distributed systems, including NoSQL databases. It states that a system can only guarantee two out of the following three properties:

- **Consistency (C):** All nodes in the system agree on the latest data value.
- **Availability (A):** Every read request receives a non-error response, even if data is inconsistent.
- **Partition Tolerance (P):** The system continues to operate even if network partitions occur.

NoSQL databases often prioritize Availability and Partition Tolerance over strict Consistency. This trade-off allows for high performance and scalability, but data may not be immediately consistent across all nodes. Let us explore three other AWS NoSQL databases:

AWS NoSQL Database Comparison:

Feature	DynamoDB	Amazon Keyspaces	Amazon Neptune	Amazon QLDB
Data Model	Key-Value	Wide-Row (Cassandra Compatible)	Graph	Appendable, Immutable Log
Use Cases	High-performance NoSQL workloads, Schemaless data, Big Data	Cassandra workloads, Scalable data, High availability	Social networks, Recommendation systems, Network analysis	Secure, traceable transactions, Audit trails, Regulatory compliance
CAP Theorem	Eventual Consistency (Availability and Partition Tolerance)	Tunable Consistency (AC or CP)	High Availability (AP)	Eventual Consistency (AP)
Data Types	Strings, Numbers, Sets, Lists, Maps	Strings, Numbers, Collections	Nodes, Edges, Properties	String, Integer, Boolean, Timestamp

Table 6.3: *AWS NoSQL Database Comparison*

Table 6.3 compares AWS NoSQL databases.

Let us explore three other AWS NoSQL databases: Amazon Keyspaces, Amazon Neptune, and Amazon Quantum Ledger Database (Amazon QLDB).

Amazon Keyspaces (for Apache Cassandra)

Amazon Keyspaces is a fully managed, scalable, and highly available NoSQL database service compatible with Apache Cassandra. It allows users to build applications using the same Cassandra application code and Apache 2.0 open-source APIs, with the added benefits of AWS-managed infrastructure. Key features of Amazon Keyspaces include:

- **Compatibility:** Amazon Keyspaces is compatible with Apache Cassandra 3.11, allowing users to seamlessly migrate existing Cassandra workloads to AWS.
- **Serverless Scaling:** Keyspaces automatically scale storage and throughput capacity based on application demand, eliminating the need for manual provisioning or management.
- **Regional Replication:** Data in Amazon Keyspaces is automatically replicated across multiple AWS Availability Zones within a region, providing high availability and durability.
- **Data Encryption:** Keyspaces encrypts data at rest using AWS Key Management Service (KMS) and encrypts data in transit using TLS encryption, ensuring data security and compliance.
- **Integration with AWS Services:** Amazon Keyspaces integrates with AWS Identity and Access Management (IAM), AWS CloudTrail, and AWS Key Management Service (KMS) for access control, auditing, and encryption key management.

Amazon Neptune

Amazon Neptune is a fully managed graph database service enabling users to build and run applications with highly connected datasets. Neptune supports Property Graph and RDF Graph models, allowing users to model complex relationships and query data using graph traversal and pattern-matching techniques. Key features of Amazon Neptune include:

- **Graph Database Engine:** Neptune provides a purpose-built graph database engine optimized for storing and querying highly connected data, such as social networks, recommendation engines, and knowledge graphs.
- **Multi-Model Support:** Neptune supports Property Graph and RDF Graph models, allowing users to choose the most suitable data model for their application requirements.
- **High Performance:** Neptune offers fast query performance and low-latency responses, even for complex graph queries spanning millions of vertices and edges.

- **High Availability:** Data in Amazon Neptune is automatically replicated across multiple Availability Zones within a region, providing high availability and fault tolerance.
- **Integration with AWS Services:** Neptune integrates with AWS Identity and Access Management (IAM), AWS CloudTrail, and AWS Key Management Service (KMS) for access control, auditing, and encryption key management.

Amazon Quantum Ledger Database (Amazon QLDB)

Amazon Quantum Ledger Database (QLDB) is a fully managed ledger database service that provides a transparent, immutable, and cryptographically verifiable transaction log. QLDB is designed to provide a central source of truth for applications that require an authoritative record of all changes to data. Key features of Amazon QLDB include:

- **Immutable Ledger:** QLDB maintains an immutable and tamper-evident transaction log, ensuring the integrity and auditability of data over time.
- **Cryptographically Verifiable:** Transactions in QLDB are cryptographically hashed and verifiable using a secure, transparent, and tamper-proof mechanism, providing assurance that data has not been altered or tampered with.
- **Transactional Model:** QLDB supports multi-document ACID (Atomicity, Consistency, Isolation, Durability) transactions, allowing users to execute complex, multi-step transactions reliably.
- **Serverless Scaling:** QLDB automatically scales storage and throughput capacity based on application demand, eliminating the need for manual provisioning or management.
- **Integration with AWS Services:** QLDB integrates with AWS Identity and Access Management (IAM), AWS CloudTrail, and AWS Key Management Service (KMS) for access control, auditing, and encryption key management.

By utilizing these AWS NoSQL databases, organizations can build scalable, high-performance, and cost-effective solutions to address diverse data management requirements, from highly connected graphs to immutable ledgers. Each database service offers unique features and capabilities, allowing users to choose the most suitable option based on their specific use case and workload demands.

Big Data and Analytics on AWS

Big Data and Analytics on Amazon Web Services (AWS) encompasses a comprehensive suite of services and tools designed to help organizations efficiently process, store, analyze, and visualize large volumes of data. AWS offers services tailored to various big data and analytics use cases, including data ingestion, storage, processing, querying, and visualization. Let us delve into the key components and capabilities of Big Data and Analytics on AWS:

- **Data Ingestion:**

  AWS provides several services for ingesting data into the platform, including Amazon Kinesis for real-time streaming data, AWS DataSync for large-scale data transfer, and AWS Snowball for offline data migration.

- **Data Storage:**

  AWS offers storage solutions optimized for big data workloads, such as Amazon S3 for scalable object storage, Amazon EBS for block storage, Amazon Glacier for long-term archival, and Amazon Elastic File System (EFS) for shared file storage.

- **Data Processing:**

  AWS provides managed services for processing and transforming large datasets, such as Amazon Elastic MapReduce (EMR) for distributed data processing using Apache Hadoop, Apache Spark, and other open-source frameworks, and AWS Glue for serverless ETL (Extract, Transform, Load) jobs.

- **Data Analytics:**

  AWS provides advanced analytics and machine learning services on big data, including Amazon Athena for interactive SQL queries on data stored in S3, Amazon QuickSight for business intelligence and visualization, and Amazon SageMaker for building, training, and deploying machine learning models.

- **Real-Time Analytics:**

  AWS offers real-time analytics solutions, such as Amazon Kinesis Data Analytics, which allows organizations to analyze streaming data in real-time and derive actionable insights for decision-making.

- **Data Governance and Security:**

  AWS provides tools and features for ensuring data governance, compliance, and security in big data environments, including AWS Identity and Access Management (IAM), AWS Key Management Service (KMS) for encryption, and AWS Lake Formation for managing data lakes.

- **Scalability and Cost Optimization:**

  AWS enables organizations to dynamically scale their big data workloads based on demand using auto-scaling capabilities. They pay only for the resources consumed, resulting in cost optimization and efficiency.

Additional AWS Services for Data Management and Analytics

Amazon Web Services (AWS) offers diverse services tailored for data management, processing, analytics, and visualization. These services empower organizations to extract actionable insights from their data, streamline data workflows, and drive data-driven decision-making. Let us explore some of the key AWS services for data management and analytics:

Amazon Athena

Overview: Amazon Athena is an interactive query service that enables users to analyze data stored in Amazon S3 using standard SQL queries. Athena eliminates the need to manage infrastructure and complex data pipelines, allowing users to query data directly from S3 without needing data loading or transformation.

Use Cases:

- **Ad-hoc Analysis:** Perform ad-hoc analysis on large datasets stored in S3 without upfront data preparation or infrastructure provisioning.
- **Log Analysis:** Analyze log data, such as server logs, application logs, and clickstream data, to extract valuable insights and patterns.
- **Data Exploration:** Explore and visualize data using popular business intelligence (BI) tools and analytics platforms integrated with Athena.

AWS Data Exchange

Overview: AWS Data Exchange is a service that simplifies the process of finding, subscribing to, and exchanging third-party data in the AWS Cloud. Data providers can publish and monetize their products, while data subscribers can discover and access a wide range of datasets from trusted providers.

Use Cases:

- **Data Monetization:** Monetize proprietary datasets by publishing them on AWS Data Exchange and offering them to a broad audience of potential subscribers.
- **Data Enrichment:** Enrich existing datasets with third-party data products, such as demographic data, market research reports, and geospatial data.
- **Data Collaboration:** Securely and competently facilitate data collaboration and exchange between organizations, providers, and consumers.

AWS Data Pipeline

Overview: AWS Data Pipeline is a web service that orchestrates and automates data-driven workflows, including data ingestion, transformation, and movement across various AWS services and on-premises environments. Data Pipeline allows users to schedule, monitor, and manage data pipelines using a visual interface or API.

Use Cases:

- **Data ETL (Extract, Transform, Load):** Build and automate ETL pipelines for processing and transforming data from source systems to target destinations.
- **Data Backup and Restore**: Schedule and manage data backup and restore operations across different storage systems and databases.
- **Data Migration:** Migrate data between on-premises data centers and AWS Cloud services, such as Amazon S3, Amazon Redshift, and Amazon RDS.

Amazon EMR

Overview: Amazon Elastic MapReduce (EMR) is a managed big data platform that simplifies the deployment and management of Apache Hadoop, Apache Spark, Apache Hive, Apache HBase, and other open-source frameworks for processing large datasets.

Use Cases:

- **Big Data Processing:** Analyze and process large volumes of structured and unstructured data using distributed computing frameworks such as Hadoop and Spark.
- **Data Transformation:** Convert raw data into actionable insights by performing complex data transformations, aggregations, and analytics.
- **Machine Learning:** Train and deploy machine learning models at scale using frameworks such as TensorFlow, PyTorch, and Apache MXNet on EMR clusters.

AWS Glue

Overview: AWS Glue is a fully managed extract, transform, and load (ETL) service that enables users to prepare and transform data for analytics and machine learning workflows. Glue automatically discovers, catalogs, and cleanses data, making it available for analysis in AWS services such as Redshift, Athena, and EMR.

Use Cases:

- **Data Integration:** Integrate data from multiple sources, including databases, data warehouses, and SaaS applications, into a unified data lake or warehouse.

- **Data Cataloging:** Catalog and index metadata about datasets, tables, and partitions, enabling easy discovery and exploration of data assets.
- **Data Preparation:** Clean, normalize, and transform raw data into a structured format suitable for analytics, reporting, and visualization.

Amazon Kinesis

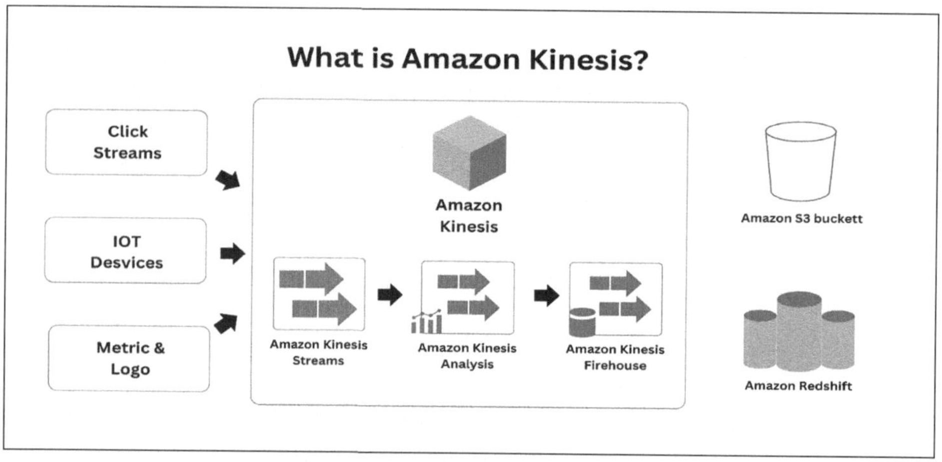

Figure 6.2: *What is Amazon Kinesis*

Figure 6.2 explains how Amazon Kinesis captures real-time data streams from various sources, processes them, and stores or delivers them to other AWS services for further analysis.

Let us look at the breakdown:

- **Data streams**: This includes various data sources that can be ingested by Amazon Kinesis, including mobile devices, websites, and IoT devices.
- **Amazon Kinesis**: This is the central component representing the Kinesis service. It continuously captures and processes the incoming data streams.
- **Amazon S3 bucket**: This represents the storage component. Amazon S3 is a storage service for objects stored on AWS. Processed data can be archived in S3 buckets for later retrieval and analysis.
- **Amazon Kinesis Firehose**: This fully managed service delivers real-time data streams to various AWS destinations, such as Amazon Elasticsearch Service and Amazon Redshift.
- **Amazon Redshift**: This data warehousing service allows you to analyze large datasets stored in S3 buckets.

Overview: Amazon Kinesis is a platform for collecting, processing, and analyzing real-time streaming data at scale. Kinesis offers three services: Kinesis Data Streams for real-time data ingestion, Kinesis Data Firehose for data delivery to AWS services, and Kinesis Data Analytics for real-time analytics.

Use Cases:

- **Real-time Data Ingestion:** Ingest and process real-time data streams from various sources, such as IoT devices, sensors, social media feeds, and application logs.
- **Real-time Analytics:** Analyze streaming data in real-time to detect anomalies, monitor performance, and trigger alerts or actions based on predefined rules.
- **Data Integration:** Integrate real-time streaming data with other AWS services, such as S3, Redshift, and Lambda, for further processing, storage, and analysis.

AWS Lake Formation

Overview: AWS Lake Formation is a service that simplifies the process of building, securing, and managing data lakes on AWS. Lake Formation provides capabilities for ingesting, cataloging, securing, and querying data lakes using a centralized management console.

Use Cases:

- **Data Lake Construction:** Build scalable and cost-effective data lakes on AWS to consolidate and analyze large volumes of structured and unstructured data from diverse sources.
- **Data Cataloging:** Catalog and index metadata about datasets, schemas, and partitions in the data lake, enabling easy discovery and exploration of data assets.
- **Data Security:** Implement fine-grained access control and encryption policies to secure sensitive data stored in the data lake and ensure compliance with regulatory requirements.

Amazon Managed Streaming for Apache Kafka (Amazon MSK)

Overview: Amazon Managed Streaming for Apache Kafka (Amazon MSK) is a fully managed service that enables users to build and run Apache Kafka-based streaming applications without managing infrastructure. MSK provides scalable, durable, and highly available Kafka clusters with automatic monitoring and management.

Use Cases:

- **Real-time Data Processing:** Ingest, process, and analyze real-time streaming data from various sources using Apache Kafka's distributed messaging capabilities.

- **Event-Driven Architectures:** Build event-driven architectures and microservices-based applications that react to changes and events in real-time.
- **Log Aggregation and Analytics:** Aggregate and analyze log data, event streams, and telemetry data from distributed systems, applications, and IoT devices using Kafka's publish-subscribe model.

Amazon OpenSearch Service

Overview: Amazon OpenSearch Service (formerly Amazon Elasticsearch Service) is a managed service that makes it easy to deploy, operate, and scale Elasticsearch clusters in the AWS Cloud. OpenSearch Service provides search, log analytics, real-time analytics, and monitoring capabilities.

Use Cases:

- **Full-Text Search:** Elasticsearch's full-text search capabilities can help you build powerful search experiences for web applications, e-commerce platforms, and content management systems.
- **Log Analytics:** Analyze and visualize log.

Amazon QuickSight

Overview: Amazon QuickSight is a fast, cloud-powered business intelligence service that enables organizations to visualize and analyze their data quickly. With QuickSight, users can create interactive dashboards, perform ad-hoc analysis, and share insights across their organization.

Use Cases:

- **Data Visualization:** Create rich, interactive dashboards and visualizations to gain insights from complex datasets. QuickSight supports various chart types, including bar charts, line charts, scatter plots, and heat maps.
- **Ad-Hoc Analysis:** Perform ad-hoc analysis by exploring data using drag-and-drop visualizations, filters, and calculations. QuickSight's intuitive interface allows users to analyze data without complex queries or programming.
- **Mobile Analytics:** QuickSight's mobile app, available for iOS and Android devices, allows users to access and interact with dashboards on the go. Users can view dashboards, explore data, and receive alerts anytime, anywhere.

Amazon Redshift

Overview: Amazon Redshift is a fully managed data warehouse service that allows organizations to analyze large datasets using standard SQL queries. Redshift is designed for high-performance, scalable analytics and offers features such as columnar storage, parallel query execution, and automatic scaling.

Use Cases:

- **Data Warehousing:** Build and manage data warehouses to store and analyze large volumes of structured data. Redshift supports petabyte-scale data warehouses and offers fast query performance, even with complex analytical workloads.
- **Business Intelligence:** Perform business intelligence and analytics tasks, such as reporting, dashboarding, and data visualization, using Redshift's SQL-based interface. Redshift integrates with popular BI tools such as Tableau, Power BI, and Looker.
- **Data Lake Integration:** Integrate Redshift with data lakes on Amazon S3 to combine structured and unstructured data for analytics. Redshift Spectrum allows users to query data directly from S3 without needing data movement or transformation.

Introduction to Caches

Caching is a fundamental concept in computer science and distributed systems that involves storing frequently accessed data in a temporary storage location to accelerate data retrieval and improve application performance. Caches are widely used in various computing environments, including web applications, databases, and content delivery networks (CDNs), to reduce latency, minimize resource consumption, and enhance scalability. Here is an in-depth exploration of caches and their significance:

- **Cache Basics:**
  - A cache is a high-speed data storage layer that stores copies of frequently accessed data, such as database queries, web pages, or application objects, for rapid retrieval.
  - Caches are typically implemented using fast-access memory technologies, such as Random Access Memory (RAM), to minimize access latency and maximize throughput.
- **Cache Use Cases:**
  - Caches are employed in various applications and systems to improve performance and efficiency. Common use cases include:
    - Web Caching: Storing web pages, images, and assets in a web cache to reduce page load times and server load.
    - Database Caching: Storing frequently accessed database query results or objects in memory to reduce database load and improve query response times.

   - Application Caching: Caching application data, such as user sessions or computed results, speeds up application performance and reduces latency.
   - Content Delivery Networks (CDNs): Distributing cached content to edge locations worldwide to accelerate content delivery and improve user experience.

- **Cache Management and Monitoring:**
  - Effective cache management involves monitoring cache utilization, hit rates, and eviction rates to optimize cache performance and resource utilization. Tools and monitoring solutions such as Amazon CloudWatch provide insights into cache metrics and performance.

A comparison of the two common cache types:

Feature	CPU Cache	Web Cache
Location	On-chip memory within the CPU	Separate server or network appliance
Data Source	Main memory (RAM)	Origin server hosting the original content
Access Speed	Fastest (nanoseconds)	Slower than CPU cache, but faster than main memory (microseconds to milliseconds)
Data	Instructions and data frequently used by the CPU	Web pages, images, and other web content
Cache Management	Automatic by the CPU	Requires configuration and monitoring
Primary Purpose	Reduce CPU access time to main memory	Reduce server load and improve website response times

Table 6.4: *A comparison of two common cache types*

Table 6.4 provides a comparison of the two common cache types.

AWS ElastiCache

This is a managed caching service offered by AWS to make deploying, operating, and scaling caches easier for your applications. It reduces the load on your databases and speeds up data retrieval for users by improving your applications' performance, scalability, and responsiveness through caching frequently accessed data.

Elasticache supports two popular in-memory data store engines:

- **Redis**: Open-source, high-performance data structure server that can be used as a database, cache, and message broker. Redis is a good choice for various applications owing to its speed and flexibility.
- **Memcached**: Simpler than Redis and is used for basic caching needs. It is an open-source, high-performance memory caching system.

Use Redis if:

- You need features such as pub/sub messaging.
- Your application needs a flexible data structure to store strings, lists, hashes, and sorted sets.

Use Memcached if:

- You need a simple and quick cache for basic key-value pairs.
- Your application does not need advanced features.

Conclusion

As we conclude this chapter on databases, it is essential to reflect on our journey, much like the careful planning and precision required in architecture. The parallels between constructing physical buildings and designing robust data infrastructures are evident, from the foundations of database systems to the intricacies of cloud-based solutions.

This chapter highlighted the critical role of databases in modern applications, contrasting SQL databases, which are used for transactional processes due to their ACID properties, with NoSQL databases, which are used for handling large volumes of unstructured data.

An architect must understand the strengths and limitations of different materials and construction techniques, and a database architect must be well-versed in the various database technologies and their applications. This chapter has highlighted the critical considerations required in both fields, emphasizing the importance of choosing the right tools for the right tasks to ensure a solid, scalable, and efficient structure.

The next chapter will explore Front-End Web and Mobile Service Offerings, where AWS Amplify, API Gateway, Device Farm, and Pinpoint facilitate seamless development, testing, and engagement for web and mobile applications. Furthermore, we delve into AWS Application Integration Services such as SQS, SNS, and Kinesis, laying the groundwork for building robust and scalable distributed systems.

Multiple Choice Questions

1. Which one of the following AWS-hosted database services services provides full management, automatic replication, and backups?
    a. Amazon RDS
    b. Amazon S3
    c. Amazon EBS
    d. AWS Lambda
2. Which of the following is a noteworthy feature of Amazon Aurora over conventional MySQL databases?
    a. Higher read/write latency
    b. Compatibility with NoSQL databases
    c. Higher performance and availability
    d. Lower cost due to fewer features
3. Which databases are optimized for key value and document storage?
    a. Amazon Redshift
    b. Amazon DynamoDB
    c. Amazon RDS
    d. Amazon Aurora
4. Which of the following services is optimized for petabyte-scale data warehousing?
    a. Amazon RDS
    b. Amazon Aurora
    c. Amazon DynamoDB
    d. Amazon Redshift
5. Which of the following AWS services is best suited for storing and analyzing large volumes of semi-structured data?
    a. Amazon DynamoDB
    b. Amazon S3
    c. Amazon Aurora
    d. Amazon RDS

6. Which of the following is a feature of Amazon RDS?
    a. Automated backup
    b. Object storage
    c. Serverless architecture
    d. Data warehousing
7. What kind of workload is Amazon DynamoDB best suited for?
    a. OLAP workloads
    b. Key-value and document store
    c. Relational database workloads
    d. Data warehousing
8. What is the best AWS database to use for a petabyte-scale data warehousing solution?
    a. Amazon Redshift
    b. Amazon DynamoDB
    c. Amazon RDS
    d. Amazon Aurora
9. What is the purpose of using Amazon ElastiCache in a Database Architecture?
    a. For storing large files
    b. Cache frequently accessed data to reduce latency
    c. For storing relational data
    d. Managing database migrations
10. Which AWS database service is designed to be compatible with MySQL and PostgreSQL, but deliver higher performance?
    a. Amazon Aurora
    b. Amazon RDS
    c. Amazon DynamoDB
    d. Amazon Redshift

Answers

1. a
2. c

3. b
4. d
5. b
6. a
7. b
8. a
9. b
10. a

References

- https://docs.aws.amazon.com/rds/index.html
- https://aws.amazon.com/rds/features/
- https://aws.amazon.com/blogs/database/choosing-the-right-rds-db-instance-class/
- https://www.geeksforgeeks.org/difference-between-olap-and-oltp-in-dbms/
- https://docs.aws.amazon.com/AmazonRDS/latest/UserGuide/Overview.Security.html
- https://docs.aws.amazon.com/vpc/latest/userguide/VPC_SecurityGroups.html
- https://docs.aws.amazon.com/vpc/latest/userguide/
- https://aws.amazon.com/architecture/security-guidance/
- https://docs.aws.amazon.com/wellarchitected/latest/security-pillar/welcome.html
- https://docs.aws.amazon.com/AmazonRDS/latest/UserGuide/Welcome.html
- https://aws.amazon.com/rds/pricing/
- https://docs.aws.amazon.com/wellarchitected/latest/reliability-pillar/welcome.html
- https://docs.aws.amazon.com/AmazonRDS/latest/UserGuide/UsingWithRDS.Securing.html
- https://aws.amazon.com/rds/performance-insights/

Chapter 7
AWS Application Services

Introduction

Imagine an architect designing a modern city. Their first step would involve creating a plan and acquiring the necessary specialized equipment. A cloud architect will use a similar method to navigate the expansive cloud environment. This chapter acts as your guide, giving a detailed summary of the crucial services provided by AWS for creating, transferring, and improving your applications using machine learning capabilities.

We will explore the world of front-end web and mobile development, exploring tools such as Amplify and API Gateway to simplify the creation and management of user interfaces. Next, we will investigate the extensive range of AWS application integration services, such as SQS and SNS queuing systems, which serve as the invisible communication pathways in your applications. Later, we will concentrate on the crucial task of migrating your current infrastructure to the cloud. AWS provides a range of services to ease this process, including identifying applications for migration and smoothly transferring data and databases. At last, we will unleash the power of machine learning using AWS. Learn how Comprehend, Forecast, and Lex tools can convert your data into valuable insights, create intelligent chatbots, and accurately analyze images and videos. This chapter will guide you and equip you with the information and insight necessary to design a solid and intelligent cloud infrastructure.

Structure

In this chapter, we will cover the following topics:

- Front-End Web and Mobile Service Offerings
- AWS Application Integration Services: Queues and More
- Machine Learning Services on AWS
- AWS Migration Services

Front-End Web and Mobile Service Offerings

In the current digital environment, you need engaging web and mobile apps to connect with your target audience. These AWS services help you simplify development, guarantee scalability, and effectively engage your users.

AWS Amplify: Build and Deploy Web and Mobile Apps

Imagine creating and deploying web and mobile apps without experiencing technical headaches–that is the essence of AWS Amplify and API Gateway.

Think of Amplify as the ultimate solution for creating full-stack apps. It manages both the front-end and the back-end. Furthermore, it can work with popular frameworks such as React, Angular, and Vue and native mobile platforms like iOS and Android.

Amplify's Tools:

- **CLI:** This tool makes setting up your app's back-end easy. Enter a few commands, and you will have user logins, data storage, and more at your fingertips.
- **Amplify Hosting**: Amplify hosts your web app, including automatic updates, custom domain names, and global reach.
- **DataStore**: This tool keeps your data in sync and handles potential conflicts.
- **Authentication**: Seamless integration with Amazon Cognito allows for safe user logins and registrations, including multi-factor authentication for added protection.
- **Storage**: Do you need to store user photos, videos, or documents? Amplify connects you to Amazon S3 for secure and scalable storage.
- **Analytics**: Track how your app is performing with Amazon Pinpoint.
- **Push Notifications**: Send targeted messages to your app users through Pinpoint, thus keeping them informed and engaged.

Benefits of Amplify:

- **Easy to Use**: Building and deploying apps becomes way more straightforward.
- **Scales with You**: Your app can handle more users as it grows, no problem.
- **Plays Well with Others**: Amplify seamlessly integrates with other AWS services.
- **Prioritize security**: Built-in features protect your app and user data.
- **Pay for what you use**: You pay for what you use; hence, it is cost-effective.

Amazon API Gateway: Manage APIs for Scalable Applications

View API Gateway as the central hub for managing your application's APIs. You can use it to generate, release, control, and protect a variety of APIs, ranging from basic RESTful APIs to live WebSocket APIs.

API Gateway's Features:

- **API Creation**: Build RESTful and WebSocket APIs to fit your app's needs.
- **Integration Powerhouse**: Connect your APIs to AWS Lambda for serverless back-ends or other AWS services such as EC2 and DynamoDB.
- **Security Matters**: Keep your APIs safe with features such as AWS IAM, Amazon Cognito, and API keys for authentication and authorization.
- **Performance Boost**: Control the flow of API calls with throttling and caching to keep things running smoothly.
- **Constantly Monitoring**: Track everything with Amazon CloudWatch to see how your APIs perform.
- **Version Control**: Manage different versions of your APIs and easily switch between them.
- **Traffic Control**: Use custom domain names and configure request/response transformations to fine-tune how your APIs work.

Benefits of API Gateway:

- **Handles the Load**: Your APIs can handle thousands of requests simultaneously and scale seamlessly.
- **Cost-Conscious**: You only pay for the API calls you receive and the data you transfer.
- **Flexible:** Build any API you need, from simple to complex.
- **Security First**: Protect your APIs from unauthorized access.
- **Developer-Friendly**: It makes managing APIs easier from start to finish.

AWS Device Farm: Test Mobile Apps Across Devices

AWS Device Farm is like a testing lab in the cloud, with real devices running on different operating systems. It lets you know if your app functions perfectly on every phone and tablet.

Benefits offered by Device Farm

- Device Farm lets you test your app on people's devices, ensuring it works as intended without emulators or simulators.
- You do not need to stack your closet with phones. Device Farm lets you access a wide range of devices.
- It lets you use popular testing frameworks to automate processes, saving time and effort.
- See exactly how your app is performing on each device. Device Farm offers in-depth reports, including logs, screenshots, and performance data, to help you pinpoint and solve any issue encountered while tracking your application's performance across all devices.
- Device Farm effortlessly integrates with your development and CI/CD pipelines, thus simplifying testing for your development process.

Amazon Pinpoint: Engage Users Through Multi-Channel Messaging

Amazon Pinpoint helps you reach your customers on their preferred channels: email, text messages, push notifications, or even voice calls!

Here's how Pinpoint helps:

- Send messages through email, SMS, push notifications, and voice messages, reaching your customers worldwide.
- Group your customers based on age, interests, and what they do on your app or website, ensuring your messages are relevant and exciting.
- Use information about your customers to generate messages that feel like they were written just for them.
- Track and view how your messages are doing with detailed reports. You can also test different versions to find what works best.

Benefits of Pinpoint:

- You can reach the right people by getting your message in front of the target customers.
- Pinpoint can handle millions of users and messages, so you can scale up as needed, helping you grow your business.
- Personalized messages lead to better customer experiences.
- You only have to pay for what you use with Pinpoint's pay-as-you-go pricing.
- Get detailed insights into your campaigns' performance.

Use cases:

- Introducing new products or features: Spread the news and build excitement.
- Keep customers updated: Send order confirmations, shipping updates, and other essential messages.
- Send exclusive offers and promotions: Make your customers feel valued.
- Reconnect with former customers: Remind them why they love your business.
- Obtain feedback: Ask questions and learn more about your customers.

AWS Application Integration Services: Queues and More

Building modern applications involves connecting different parts that run independently. AWS Application Integration Services will assist you in accomplishing this smoothly and effectively. Imagine it as a set of tools enabling your applications to talk to each other, regardless of their technological differences and platform variety, making it easier to develop and manage complex systems.

Amazon Simple Queue Service (SQS)

SQS acts like a reliable message queue, allowing you to send and receive messages between different parts of your application. It is excellent for decoupling tasks and processing messages, even if one part is down.

Introduction and Message Queuing Concepts

Imagine you have a busy restaurant kitchen. Orders arrive, but the cooks can only handle one at a time. SQS is like a waiter taking orders and putting them on a list (the queue) for the cooks (consumers) to handle individually.

Here's how SQS works:

- **Messages**: These are the orders with instructions or data (up to 256 KB) that must be processed.
- **Queue:** This is the list where messages wait. Producers (like the waiter) add messages, and consumers (like the cooks) remove them.
- **Producers**: These are the parts of your application that send messages to the queue.
- **Consumers**: These are the parts of your application that receive and process messages from the queue.
- **Visibility Timeout**: This is like giving the cook a few minutes to focus on one

order before checking if others are waiting. It prevents confusion and ensures each message gets appropriately processed.

- **Dead-Letter Queue**: This is like a "hold bin" for orders that cannot be completed (due to errors). It allows you to investigate and fix any issues before trying again.

Benefits of SQS:

- **Decoupling**: Multiple parts of your application can work independently without worrying about each other's availability.
- **Scalability:** You can easily add more consumers to handle more messages as your application scales.
- **Reliability**: Messages are delivered even if the consumer is temporarily unavailable.
- **Flexibility:** Supports various message formats and processing options.

Types of Queues (Standard, FIFO, and more)

The standard queue is best suited for high-volume situations where an order might not be critical, such as processing social media posts or sending marketing emails. On the other hand, FIFO queues are perfect for scenarios where order matters and duplicates cannot be tolerated, such as processing financial transactions or handling critical system updates.

Let us understand this with an analogy;

Imagine you have two types of queues at a restaurant:

- **Standard Queue:** This is like a busy lunch rush. Orders can pile up quickly; sometimes, the same order might be accidentally processed twice. But overall, things get done.
  - **High Throughput**: Handles many orders at once, perfect for busy situations.
  - **At-Least-Once Delivery**: Ensures each order gets called at least once, but there might be duplicates.
  - **Best-Effort Ordering**: Orders are usually processed in the order they came in, but sometimes they need clarification.
- **FIFO Queue:** This is like a carefully numbered queue for a limited-edition sneaker release. Each person gets their turn in the exact order they arrived.
  - **Exactly-Once Processing**: Ensures each order is served precisely once, with no duplicates.
  - **Preserved Message Order**: People are served in the strict order in which they joined the line.

   - **Limited Throughput**: Handles fewer orders simultaneously but with perfect accuracy.

Sending and Receiving Messages

Let us understand this with the same restaurant analogy:

Sending Messages:

- Think of the **"`SendMessage API`"** as the waiter taking your order. You give them the message (up to 256 KB of data), and they add it to the queue.
- **"`Message Attributes`"** are like extra notes on the order. You can add timestamps, special instructions, or a priority level.
- **"`Delay Seconds`"** is like asking the waiter to hold your order for a bit. It is useful if you want the message to be processed later, at a specific time.

Receiving Messages:

- The **"`ReceiveMessage API`"** is like the cooks checking the queue for orders. They can retrieve up to 10 messages at a time.
- **"`Visibility Timeout`"** is like giving the cook a few minutes to focus on one order. It prevents other cooks from grabbing the same order, causing confusion.

Once the order is complete, the cook uses the **"`DeleteMessage API`"** to remove it from the queue, ensuring it is not processed again by mistake.

So, SQS keeps your application running smoothly, just like a well-organized restaurant kitchen.

Use Cases for SQS

This section provides some use cases of SQS, explaining how it can transform your applications for the better.

- **Decoupling Microservices**: SQS allows microservices to communicate asynchronously, which means they can send and receive messages without directly waiting for each other. This reduces dependencies, making the overall system more flexible and resilient.
- **Batch Processing**: SQS can collect and aggregate data for batch processing, efficiently handling large volumes of data, such as logs or transactional records.
- **Load Leveling**: SQS is a buffer for incoming messages during peak traffic. Load leveling prevents system overload and ensures a consistent processing rate, improving overall system stability.
- **Asynchronous Workflows**: SQS is ideal for managing tasks that do not require

immediate processing, including sending email notifications, generating reports, or transcoding videos. These tasks can be handled in the background without impacting the main flow of work.

- **Event Sourcing**: SQS helps capture and store events in a system for future analysis or auditing. This tracks changes, identifies issues, and understands system behavior over time.
- **Serverless Applications**: SQS integrates with AWS Lambda effortlessly, helping you build serverless applications. Messages arriving in the queue can trigger Lambda functions, enabling efficient and scalable processing without managing servers.

Amazon Simple Notification Service (SNS)

This publish-subscribe system lets you send messages to multiple recipients, where the recipients are other services listening for specific notifications at once. It is perfect for sending notifications, triggering workflows, or fanning data to different services. It follows a publish-subscribe (pub/sub) messaging pattern, allowing you to simultaneously send messages to multiple recipients.

Introduction and Elements (Topics, Subscribers)

Imagine that you must send the same message to multiple people or systems simultaneously. SNS acts like a central hub, making it easy and efficient to do this. The critical elements of SNS are topics, subscribers, and publishers.

Topics:

- Topics are logical access points that act as a communication channel.
- Publishers send messages to topics, and SNS distributes these messages to all subscribers.
- Topics simplify the management of message distribution by handling message delivery to multiple subscribers.

Subscribers:

- Subscribers are the endpoints that receive messages from the topics.
- Different types of subscribers include AWS Lambda functions, HTTP/S endpoints, email addresses, SQS queues, and mobile devices (via SMS, mobile push, and more).
- Each subscriber must subscribe to a topic to receive messages that are published.

Managing and Publishing to SNS Topics

The steps for managing and publishing are:

1. **Creating a topic**
    a. You can generate a fresh SNS topic using the AWS Management Console, CLI, or SDKs.
    b. Subjects can be designated and set up with characteristics such as delivery policy, access policy, and more.
2. **Managing subscriptions**
    a. Subscribers can subscribe to a topic using the AWS Management Console, CLI, or SDKs.
    b. Every subscription can be customized to indicate the protocol and endpoint.
    c. Confirmation of subscriptions is required before messages can be received, as per the protocol.
3. **Publishing messages**
    a. Publishers can send messages to a topic by indicating the Amazon Resource Name (ARN).
    b. Messages can be transmitted using the AWS Management Console, CLI, SDKs, or by making API calls.
    c. SNS can handle various types of messages, such as text and JSON, and enables message attributes for extra metadata.

Use Cases for SNS

This section provides some use cases of SNS, explaining how it can transform your applications for the better.

- **Notification Systems**: To send notifications about security alerts, application updates, or system failures and notify users about account activities, order statuses, and promotions through SMS or push notifications.
- **Triggering Workflows**: SNS can trigger AWS lambda functions or other microservices and manage workflows by triggering different services.
- **Workflow Automation**: An SNS notification can trigger actions in different applications or systems based on events.
- **Application and System Alerts**: To receive critical event notifications from your applications or infrastructure.

Amazon Simple Email Service (SES): Send Bulk Emails

Amazon SES is a super reliable and affordable email delivery service built on the same technology Amazon uses for its emails. It helps businesses send those emails without worrying about getting stuck in spam folders.

Here is what makes SES advantageous for sending bulk emails:

- **Can handle big crowds**: No matter how many emails you need to send, SES can handle it.
- **Keeps your reputation clean**: SES helps protect your sender reputation (think of it as your email-sending track record) by giving you tools to manage bounces and complaints.
- **Personalize your message**: SES lets you use fancy templates or add custom details to your emails.
- **Get your emails delivered**: SES provides features to track how well your emails are delivered and even gives you dedicated IP addresses to improve your sender score.

SES also offers multiple ways to send your bulk emails:

- **Through your app**: SES can connect with your app directly to send emails.
- **Using code**: Developers can use SES's special codes to send emails programmatically.
- **The AWS dashboard**: You can send emails directly from the AWS website for more straightforward needs.

Some extra features that make SES even better for bulk emails:

- **Email templates**: Create reusable templates to save time and keep your emails consistent.
- **Fine-tune your settings**: Manage different email-sending configurations and track their performance.
- **Dedicated IP addresses**: You can use a dedicated IP address with SES to gain more control over your sender reputation.
- **Stay informed**: SES can update your emails' performance by sending notifications to other AWS services you use.

Use Cases for SES

This section looks into the use cases of SES.

- **Account Activity**: To send account verification emails, password reset notifications, and other critical account-related messages using SES.
- **Order Statuses**: To email customers about order confirmations, shipping updates, and delivery notifications.
- **Promotions**: To run targeted email marketing campaigns or send promotional offers to your customer base.

Tabular Comparison of SQS, SNS, and SES

Now that we have examined each queue service independently, let us compare their brief features in *Table* 7.1.

Feature /Service	AWS SQS	AWS SNS	AWS SES
Service Type	Message Queue	Notification Service	Email Service
Primary Use Case	Decoupling and scaling microservices, distributed systems, and serverless applications	Sending notifications and messaging between distributed systems	Sending bulk and transactional emails
Message Delivery	At-least-once delivery, FIFO (First-In-First-Out) queues available	At-least-once delivery	Best-effort delivery, built-in retry mechanism
Message Retention	Up to 14 days	Not applicable	Not applicable
Message Size	Up to 256 KB per message	Up to 256 KB per message	Up to 10 MB per email
Message Ordering	FIFO queues available for strict message ordering	No built-in ordering	Not applicable
Throughput	Virtually unlimited, with a limit of 120,000 in-flight messages	High throughput, 1 million deliveries per second	Scalable to handle millions of emails per day
Integration with Other AWS Services	AWS Lambda, Amazon EC2, Amazon ECS, Amazon S3, Amazon RDS	AWS Lambda, Amazon EC2, Amazon S3, Amazon RDS	Amazon CloudWatch, AWS Lambda, Amazon S3
Reliability	Highly reliable with redundant data storage	Highly reliable with redundant data storage	Highly reliable with redundant data storage

Delivery Mechanism	Polling or long-polling	Push-based (HTTP/S, email, SMS, Lambda)	SMTP, API-based
Security	IAM roles and policies, encryption (in transit and at rest)	IAM roles and policies, encryption (in transit and at rest)	IAM roles and policies, TLS for data in transit
Cost	Based on the number of requests and data transfer	Based on the number of requests and data transfer	Based on the number of emails sent and data transfer

Table 7.1: *Comparison between SQS, SNS, SES*

AWS Step Functions (SWF)

This service simplifies coordinating different parts of your software (distributed applications and microservices). It uses visual workflows, so you can see the steps laid out clearly. Step Functions works with many other AWS services, allowing you to build intricate workflows that involve various functionalities.

Building Workflows with SWF

The process of building workflows with SWF can be broken down into three steps:

Step 1: Define Workflow:

- Define a workflow type, specifying the unique name, version, and task list.
- Define activities and decisions (tasks) during the workflow execution.
- Manage tasks using task lists, which help queue and dispatch tasks to workers.

Step 2: Workflow Execution:

- Initiate workflow execution by specifying the workflow type and input parameters.
- Implement activity workers that perform the actual work of the tasks. These workers poll SWF for functions, execute them, and return results.
- Implement deciders, which dictate the logical flow of the workflow by making decisions based on the current workflow state and task outcomes.

Step 3: Monitoring and Scaling:

- Use CloudWatch to monitor workflow executions and set up alarms.
- Scale workers horizontally to handle high loads by adding more worker instances.

Amazon Kinesis: Stream Processing Made Easy

Amazon Kinesis lets you collect, process, and analyze large streams of data in real-time effortlessly. This helps your applications react to new information. This section demonstrates how Amazon Kinesis can transform your data processing capabilities.

Working with Data Streams

Amazon Kinesis Data Streams is a service for real-time data streaming at a massive scale.

Here is how it works:

- **Data Chunks (Shards):** Every stream is divided into manageable chunks called shards. Each shard holds a specific sequence of data records.
- **Data Records**: Each record is like a piece of information in the stream. It has a unique ID (sequence number), a label (partition key) to categorize it, and the actual data.
- **Data Flow (Producers and Consumers):** Producers constantly push data into the stream, such as device sensor readings or website clicks. Conversely, influential consumers, such as real-time dashboards or pricing algorithms, process this data as it arrives.

Processing the stream:

- **Kinesis API**: This is a library that pours data into the stream. Developers can use the Kinesis API to feed data into the system continuously.
- **Consumer Applications**: These are the tools that analyze the data stream. They might be real-time dashboards that display website traffic or automated systems that adjust product prices based on demand. Kinesis makes this data readily available for use in these applications.
- **Stream Processing Made Easy**: Building applications to handle this data stream can be complex. Kinesis Client Library (KCL) acts like a pre-built toolbox. It simplifies the process by automatically balancing the workload and ensuring data is processed despite hiccups.
- **Lambda Integration:** Imagine having robots programmed to react to specific data in the stream. Lambda integration allows you to connect AWS Lambda functions to the stream. These functions are like mini-programs that can be triggered automatically whenever specific data appears in the stream, enabling real-time actions.

Processing Video Streams

Amazon Kinesis Video Streams allows you to securely stream video from connected devices to AWS for analytical, machine learning, and processing purposes.

Its features are:

- Encrypting video data during both transportation and at rest.
- Supporting real-time and batch processing for analytics or machine learning tasks.
- Storing video streams with time-indexed data facilitates easier search and retrieval of specific segments.

Use cases:

- Monitoring home security cameras.
- Analyzing video streams from factory equipment to detect anomalies.
- Streaming and analyzing patient monitoring data.

Using Kinesis Firehose for Delivery

Imagine a fire hose constantly spraying valuable information–sensor readings from your smart home, website visitor clicks, or even live chat logs. The Kinesis Firehose is like a super-powered attachment for this fire hose. It helps you send this real-time data stream to its exact destination quickly and securely.

Exploring Amazon Kinesis Delivery Options

- **Data Lakes**: These are giant storage bins for all your data. Firehose can deliver your data stream to Amazon S3, a massive storage service, so that you can analyze it later.
- **Analysis Tools**: Like a robust magnifying glass, Firehose can send your data to services such as Amazon Redshift or Elasticsearch. These tools help you uncover hidden patterns and trends in your data stream.
- **Custom Services**: You can also send your data to other services, such as Splunk, for even more specialized analysis.

Preparing the Data for Delivery:

Firehose is like a helpful assistant before it sends the data. It can:

- **Clean and Organize**: Firehose can transform your data stream using Lambda functions, such as mini-programs. This can involve removing unnecessary parts or making it easier to understand the destination service.
- **Shrink It Down**: Firehose can compress your data stream, saving storage space. It is like packing your data efficiently before sending it off.

- **Add Security**: Firehose can encrypt your data stream, ensuring only authorized users can access it. It is like adding a lock to your data package.
- **Scalable and reliable**: Firehose automatically scales up or down to keep up with the data flow. If there is ever a hiccup, it has built-in retries and error logging to ensure your data gets delivered safely and securely.

Leveraging Kinesis Data Analytics

Amazon Kinesis Data Analytics helps you to process and analyze streaming data in real-time using standard SQL.

- **Real-time Processing:**
  - SQL is used to query streaming data, allowing real-time analysis without learning new programming languages.
  - Perform operations on data within specified time windows, such as tumbling, sliding, and session windows.
- **Integration:**
  - **Data Sources**: Read data from Kinesis Data Streams or Kinesis Data Firehose.
  - **Outputs**: Processed data is transferred to various destinations, such as Kinesis Data Streams, Kinesis Data Firehose, or AWS Lambda, for further processing.
- **Use Cases:**
  - **Real-time Analytics**: Monitor and analyze real-time application logs, clickstream, or sensor data.
  - **Anomaly Detection**: Identify and respond to unusual patterns in the data stream immediately.

Amazon MQ: Manage Message Queuing

Amazon MQ is a managed message broker service for Apache ActiveMQ and RabbitMQ in the cloud. It handles the behind-the-scenes tasks, freeing you to focus on building your applications.

Key Features:

- It handles everything, including server setup, updates, and maintenance.
- It supports industry-standard messaging protocols, so your applications can easily connect and exchange messages.
- It is highly reliable and can automatically failover and deploy across multiple zones to ensure continuous operation.

- It automatically adjusts to your application's needs, so you are never under or over-provisioned.
- It works with AWS security services to keep your messages safe, both in transit and at rest.
- It provides detailed insights into your broker's health and performance using CloudWatch.

Benefits:

- **Fast Setup**: You can create a new message broker in minutes with just a few clicks; no complex configuration is needed.
- **Focus on Development**: Offload infrastructure management to AWS, allowing developers to concentrate on building great software.
- **Works with What You Have**: Supports multiple protocols for seamless integration with existing systems.
- **Cost-Effective**: Pay-as-you-go pricing ensures you only pay for what you use.

Use Cases:

- **Microservice Communication:** Ensures reliable message delivery between microservices, even with temporary outages.
- **Decoupled Architectures:** Enables building loosely coupled systems that communicate asynchronously for improved scalability and resilience.
- **Event-Driven Architectures**: Facilitates real-time responses to events, creating dynamic and scalable applications.

Getting Started:

1. **Create a Broker**: Create a new broker using the AWS Management Console, command-line tools, or SDKs. Choose your preferred engine (ActiveMQ or RabbitMQ), instance size, and other settings.

2. **Connect Your Applications**: Use the provided connection information to connect your applications to the broker. Standard messaging protocols are supported for easy integration with various tools and libraries.

3. **Monitor and Manage**: Utilize CloudWatch to monitor your broker's performance, set up alerts for critical metrics, and track events for troubleshooting and auditing.

Machine Learning Services on AWS

AWS provides a wide range of machine learning (ML) services and tools that empower developers, data scientists, and researchers to create, train, and implement ML models effectively and on a large scale. These services span the entire process, from data preparation to model deployment and monitoring.

Amazon Comprehend: Process Textual Data

Amazon Comprehend is a cloud-based natural language processing (NLP) service powered by machine learning. It helps you extract meaning and gain valuable insights from your text data.

Here is what Comprehend can do:

- Comprehend can identify and categorize specific entities within your text. This could be people's names, locations, dates, organizations, or product mentions.
- It can analyze the overall tone of the text by understanding whether it is expressing positive, negative, or neutral sentiments.
- It can pinpoint the most important phrases that capture the essence of the text.
- It can identify the primary language used in a document, making it helpful in processing multilingual content.
- It can break down the text structure, identifying parts of speech like nouns, verbs, and adjectives, which can be valuable for tasks such as information extraction or machine translation.

Use Cases:

- **Customer Feedback Analysis**: This analyzes customer reviews, emails, and social media posts to understand customer sentiment toward a product or service.
- **Automating Document Processing**: It speeds up tasks such as segregating documents, extracting key information, or filtering irrelevant data.
- **Enhanced Search Functionality:** Improve your search capabilities by using Comprehend to identify the most relevant documents based on user queries.

Amazon Forecast: Forecast Future Trends

Amazon Forecast is like a crystal ball that predicts future trends. It is powered by cutting-edge machine learning (ML). It analyzes your past data to generate extremely accurate forecasts for your needs.

Working of Forecast:

- **Automated Machine Learning**: Forecast takes care of the technical details. It automatically analyzes your data, selects the best ML algorithms, and fine-tunes them to create the most accurate forecast model.

- **Advanced Predictions:** Forecast goes beyond simple guesses. It leverages sophisticated machine learning models to predict future outcomes with surprising accuracy.
- **Seamless Integration:** Forecast integrates smoothly with other AWS services you might already be using, such as S3 for data storage, Redshift for data warehousing, and RDS for relational databases.

Use cases:

- **Demand Planning:** Forecast can predict customer demand for your products, helping you optimize your inventory levels, reducing the risk of stockouts and overstocking.
- **Inventory Management**: Forecast empowers you to plan your inventory more efficiently by anticipating future demand.
- **Financial Planning**: Accurate forecasts can guide your financial planning decisions, allowing you to allocate resources effectively and make data-driven financial decisions.

Amazon Forecast is thus a powerful tool for unlocking the predictive power of your data. It helps you anticipate future trends and optimize your operations.

Amazon Fraud Detector: Identify Fraudulent Activities

Amazon Fraud Detector is a real-time service that uses machine learning to detect potentially fraudulent activities.

Its features are:

- **Automated model building**: It automates the entire model-building process by creating a custom model tailored to your needs.
- **Real-time fraud detection:** Fraud detector analyzes transactions as they happen, allowing to catch fraudulent activity immediately before any damage is done.
- **Highly customizable:** A fraud detector allows you to customize your model to focus on the types of fraud most relevant to your industry.

Use cases:

- **Credit card fraud:** Fraud Detectors can identify suspicious credit card transactions based on factors such as unusual purchase locations, high transaction amounts, or inconsistencies in billing information.
- **Fake payments:** It can also help detect fake online payments from stolen accounts or fraudulent sources.

- **Account Takeovers**: Fraud Detectors can analyze login attempts and identify patterns that might suggest an account takeover attempt by unauthorized individuals.

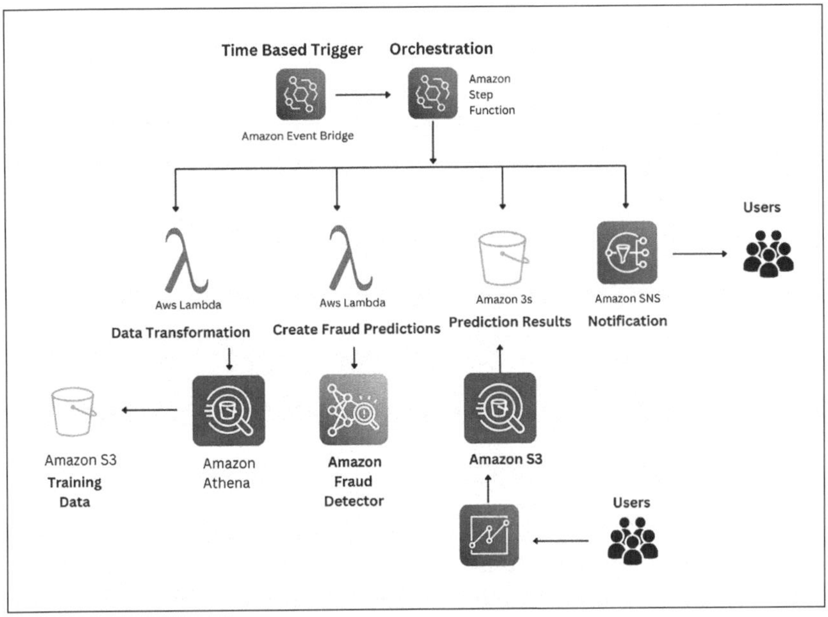

Figure 7.1: *Amazon Fraud Detector*

Figure 7.1 depicts the steps involved in automatically responding to fraudulent activities. The process can be broken down into:

1. **Trigger:** The process starts with a trigger for identifying suspicious activities based on predefined criteria.
2. **Amazon EventBridge:** This service acts as the event routing engine. It monitors for triggers and routes them to the appropriate AWS Lambda functions for processing.
3. **Data Transformation:** This step involves modifying the data format or structure to ensure compatibility (in some cases).
4. **Amazon S3:** This service acts as a storage repository for training data used to build fraud detection models and the results generated by those models.
5. **Amazon Athena:** Amazon Athena can be used to perform ad hoc analyses if fraud analysis involves querying historical data stored in S3.
6. **Amazon Fraud Detector:** This core service leverages machine learning models to analyzc incoming data and identify potentially fraudulent activities.
7. **Generate Fraud Prediction Results:** Amazon Fraud Detector generates

predictions based on analyzed data, which include a risk score indicating the likelihood of fraud and other relevant details.

8. **Amazon SNS:** Amazon Simple Notification Service distributes fraud prediction results to various destinations, such as Amazon S3 for storage or AWS Lambda functions for further processing.
9. **AWS Lambda Functions:** These serverless functions can be customized to execute specific actions based on the received fraud prediction results.
10. **Amazon S3:** The results of actions taken by AWS Lambda functions can be stored in Amazon S3 for auditing purposes.
11. **Users:** Users can interact with the system at various points throughout the process and monitor the Amazon Fraud Detector console.

Amazon Kendra: Intelligent Search for Your Data

Amazon Kendra is a cloud-based search service designed to help you find information across numerous data sources. It uses advanced machine learning algorithms to understand your requirements and deliver relevant results. Figure 7.2 describes how Amazon Kendra works.

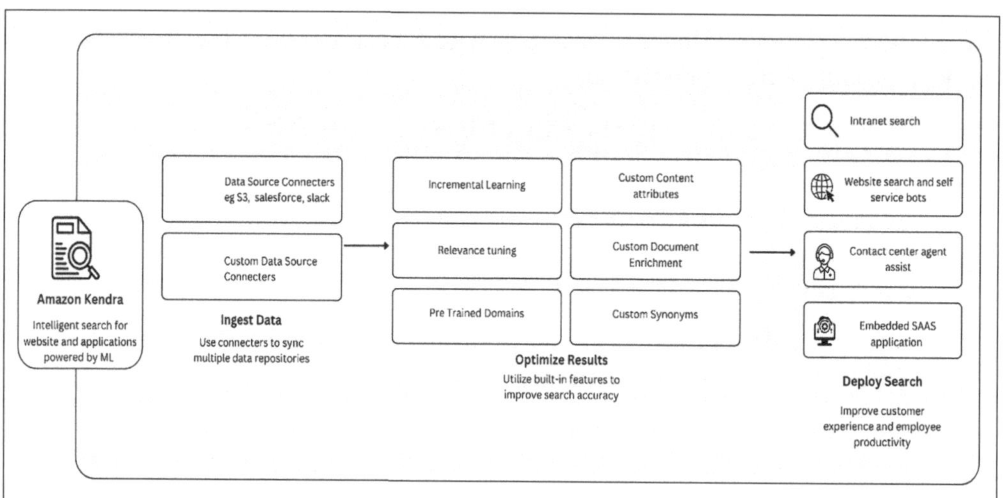

Figure 7.2: *Amazon Kendra*

Features:

- It connects to your documents stored in AWS services such as S3, SharePoint, and Salesforce.

- It uses natural language processing to understand the intent behind your searches.
- It provides faceted search options to filter results based on specific criteria.
- It offers machine learning-powered ranking to prioritize the most relevant results.
- It integrates with chatbots and applications for seamless information access.

Use Cases:

- Enterprise knowledge management lets employees quickly find internal documents, policies, and FAQs.
- Customer self-service portals: It allows customers to find answers to their questions within a knowledge base.
- Legal document search: It simplifies searching through legal contracts and case files.
- Research and development: It facilitates information retrieval for research on specific projects.

Amazon Lex: Build Chatbots with Conversational AI

Amazon Lex allows you to build chatbots with natural language understanding capabilities. These chatbots can interact with users through text or voice interfaces to simulate conversations, provide information, or complete tasks.

Features:

- It offers pre-built conversation flows for everyday tasks such as scheduling appointments or answering FAQs.
- It lets you define custom conversation flows with decision points and branching logic.
- It integrates with other AWS services, such as DynamoDB, to access and update data.
- It provides real-time sentiment analysis to understand user intent and emotions.

Use Cases:

- **Customer service chatbots**: These are used to answer customer questions, resolve issues, and collect feedback.
- **HR chatbots:** These are used to assist employees with onboarding, benefits information, and scheduling.

- **IT support chatbots**: To provide troubleshooting steps and reset passwords.
- **Marketing chatbots**: For qualifying leads, scheduling meetings, and gathering customer data.

Amazon Polly: Text-to-Speech Conversion

Amazon Polly converts text into realistic-sounding speech. You can choose from various voices and languages to create spoken audio content from your written text.

Features:

- It offers a variety of lifelike voices with different accents and speaking styles.
- It supports Speech Synthesis Markup Language (SSML) for fine-tuning pronunciation and emphasis.
- It integrates with applications for creating voice-enabled features such as audiobooks or eLearning materials.
- It can be used to generate audio descriptions for images to improve accessibility.

Use Cases:

- For creating audio content for podcasts, audiobooks, and educational materials.
- Enhancing accessibility by providing audio descriptions for web content and mobile apps.
- For adding voice prompts to interactive voice response (IVR) systems.
- It converts text messages or notifications to speech for hands-free consumption.

Amazon Rekognition: Image and Video Analysis

Amazon Rekognition uses deep learning to analyze images and videos. It can detect objects, people, scenes, faces, and text within visual content, extracting valuable information for various applications.

Features:

- **Object and scene detection**: It identifies objects such as cars, people, furniture, and activities such as sports or cooking within images and videos.
- **Facial analysis**: It recognizes faces, detects emotions, and estimates age and gender in images.
- **Text-in-image extraction:** It extracts text-embedded images such as digital signs or storefronts.

- **Content moderation**: It detects inappropriate content in images and videos to ensure website or application safety.

Use Cases:

- **Image and video categorization**: It automatically classifies images based on their content for better organization and search.
- **Security and surveillance**: This is used to identify objects and people in video feeds for anomaly detection or security monitoring.
- **Media and entertainment**: Analyzing video content to generate captions, personalize recommendations, or identify scenes.
- **E-commerce**: For extracting text from product images for product search and automatic tagging.

Amazon SageMaker: Build, Train, and Deploy Models

Amazon SageMaker is a cloud platform designed to simplify the process of building, training, and deploying machine learning models. It provides tools and features to manage the entire machine-learning lifecycle in a single environment.

Features:

- **Pre-built algorithms**: It offers a library of pre-built machine learning algorithms for everyday tasks such as classification, regression, and forecasting.
- **Notebook environment**: It provides Jupyter notebooks for writing and experimenting with your machine-learning code.
- **Training infrastructure**: It manages the infrastructure needed to train your models, allowing you to scale resources up or down as needed.
- **Model deployment**: It offers tools to deploy your trained models as web services that can be integrated into applications.
- **Model monitoring**: It allows you to monitor the performance of your deployed models and identify any issues.

Use Cases:

- **Predictive maintenance**: This involves analyzing sensor data from equipment to predict potential failures and schedule maintenance proactively.
- **Fraud detection**: This is used to identify fraudulent transactions in real-time using machine learning models.
- **Customer churn prediction**: This is used to predict which customers are at risk of churning and take steps to retain them.

- **Image and video recognition**: For building models to recognize objects, scenes, and activities within images and videos for various applications.

Amazon Textract: Extract Text from Documents (Version 1.1)

Amazon Textract is a service powered by machine learning that streamlines the process of extracting text and data from scanned documents. It can process various document types, such as PDFs, images, and forms, transforming the data into a structured layout that is simple to handle.

Features:

- **Optical Character Recognition (OCR):** It accurately extracts printed text from scanned documents, even with challenging layouts or handwriting.
- **Form understanding**: It identifies and extracts data from specific fields within forms, such as invoices, receipts, or applications.
- **Table understanding**: It recognizes and extracts data from tables embedded within documents, preserving the table structure for easy analysis.
- **Text Location**: It identifies the location of the text within documents, allowing for focused processing or redaction of sensitive information.

Use Cases:

- **Automating data entry**: To eliminate manual data entry tasks by automatically extracting data from invoices, receipts, and other forms.
- **Document processing pipelines:** Integrate Textract into workflows to process large volumes of scanned documents for further analysis.
- **Legal document review**: For extracting critical information from contracts, agreements, and other legal documents for efficient review.
- **Historical document archiving**: This process extracts text from historical documents for digital preservation and more accessible search capabilities.

Amazon Transcribe: Speech-to-Text Conversion

Amazon Transcribe converts spoken audio into text. It uses advanced speech recognition technology to handle various audio formats and accents, providing accurate transcripts for further processing or analysis.

Features:

- **Real-time transcription:** It transcribes speech into the text as it happens, which is ideal for applications like live captioning or voice-enabled dictation.

- **Batch transcription**: It transcribes audio files stored in S3 buckets, suitable for processing pre-recorded audio content.
- **Speaker advancement**: It identifies speakers within a recording, allowing you to differentiate who is saying what.
- **Custom vocabulary support**: Trains the service to recognize domain-specific terms or jargon for improved accuracy.

Use Cases:

- **Generating captions for videos and podcasts**: Creating subtitles for multimedia content to improve accessibility and searchability.
- **Transcription for meetings and conferences:** Transforming recorded meetings and lectures into text for easy review and information sharing.
- **Voice-enabled applications:** To power voice-driven interfaces for dictation software, customer service chatbots, or voice assistants.
- **Media and entertainment:** For Transcribing interviews, speeches, or historical recordings for research or content production.

Amazon Translate: Language Translation Services

Amazon Translate is a machine learning service that offers real-time translation between dozens of languages. It utilizes neural machine translation technology to provide high-quality, natural-sounding translations for various content types.

Features:

- **Supports a wide range of languages**: It provides translation between dozens of languages, catering to a global audience.
- **Batch translation:** It efficiently translates large volumes of text stored in S3 buckets.
- **Real-time translation**: Enables real-time translation for applications such as chatbots or multilingual websites.
- **Custom translation models:** Allows you to train custom translation models for specialized domains or terminology.

Use Cases:

- **Creating multilingual websites and applications**: For delivering content to a global audience.
- **Customer Support**: By offering real-time translation for customer service chats and emails, this enables communication with a broader customer base.
- **Content Localization**: To localize marketing materials, brochures, and training documents for international audiences.

AWS Migration Services

Imagine you are shifting into a new house, but this house is a whole new way of living. You used to have everything under one roof, but now it is spread across different, connected spaces. Moving your computer systems and data to the cloud can feel like that. An AWS Migration Strategy is your roadmap for this significant change. You plan to pack up your applications, data, and IT infrastructure (such as your servers and databases) from your current setup, maybe your own data center, and unpack them efficiently in the AWS cloud.

This strategy is not just about the physical move, though. It also ensures everything works well in its new, digital home. Here is where your AWS Migration Strategy gets even more helpful. It considers things like:

- **The scale and complexity of your IT environment**: A small company with a handful of programs could experience an easier transition than a big corporation with numerous interconnected systems.
- **Your application category**: Certain applications may require a full reconstruction to utilize the cloud, whereas others can be transferred with limited adjustments.
- **Your budget and timeline**: Due to your budget and timeline constraints, moving all items at once may not be possible. Your plan can assist you in organizing and scheduling the migration according to your needs.
- **Security**: Security is essential for ensuring the safety of your data while transitioning to the cloud and after it has been successfully integrated. Your strategy will address how to maintain security throughout the process.

Before we dive deep into migration services, let us look at the migration strategies:

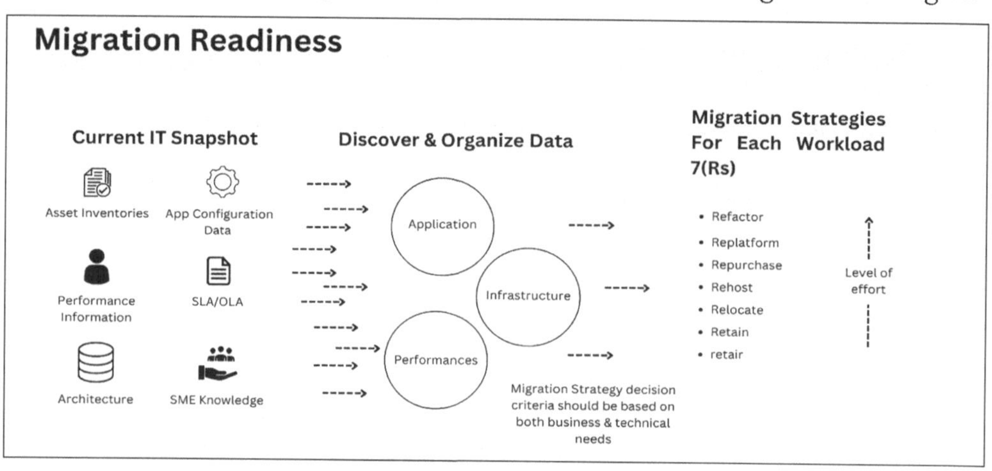

Figure 7.3: *Migration readiness*

Figure 7.3 explains the migration strategy decision process:

- **Current IT Snapshot**: This refers to the starting point for the migration, which includes information about the current IT infrastructure, applications, and data.
- **Migration Strategies**: Several migration strategies are outlined, including refactor, replatform, repurchase, rehost, relocate, and retain. The most suitable strategy depends on the application architecture, performance requirements, and cost considerations.
- **Discover and Organize Data**: This step involves gathering and organizing all relevant data about the IT workloads to be migrated.
- **Decision Criteria**: The decision on which migration strategy to use should consider business needs (example, cost, time to migrate) and technical needs (example, application architecture, performance requirements).

The 7Rs can be briefly explained as:

1. **Retire**: Move or retire old applications to address compatibility issues.
2. **Replace**: Take advantage of the cloud by replacing on-premise systems with SaaS or cloud-native versions.
3. **Relocate (Rehost):** Transfer data to new locations within data centers for high availability and disaster recovery.
4. **Replatform**: Migrate the entire IT stack to cloud-aligned technology and services.
5. **Rebuild**: Develop and code applications from a cloud-native standpoint for faster development and lower costs.
6. **Re-use**: Reuse code across projects to reduce development effort.
7. **Re-architect**: Change legacy application architecture to fit cloud infrastructure needs.

By considering these factors and creating a detailed plan, your AWS Migration Strategy will serve as a roadmap for a seamless and prosperous shift to the cloud. It assists in preventing unexpected issues, reducing periods of inactivity, and allowing you to concentrate on the advantages of cloud technology, such as scalability, cost-effectiveness, and enhanced performance. It is similar to having a specialized moving company for high-tech relocations, guaranteeing a safe arrival and flawless setup in the new location.

AWS Application Discovery Service: Identify Applications for Migration

AWS Application Discovery Service (ADS) helps you identify and inventory your on-premises applications. It scans your environment and gathers information about applications, their dependencies, and infrastructure usage.

Features:

- Discovers running applications and servers in your on-premises environment.
- Auto-collects data on application dependencies and infrastructure configurations.
- Provides insights into application usage patterns and resource consumption.

Use Cases:

- Planning your cloud migration strategy requires understanding your application landscape.
- Estimating potential migration costs and resource requirements on AWS.
- Identifying dependencies between applications is necessary to ensure a smooth migration process.

AWS Application Migration Service: Simplify Application Migration

AWS Application Migration Service (AMS) is designed to simplify the migration of applications from on-premises environments or other clouds to AWS. It automates server conversion and migration planning, reducing manual effort and migration time.

Features:

- Converts on-premises applications to a format compatible with AWS cloud infrastructure.
- Automates server replication and migration to AWS instances.
- Minimizes downtime during application cutovers to AWS.

Use Cases:

- To Migrating mission-critical applications to AWS with minimal disruption.
- To simplify application migration for teams with limited cloud expertise.
- Enables faster time-to-value by accelerating application deployment on AWS.

AWS Database Migration Service (DMS): Move Databases to AWS

AWS Database Migration Service (DMS) is a service that helps you migrate your existing databases to AWS cloud databases. It supports various database engines and migration scenarios, offering a flexible solution for database transfers.

Features:

- Supports migration from database engines such as MySQL, PostgreSQL, Oracle, and SQL Server.
- Enables homogeneous (like-to-like) or heterogeneous (different engines) database migration.
- To provide continuous data replication to keep your AWS database synchronized with the source.

Use Cases:

- To move existing databases from on-premises environments to managed database services on AWS.
- To consolidate multiple databases into a single, centralized database on AWS.
- To enable easier database scaling and management by leveraging AWS cloud capabilities.

AWS DataSync: Transfer On-Premises Data to AWS

AWS DataSync lets you quickly transfer data between on-premises storage systems and AWS storage services. It provides a secure and efficient way to migrate large datasets to the cloud.

Features:

- Transfers data between on-premises storage such as Network Attached Storage (NAS) and cloud storage services such as Simple Storage Service (S3).
- Supports scheduled and ongoing data transfers for continuous data replication.
- Offers features such as data filtering and transformation during the transfer process.

Use Cases:

- To migrate extensive data archives, backups, or file shares to AWS storage for centralized management.
- To offload data storage and management from on-premises infrastructure to AWS cloud storage.
- Enables data lakes and analytics pipelines by transferring data to AWS data storage services.

AWS Migration Hub: Centralized Migration Management

AWS Migration Hub is a central dashboard for overseeing your cloud migration procedure. It offers a consolidated perspective on your current migrations, enabling you to monitor advancement, spot possible problems, and handle resources effectively.

Features:

- It provides a single dashboard to view the status of all ongoing migrations across different AWS tools and services.
- It integrates with various migration tools for centralized management, such as the AWS Database Migration Service (DMS) and the AWS Server Migration Service (SMS).
- It offers reporting and analytics to track migration progress and identify areas for improvement.
- It allows you to collaborate with different teams involved in the migration process.

Use Cases:

- For managing large-scale cloud migrations with multiple applications and data sources.
- To track the progress of individual migration tasks and identify dependencies.
- For collaborating with different teams involved in various stages of the migration.
- To monitor resource utilization and ensure smooth execution of the migration plan.

AWS Snow Family: Data Migration Appliances

The AWS Snow Family consists of physical data migration devices created to securely move large datasets to the AWS cloud. These devices are perfect for scenarios where transferring large data volumes via the Internet is sluggish or impossible.

Features:

- It offers various appliance sizes to accommodate data transfers of varying capacities (from terabytes to petabytes).
- It provides secure data encryption and tamper-evident seals to ensure data confidentiality during transfer.
- It simplifies the data transfer process with easy-to-use setup and configuration.

- It integrates seamlessly with AWS storage services like S3 for efficient data ingestion.

Use Cases:

- For migrating extensive data archives, such as medical records or video libraries, to AWS cloud storage.
- To transfer backup data sets to the cloud for disaster recovery purposes.
- To offload data migration tasks from your internet connection to avoid network congestion.
- To move large datasets from geographically remote locations to AWS with lower latency.

AWS Transfer Family: Secure File Transfer Solutions

The AWS Transfer Family offers managed file transfer services that provide secure and reliable ways to move files between your on-premises environments and the AWS cloud.

Features:

- It supports file transfer protocols such as FTP, SFTP, and FTPS for secure and familiar data transfers.
- It offers user authentication and access controls to restrict unauthorized file access.
- It integrates with AWS IAM for centralized identity and access management.
- It provides activity logging and auditing for tracking file transfer operations.

Use Cases:

- To securely transfer sensitive data files between on-premises servers and AWS cloud storage.
- To automate routine file transfers between different locations for data synchronization.
- To enable secure file sharing between internal teams or external partners.
- For providing a user-friendly interface for file transfers without requiring complex configuration.

Conclusion

We have explored a flexible range of services that can meet various needs, from using Comprehend for text analysis to detecting fraud with Fraud Detector, from utilizing

Kendra for intelligent search to creating chatbots with Lex. Polly, Rekognition, and Textract can improve your apps by converting text into audio, examining visual elements, and pulling data from files. Ultimately, SageMaker offers an extensive platform for creating, educating, and implementing your machine learning models, demonstrating the adaptability of AWS machine learning offerings.

The section also dives into AWS Migration Services, a suite of tools meticulously designed to facilitate the seamless transition of your applications and data to the cloud. From identifying migration use cases to transferring databases and data sets, these services streamline the process, making it more efficient and minimizing downtime.

Utilizing the range of services discussed in this chapter allows you to create scalable, intelligent, and user-friendly applications on AWS. Get ready to delve further into the upcoming chapter as we explore AWS Management and Governance, which will provide you with the resources necessary to oversee and protect your cloud infrastructure efficiently.

Multiple Choice Questions

1. Which services are used to build and deploy highly scalable and secure front-end web and mobile applications?
   a. Amazon CloudFront
   b. AWS Amplify
   c. Amazon EC2
   d. AWS Lambda
2. Which of the following provides managed message queuing for decoupling microservices?
   a. Amazon SNS
   b. Amazon SQS
   c. Amazon MQ
   d. AWS Step Functions
3. Which services lets developers add AI capabilities such as speech recognition and text-to-speech to their applications?
   a. Amazon Lex
   b. Amazon Polly
   c. Amazon SageMaker
   d. AWS Comprehend

4. Which of the following is an AWS service with the sole purpose of migrating databases to AWS?
    a. AWS Database Migration Service (DMS)
    b. AWS Snowball
    c. AWS DataSync
    d. AWS Glue
5. Which of the following is an AWS service that will automate containerized application deployment, scaling, and operations?
    a. Amazon ECS
    b. AWS Elastic Beanstalk
    c. AWS Fargate
    d. Amazon EKS
6. Which of the following is an AWS service that can integrate microservices and create workflows using a simple drag-and-drop interface?
    a. AWS Step Functions
    b. AWS Lambda
    c. Amazon SQS
    d. Amazon CloudWatch
7. What is the primary use case for AWS AppSync?
    a. Serverless compute service
    b. Real-time data synchronization and offline data management
    c. Data warehousing
    d. Machine learning model training
8. Which services should be used while developing an application requiring real-time video and audio processing?
    a. Amazon Rekognition
    b. Amazon Kinesis Video Streams
    c. Amazon Transcribe
    d. Amazon Polly

9. Which AWS services can be used to deploy web applications while managing minimal infrastructure?
   a. AWS Elastic Beanstalk
   b. Amazon EC2
   c. Amazon RDS
   d. Amazon S3
10. Which among the following is an AWS service that has complete machine learning model training, tuning, and deployment?
    a. Amazon Comprehend
    b. Amazon SageMaker
    c. AWS Lambda
    d. Amazon Rekognition

Answers

1. b
2. b
3. b
4. a
5. d
6. a
7. b
8. b
9. a
10. b

References

- https://docs.aws.amazon.com/amplify/
- https://docs.aws.amazon.com/apigateway/
- https://docs.aws.amazon.com/devicefarm/
- https://docs.aws.amazon.com/pinpoint/

- https://docs.aws.amazon.com/sqs/
- https://docs.aws.amazon.com/sns/
- https://docs.aws.amazon.com/ses/
- https://docs.aws.amazon.com/step-functions/
- https://docs.aws.amazon.com/amazonswf/
- https://docs.aws.amazon.com/kinesis/
- https://docs.aws.amazon.com/amazon-mq/
- https://docs.aws.amazon.com/comprehend/
- https://docs.aws.amazon.com/forecast/
- https://docs.aws.amazon.com/frauddetector/
- https://docs.aws.amazon.com/kendra/
- https://docs.aws.amazon.com/lex/
- https://docs.aws.amazon.com/polly/
- https://docs.aws.amazon.com/rekognition/
- https://docs.aws.amazon.com/sagemaker/
- https://docs.aws.amazon.com/textract/
- https://docs.aws.amazon.com/transcribe/
- https://docs.aws.amazon.com/translate/
- https://docs.aws.amazon.com/application-discovery/
- https://docs.aws.amazon.com/mgn/
- https://docs.aws.amazon.com/dms/
- https://docs.aws.amazon.com/datasync/
- https://docs.aws.amazon.com/migrationhub/
- https://docs.aws.amazon.com/snowball/
- https://docs.aws.amazon.com/transfer/

CHAPTER 8
AWS Management and Governance Services

Introduction

Imagine a vibrant architect's studio filled with a dynamic atmosphere of creativity. However, simultaneously managing many projects might be chaotic. The city's best architects saw they needed more than competency to maintain a competitive edge. A system was required to raise efficiency, ensure consistency, and enable automation.

Enter the Amazon Web Services (AWS) platform. AWS provides a set of tools to optimize the studio's workflow. By using solutions, such as Infrastructure as Code (IaC) and DevOps, architects can generate detailed plans for their projects, guaranteeing uniformity and dependability. The blueprints are represented as code, enabling automation and easy duplication. CI/CD pipelines significantly increase efficiency. These pipelines make building, assessing, and executing projects easier, leading to completion and better design outcomes.

To ensure security and compliance with regulations, the studio has integrated monitoring and logging tools, such as AWS CloudWatch, AWS X-Ray, and AWS CloudTrail. These tools offer real-time insights into project status and performance, allowing architects to promptly identify and address any issues.

Using these AWS services, the architect's studio constructed a resilient, effective, and expandable infrastructure. This solid basis provides the platform for ongoing expansion and achievement. In this chapter, we will explore these ideas in depth.

Structure

In this chapter, we will cover the following topics:

- Introduction
- Infrastructure Provisioning and Management
- Monitoring and Logging

- Security and Compliance: Tracking User Activity and API Calls using CloudTrail
- Additional Management and Governance Services
- Real-world Use Cases

Cloud Infrastructure for Growth

Establishing an effective cloud infrastructure supporting future growth is crucial in today's rapidly evolving tech landscape. Your cloud infrastructure may be optimized to excel in a dynamic environment, similar to how an architect methodically plans to deliver optimal performance.

By exploring the following essential subjects, you will get the knowledge and skills to build a robust personalized cloud ecosystem that fulfills your precise needs.

To secure your cloud-based future with certainty, it's crucial to understand concepts like enhancing security protocols, improving effectiveness, and guaranteeing scalability.

Infrastructure as Code (IaC)

This involves controlling and transmitting computer infrastructure via specification files that machines can understand, emphasizing automated procedures over human intervention. Configuration files help you define your infrastructure resources, including servers, databases, and networks. These files may be subjected to version control, making straightforward tracking alterations and deployments possible.

Let's consider the example of an e-commerce website using AWS CloudFormation templates to automate provisioning and managing infrastructure. It ensures consistency and reduces manual errors. During peak shopping hours, the website must increase its capacity. With Infrastructure as Code (IaC), they can automatically deploy new servers and resources utilizing predefined templates, which guarantees consistency and minimizes the chances of configuration drift.

Benefits of Infrastructure as Code (IaC):

- Infrastructure as Code (IaC) guarantees that the creation and configuration of your infrastructure stay consistent across all environments to reduce undesired variations and mistakes.
- It records modifications made to your infrastructure in the document, enabling you to revert to known-good configurations when necessary.
- Once written, it simplifies infrastructure setup and execution to expedite deployments and decrease errors.

Amazon Web Services (AWS) offers Infrastructure as Code (IaC) services:

- Using AWS Service Catalog enables the establishment and handling of service collections that customers can easily deploy.
- AWS CloudTrail is a monitoring tool that logs and documents all AWS API requests made from your account and maintains a history of any modifications made to your infrastructure.

AWS Infrastructure as Code (IaC) Services:

- **AWS CloudFormation**: To create and manage AWS resources through IaC.
- **AWS Service Catalog**: This is for managing service portfolios for users to deploy.
- **AWS CloudTrail**: This is to keep track of all API requests you make on AWS, giving you a record of infrastructure changes.

DevOps

DevOps is a philosophy centered on the knowledge sharing and tooling necessary in a high-performing, reliable, and collaborative engineering organization. It speeds up development processes, enhances teamwork, and establishes practices for creating, maintaining, and improving technical infrastructure. It also highlights teamwork among development, operations, and security groups.

Let's consider a software development team following DevOps methodologies by utilizing AWS tools, such as CodePipeline and CodeBuild to improve teamwork between development and operations. This results in quicker and more dependable software deployments. DevOps lets the team break silos which enables CI/CD to take place continuously. This leads to faster feature implementation, fixes bugs, and improves user satisfaction.

Benefits of Adopting DevOps:

- Streamlined procedures provide accelerated development, testing, and deployment cycles.
- When teams work together, the quality of the code is boosted enhancing the reliability of the infrastructure.
- We can accelerate the pace of developing and testing new concepts by speeding up deployments and feedback cycles.

Continuous Integration/ Continuous Delivery (CI/CD) Pipelines

Continuous Integration/Continuous Deployment (CI/CD) pipelines handle tasks like merging code, conducting tests, and deploying software automatically. This process enables faster feedback loops and reduces the chances of introducing mistakes in production scenarios.

If a company implements CI/CD pipelines with AWS CodePipeline to automate the testing and deployment of their applications, it reduces manual intervention, minimizes errors, and ensures compliance with financial regulations.

Benefits of Continuous Integration and Continuous Deployment (CI/CD):

- Delivering new features and bug fixes to users is possible by utilizing automated deployment techniques to accelerate releases.
- The use of regular integration and testing facilitates the early identification of bugs throughout the development process.
- Automated deployments minimize the possibility of human mistakes and ensure consistent configurations.

Amazon Web Services (AWS) provides a range of DevOps and CI/CD services:

- AWS CodePipeline helps you effortlessly create and oversee integration and deployment pipelines, thus coordinating the CI/CD process across multiple AWS services.
- AWS CodeBuild lets you automate compiling source code and conducting tests for deployment by integrating with CodePipeline
- AWS CodeDeploy also simplifies the deployment of code across various AWS services.

The Significance of Monitoring and its Optimal Approaches

Maintaining your cloud infrastructure's well-being, efficiency, and safety requires monitoring. Effective monitoring lets you catch problems early to prevent disruptions to your users.

For example, a healthcare provider monitors their AWS infrastructure using Amazon CloudWatch to ensure the availability and performance of critical applications, setting up alarms to detect and respond to issues. CloudWatch monitors server health, application performance, and network traffic. If any critical metrics exceed the threshold, it notifies the operations team, thus ensuring the high availability of healthcare services.

Benefits of Monitoring:

- **Proactive Problem Detection:** Address problems early to reduce their impact on users or applications.
- **Performance Optimisation:** Assess resource utilization to upgrade your infrastructure for cost efficiency and effectiveness.

- **Security Vigilance:** Strengthen security comprehension by actively monitoring occurrences and identifying vulnerabilities to your infrastructure.

Effective Observability Methods:

Observability is critical as cloud-native environments are becoming more complex by the day. It helps in improving team efficiency and leads to better decisions. For instance, network monitoring software can help identify network-related issues that could have been otherwise blamed on other teams. Engineers use tools to analyze data about programs and modules and to communicate between components. Some data sources include:

- Metrics are indicators that offer insights into the condition and effectiveness of your infrastructure with numerical data.
- Thresholds refer to values for measurements that prompt alerts when there is a deviation from the expected performance.
- Logs include written pieces of information from applications.

Services for Monitoring AWS:

- Amazon CloudWatch is a hub for monitoring and analyzing your AWS resources, applications, and logs.
- AWS CloudTrail is a tool that records and tracks all API requests directed toward your AWS account, enabling user activity monitoring and identifying security risks.
- The AWS Health Dashboard offers a gateway to access service health data for various AWS services.

Record-keeping and Tracking

Logging and tracing provide extensive information about your applications and infrastructure which is essential for issue resolution and code debugging.

Advantages of Utilizing AWS Cloud:

- **Enhanced Problem Solving**: Logs and traces facilitate rapid issue identification, saving time and frustration.
- **Improved Efficiency**: By identifying areas of congestion, you may optimize the use of AWS resources and guarantee seamless functionality.
- **Security**: Logs serve as a record of security occurrences, aiding in maintaining a secure cloud environment.

AWS Logging and Tracing Services:

- Amazon CloudWatch is a hub where you can collect and inspect logs and monitor data from your AWS services.

- AWS X-Ray is a tool designed to track requests throughout your AWS services and detect performance issues.

By utilizing logging and tracing mechanisms, you can gain insights into how your AWS cloud operates and ensure it performs optimally. For example, the media streaming service uses AWS CloudWatch Logs and AWS X-Ray to collect, analyze, and trace log data across its microservices architecture. This helps troubleshoot issues and improve performance. Whenever the users experience buffering issues, the streaming service uses CloudWatch Logs to analyze server logs and X-Ray to trace request paths across microservices.

Key Insights

Managing and overseeing your AWS cloud setup ensures a scalable and efficient infrastructure. By using the range of services offered by AWS and following practices, you can simplify your operations and enhance your operational abilities.

Key tactics, such as Infrastructure as Code (IaC), DevOps principles, and Continuous Integration/Continuous Delivery (CI/CD) pipelines, are essential in this endeavor. You can build a cloud infrastructure by integrating these techniques and leveraging AWS services in your management and governance practices. Employ these tools and strategies to enhance your setup and establish a foundation for future growth and innovation.

Infrastructure Provisioning and Management

In cloud computing, it's crucial to handle infrastructure setup and management. This includes getting everything ready for applications and services to run smoothly. Regarding AWS, these responsibilities involve setting up and organizing resources, such as machines, databases, networking elements, and other essentials.

- **Infrastructure Provisioning:** Build and configure cloud resources automatically to ensure the required infrastructure is ready for deploying applications, conducting tests, and scaling as and when needed.
- **Infrastructure Management**: Includes activities needed to enhance the established infrastructure, such as monitoring performance, ensuring security measures, managing updates, and adjusting resource scale.

By utilizing AWS services and following industry practices, companies can achieve dependable and scalable infrastructure setup and maintenance. These aspects are essential for supporting resilient cloud environments.

Let's explore the key AWS services and practices that streamline these processes.

CloudFormation

AWS CloudFormation lets you outline and set up AWS infrastructure components in an automated manner through code.

Template Overview

A CloudFormation template (depicted in *Figure* 8.1) is a text document detailing an application's AWS resources. It empowers you to establish and oversee interconnected AWS resources efficiently. Let us consider a startup that uses AWS CloudFormation to create and manage resources, such as VPCs, EC2 instances, and RDS databases, ensuring infrastructure consistency and version control. The company can easily replicate development, testing, and production environments by managing infrastructure as code.

A CloudFormation template consists of several key sections:

- **Parameters**: Input values that can be provided when the stack is created or updated, allowing customization without changing the template.
- **Mappings**: Key-value pairs that can specify conditional values such as regional settings.
- **Conditions**: Statements that determine whether certain resources are created or certain properties are assigned based on input parameter values.
- **Resources**: The AWS resources you want to create, the only required section, include EC2 instances, S3 buckets, or IAM roles.
- **Outputs**: Values that are returned when you view the properties of your stack include resource attributes, such as instance IDs or IP addresses.

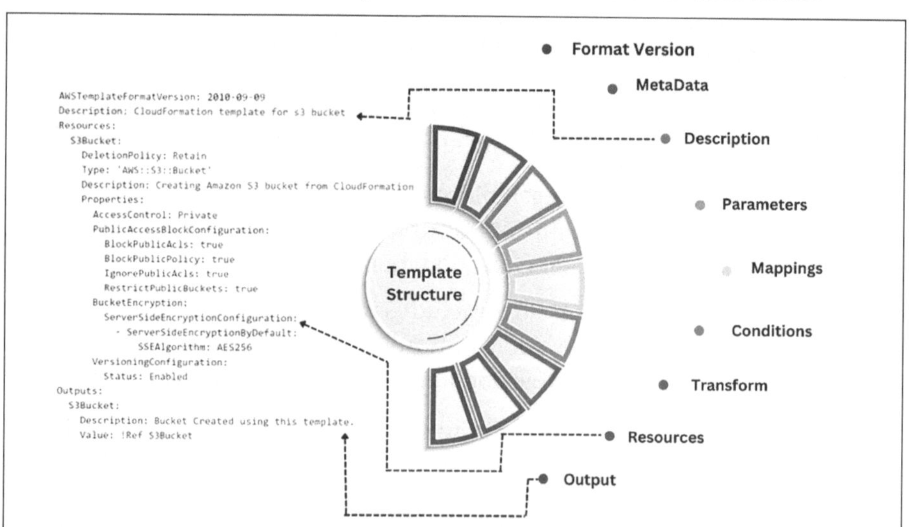

Figure 8.1: *Sample CloudFormation Template*

Best Practices for CloudFormation Templates

- **Use Modular Templates**: Break down large templates into smaller, reusable modules.
- **Parameterize as Much as Possible**: Use parameters to increase the reusability of templates.
- **Leverage Mappings and Conditions**: Use mappings for region-specific settings and conditions for optional resources.
- **Version Control Your Templates**: Store templates in a version control system like Git to track changes and manage versions.
- **Regularly Validate Templates**: Use tools like AWS CloudFormation Linter (cfn-lint) to validate templates before deploying.
- **Document Your Templates**: Include descriptions and comments to make templates easier to understand and maintain.

AWS CodePipeline: Your CI/CD Solution on AWS

AWS CodePipeline integrates and continuously delivers in an automated manner to streamline the process of application updates and infrastructure. *Figure* 8.2 depicts continuous integration and continuous deployment.

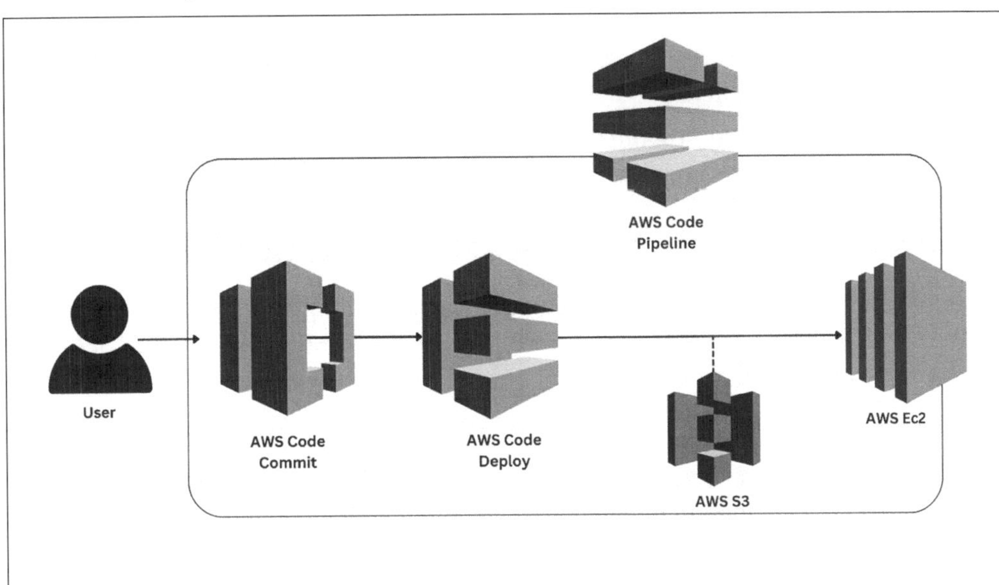

Figure 8.2: *AWS CodePipeline*

CodeCommit: Secure Source Code Management

AWS CodeCommit is a scalable source control service that securely hosts Git repositories. It enables teams to store and track source code versions effortlessly and seamlessly integrate with CodePipeline for CI/CD processes.

Key features include:

- **Unlimited Repositories**: For an unlimited number of repositories.
- **Encryption**: Used for data encryption in transit and at rest.
- **Access Control**: Used for managing access with AWS IAM policies.
- **Integration with Other AWS Services**: Integrates with AWS Lambda, AWS CodeBuild, and other services for a complete CI/CD pipeline.

Build Stage: Building and Preparing Your Application

During the build phase of CodePipeline, AWS CodeBuild is usually employed. It is a build service that compiles source code, conducts tests, and generates artifacts.

Key steps include:

- **Source Code Retrieval**: CodeBuild retrieves the latest source code from CodeCommit or other source repositories.
- **Build Specification**: A buildspec.yml file defines the build commands and settings.
- **Compilation and Testing**: CodeBuild compiles the code and runs unit tests to ensure code quality.
- **Artifact Creation**: The built and tested code is packaged into artifacts, which can be stored in S3 or pushed to container registries.

Deploy Stage: Automating Deployment to AWS

The deployment phase in CodePipeline automates sending the created components to AWS services, such as AWS Elastic Beanstalk, AWS Lambda, Amazon ECS, or local in-house servers.

Key components:

- **Deploy Actions**: Actions in this stage define how and where to deploy the artifacts. For instance, an Elastic Beanstalk deploy action can update an application running on Beanstalk.
- **Approval Actions**: Manual approval actions can be added to the pipeline to require human intervention before deployment.

- **Notifications**: Integration with AWS SNS or other notification services alerts teams on deployment status.

Key Insights

By integrating these stages, AWS CodePipeline provides a robust and automated solution for continuously integrating and delivering applications, ensuring that updates are deployed quickly and reliably.

Monitoring and Logging

In the changing realm of cloud infrastructure, managing and recording activities are crucial to ensure your setup's well-being, efficiency, and safety. AWS provides a range of services tailored to offer in-depth understanding and management.

AWS CloudWatch enables real-time monitoring of resource metrics and application logs, while AWS CloudTrail provides detailed logging of user activity and API calls for compliance and security.

Implementing best practices such as setting up CloudWatch Alarms for proactive alerts, using centralized logging with CloudTrail, and ensuring log integrity with AWS KMS encryption, ensures efficient and effective management of your AWS infrastructure.

CloudWatch: The Vigilant Guardian of Your AWS Environment

CloudWatch protects your AWS setup, monitoring metrics, and providing insights. It is the cornerstone of observability, ensuring your resources operate optimally. Let us consider an IoT solution provider that uses Amazon CloudWatch to monitor the health and performance of its IoT devices, setting up alarms to notify the operations team of any anomalies. Herein, the alarms trigger if devices go offline, allowing for troubleshooting and maintenance.

Key Elements

Amazon CloudWatch provides a range of monitoring features for AWS resources and applications, offering real-time information and practical insights. As a monitoring center, CloudWatch allows you to gather and monitor metrics, track log files, and establish alarms. This tool guarantees that you have the visibility to uphold and enhance the efficiency of your setup.

- **Comprehensive Monitoring**: CloudWatch collaborates with various AWS services to gather data on metrics, such as CPU usage, memory consumption, and network activity.

- **Real-Time Data**: You will gain access to both past and current data, empowering you to make informed choices using the latest information available.
- **Actionable Insights:** CloudWatch equips you with the resources to examine data effectively and derive insights to enhance system efficiency and address problems.

Monitoring Metrics (Basic, Detailed, and Custom)

CloudWatch enables you to keep an eye on different metrics, allowing you to monitor and analyze performance data in various ways.

- **Basic Metrics:** CloudWatch offers metrics without charge by default. These metrics cover performance indicators, such as CPU usage, disk I/O, and network activity.
- **Detailed Metrics:** For more gritty monitoring, you can activate detailed monitoring. This feature provides data at a higher frequency (every minute) than monitoring (every five minutes), allowing for more precise analysis and quicker responses to performance issues.
- **Custom Metrics:** CloudWatch allows for custom metrics, allowing you to create and track metrics related to your application or infrastructure. These custom metrics can include data points related to your application, such as transaction volumes, error rates, or customized business performance indicators.

Setting Up Alarms and Alerts for Proactive Monitoring

Setting up alarms and notifications allows you to tackle problems in advance, preventing user disruptions and maintaining operations.

- **Alarms**: CloudWatch alarms are customizable and help you monitor data points and take action when they cross set limits. For instance, you can create an alarm to inform you if CPU usage goes above 80% for a period.
- **Alerting**: Alerts can be linked with notification services like Amazon SNS (Simple Notification Service), which can send messages through email, text, or other communication methods. This ensures that the appropriate individuals are informed promptly about the steps.
- **Automated Responses**: CloudWatch alerts can also trigger automated actions, such as adjusting resources in Auto Scaling, group activating an AWS Lambda function for resolution, or generating an incident in an IT service management platform.

Building Informative Dashboards for Resource Visualization

Develop user dashboards that display resource performance and overall health, making it easier to spot issues or slowdowns in performance.

- **Custom Dashboards**: CloudWatch dashboards offer customization options, allowing you to design representations of your metrics. You can include widgets that showcase graphs, charts, and numerical data points.
- **Multiple View**: Dashboards can be set up to show perspectives of your data, giving you an overview of your infrastructure status. This may involve views of metrics or detailed views focusing on specific resources.
- **Interactive Graphs**: Interactive charts allow you to zoom in on periods, compare metrics, and track trends over time. This feature is essential for spotting patterns and troubleshooting problems.
- **Grouping Resources**: Grouping resources and their metrics on one dashboard makes monitoring easier for complex environments with multiple interconnected services.

By utilizing CloudWatch's monitoring features, establishing alarms and alerts, and creating informative dashboards, you can guarantee your AWS setup's well-being, performance, and durability. This thorough monitoring strategy not only aids in sustaining top-notch operations but also enables you to make informed choices based on data to improve the effectiveness and dependability of your cloud system.

CloudWatch Logs: The Chronicle of Your AWS Environment

Amazon CloudWatch Logs is a centralized platform for logging purposes, aiding the organization to, retrieve and examine log information from your AWS assets. It functions as a record keeper for your AWS setup, gathering logs that offer information on your software and infrastructure's functionality, well-being, and protection. *Figure 8.3* explains how CloudWatch interacts with AWS services.

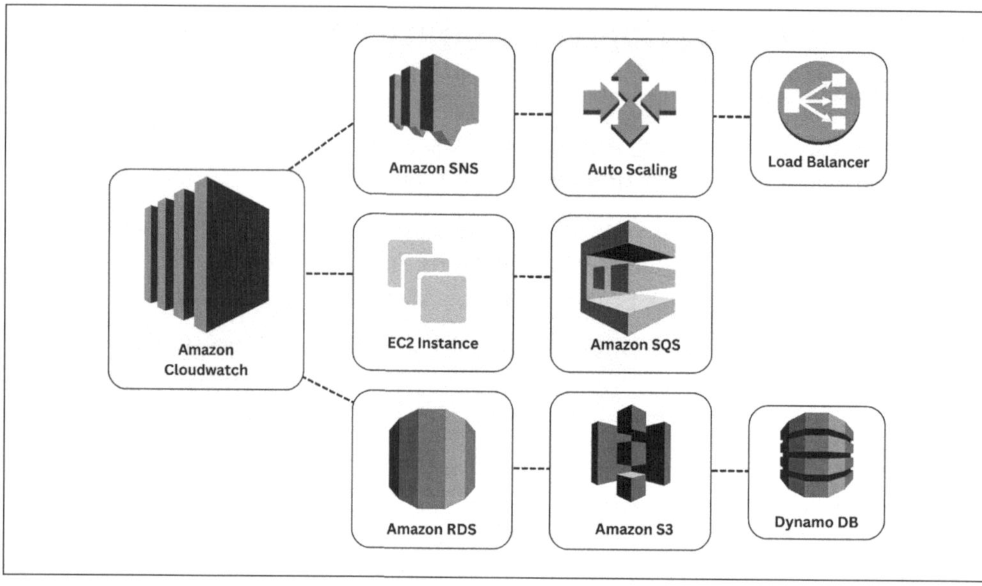

Figure 8.3: *Amazon CloudWatch*

Logging Best Practices for Efficient Log Management

It is really important to follow the practices when logging for log management. These practices are key to managing a large amount of log data, making it easier to find and analyze the necessary information quickly.

- **Setting Retention Policies:** Establish guidelines for retaining logs to remove log entries automatically. This practice aids in controlling storage expenses and ensures that your log information remains pertinent and valuable.
- **Enabling Log Filtering**: By applying filters, you can concentrate on events, errors or patterns in your log data, simplifying issue diagnosis and comprehension of system operations.
- **Indexing for Faster Searches**: Indexing enhances the speed of searches and queries, allowing you to swiftly locate log records based on keywords, timestamps, or other criteria. This improves your ability to analyze logs promptly.

Security and Compliance: Tracking User Activity and API Calls with CloudTrail

Ensuring security and compliance is crucial in any cloud setting, and AWS CloudTrail plays an important role in upholding both aspects. AWS CloudTrail offers a logging solution to monitor user actions and API requests, promoting transparency and responsibility within your AWS system. By recording data on each API request, CloudTrail helps maintain a compliant environment.

When integrated with AWS Organizations, CloudTrail enables centralized logging across accounts, simplifying governance and compliance oversight. Following recommended practices, such as enabling log file validation, encrypting logs using AWS KMS, and configuring region trails, helps uphold the security and resilience of your logging setup. *Figure* 8.4 explains how CloudTrail works.

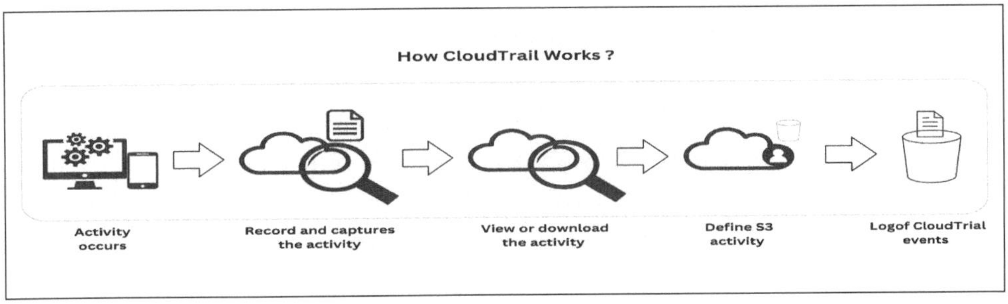

Figure 8.4: *How CloudTrail works*

Understanding CloudTrail Events

CloudTrail logs every API call in your AWS account, capturing detailed information about each request. This includes:

- **Who Made the Call:** Identifies the user, role, or service that initiated the API request, providing accountability and traceability.
- **Services Used:** This logs the AWS services accessed during the API call, helping you understand the interaction between different infrastructure components.
- **Actions Performed:** Records the specific actions taken, such as creating, modifying, or deleting resources. This helps track changes and understand the impact of various operations on your environment.

Integrating CloudTrail with AWS Organizations

Integrate CloudTrail to AWS Organizations for logging across accounts, streamlining governance and compliance tasks by merging log information from all accounts into one central repository.

- **Centralized Logging:** Gather logs from AWS accounts and regions and store them in a central S3 bucket for simplified log data management and analysis.

- **Cross Account Insights**: It allows you to monitor and ensure compliance by providing visibility into activities across all organization accounts.
- **Simplified Compliance:** Streamline your compliance reporting with a unified view of user activity and API calls across your AWS environment.

Best Practices for Secure CloudTrail Configuration

Ensuring that you follow the recommended guidelines for setting up CloudTrail guarantees the security and durability of your logging system.

- **Enabling Log File Validation:** Enable log file validation to maintain the integrity of your log files. This function utilizes a hash algorithm to generate and confirm hash digests for each log file, safeguarding them against any alterations.
- **Encrypting Logs With AWS KMS**: To secure your CloudTrail logs, consider encrypting them with AWS Key Management Service (KMS). This additional security layer ensures only authorized users and services can access your log data.
- **Setting Up Multi-Region Trail:** Implement multi-region trails to capture log data from all regions where your AWS resources are active. This approach offers an overview of user activities and API calls, preventing any actions from going unnoticed.

Key Insights

You can acquire information about your AWS setup when you utilize CloudWatch Logs and CloudTrail while following logging and monitoring practices. These tools help ensure your cloud infrastructure's secure and dependable operation, enabling you to uphold top-notch performance and compliance standards. Whether you're observing metrics, configuring alerts, displaying data using dashboards, or monitoring user actions and API calls, these resources offer the transparency and authority required to oversee your AWS environment.

Deep Dive into AWS Management and Governance Services

AWS provides various services to improve your setup's organization, automation, and oversight. These services offer functions such as streamlining tasks with AWS Systems Manager, utilizing AWS CLI for command-line operations, and ensuring continuous resource monitoring through AWS Config. AWS Health Dashboard provides proactive service health updates, while AWS License Manager simplifies software license compliance.

The AWS Management Console provides a user-friendly interface for managing resources, while AWS Proton supports the development of serverless applications. With the AWS Service Catalog, users can easily provision self-services. AWS Trusted Advisor helps optimize costs and enhance security. Additionally, AWS X-Ray aids in debugging and analyzing performance. Understanding these services allows you to manage and optimize your AWS environment effectively.

Here's a breakdown of the AWS services to help you understand their functionalities in managing and governing your cloud resources:

AWS Systems Manager: Fleet Management and Automation

AWS Systems Manager is a featured service created to offer a platform for effectively managing AWS resources. It provides utilities for automating duties and simplifying resource oversight throughout your AWS setup. Let us understand this with an example. An enterprise uses Systems Manager to automate routine maintenance tasks, such as patching, software updates, and configuration management across thousands of EC2 instances and on-premises servers, ensuring consistency and reducing manual effort.

Fleet Management: AWS Systems Manager makes handling many instances easier, whether on AWS or on-premises. It streamlines tasks, such as setting up, updating, and installing software, making managing a group of servers easier. With AWS Systems Manager, you can automate tasks to maintain setups and minimize the risk of mistakes.

Automation: The service provides an Automation function that lets you automate maintenance and deployment tasks. Through Automation documents (also known as playbooks) you can create instances, install software, and apply patches without input. This automation helps decrease burdens and enhances productivity.

Key Features: The package consists of Patch Manager to automate patching procedures, State Manager to uphold configuration, Automation for task automation, Inventory for overseeing resource inventory, and Session Manager for traceable access to instances.

AWS Command Line Interface (AWS CLI): Command-Line Access to AWS Services

The AWS Command Line Interface (CLI) is a tool that allows users to manage AWS services using command-line instructions. The tool makes it easier to automate and script tasks. It offers a way to interact with and oversee AWS assets. A DevOps engineer creates shell scripts using AWS CLI commands to automate the deployment of infrastructure and backups and reduce the risk of manual errors.

- **Command-Line Access:** The AWS Command Line Interface (CLI) provides a command-line tool to engage with AWS services, granting you the freedom and authority to oversee your AWS setup. You can execute various tasks from the terminal, such as starting EC2 instances, overseeing S3 buckets, and setting up IAM roles.
- **Automation:** The AWS CLI's ability to access the command line makes it easier to automate tasks using scripts. This feature is essential for incorporating AWS tasks into development and deployment pipelines, ultimately improving the effectiveness and dependability of your DevOps practices.
- **Key Features:** The guide contains instructions for various AWS services, setup profiles, handling environments, and the option to run commands directly from the terminal.

AWS Config: Resource Configuration Management and Change Tracking

AWS Config is a tool for monitoring, assessing, and reviewing configurations for AWS resources. By tracking configuration changes, it helps ensure compliance and security. For example, an insurance company sets up AWS Config rules to monitor resource configurations and automatically notify administrators of non-compliant changes. This helps in maintaining security and compliance with industry standards.

- **Configuration Management:** AWS Configuration consistently logs the setups of your AWS assets and keeps a record of modifications. This assists in comprehending the condition of your surroundings over time and confirming that resources adhere to company policies.
- **Change Tracking:** The service tracks changes in resource configurations, offering detailed information about modifications. This visibility helps you detect unexpected changes, investigate issues, and ensure compliance with governance policies.
- **Key features:** Include configuration snapshots, which provide point-in-time views of your resource configurations, compliance auditing to evaluate resource configurations against desired states, and detailed resource relationships.

AWS Health Dashboard: Proactive Monitoring for AWS Service Health

The AWS Health Dashboard customizes your view of the status of AWS services and resources. It provides up-to-date and past data on service interruptions and planned maintenance activities that could affect your setup. An example could be a SaaS provider using the Health Dashboard to receive alerts about AWS service issues. They ensure continuous service delivery during outages by implementing contingency plans.

- **Proactive Monitoring:** The dashboard sends you alerts about events that might impact your AWS services, allowing you to take measures to address potential problems. This assists in upholding the accessibility and dependability of your applications.
- **Service Health**: The AWS Health Dashboard provides in-depth information on the condition of AWS services in regions and accounts. It details resolved incidents, scheduled maintenance activities, and other occurrences influencing your AWS setup.
- **Key Features:** The Health dashboard includes a personalized dashboard for monitoring service health, health alerts for real-time notifications, and detailed event descriptions for understanding the impact and remediation steps.

AWS License Manager: Streamlined License Management for Your Software

AWS License Manager helps manage software licenses from companies, such as Microsoft, SAP, Oracle, and IBM in AWS and on-premises environments.

- **Streamlined Management**: This tool simplifies the process of monitoring and managing software licenses, reducing the risk of exceeding license limits and ensuring compliance with regulations. It offers resources for license management, enabling you to keep an up-to-date record and prevent expenses.
- **Centralized Control**: Manage all your software licenses with AWS License Manager, which gives you a hub for visibility and control over license usage. This streamlined approach helps organizations uphold licensing rules and comply with vendor agreements.
- **Key Features:** License Manager custom licensing rules to define how licenses are used and automate license discovery to track usage and integration with AWS Systems Manager for broader resource management.

AWS Management Console: Web-Based Interface for AWS Service Management

The AWS Management Console is a user web interface that allows individuals to control and set up AWS services easily and provides an interface for accessing different AWS services and resources.

- **Web-based Interface:** The console offers a user-friendly interface for handling AWS services, even for users with limited technical expertise. It streamlines the setup and management of AWS resources using a visual interface.

- **Service Management:** The AWS Management Console provides a hub for overseeing your AWS setup. It lets you launch and configure instances, handle storage, and track resource usage. It works seamlessly with AWS services to offer a complete suite of management features.
- **Key Features:** The management console includes a resource management interface for managing AWS resources, a billing dashboard for monitoring costs, and service-specific consoles for detailed service management.

AWS Proton: Serverless Application Management for Faster Development

AWS Proton is a service that helps teams deploy and manage serverless and container-based applications easily. It allows developers to build and launch applications swiftly using defined infrastructure templates. A development team can use AWS Proton to define standard templates for microservices and manage those consistently, reducing the time and effort spent on manual configuration.

- **Application Management:** AWS Proton makes setting up, deploying, and keeping track of serverless and containerized applications easier. It offers a system for overseeing an application's life cycle, from development to production.
- **Faster Development**: Infrastructure templates help AWS Proton developers concentrate on coding rather than handling infrastructure tasks. This speeds up the development process and guarantees dependable deployments.
- **Key Features:** It involves setting up automated infrastructure to facilitate resource setup, creating pipelines to improve application delivery and incorporating monitoring tools to guarantee application performance and reliability.

AWS Service Catalog: Self-Service Provisioning of Approved IT Resources

Organizations can utilize the AWS Service Catalog to establish and manage lists of IT services. It offers a self-service portal for individuals to request IT resources that adhere to guidelines.

- **Self-service Provisioning:** Users can easily access and provision IT resources from a list of authorized services using the platform. This accelerates the deployment process and reduces the need for IT intervention.
- **Approved Resources:** AWS Service Catalog ensures that only compliant and approved resources are deployed, maintaining governance and compliance. It provides controls for defining and enforcing policies on resource usage.

- **Key Features:** It consists of product collections for arranging and managing IT services control, access to regulate resource provisioning permissions, and monitoring usage to monitor resource consumption.

AWS Trusted Advisor: Real-Time Recommendations for Cost Optimization and Best Practices

AWS Trusted Advisor is a service that provides suggestions for improving your AWS setup. It covers advice on saving costs, enhancing performance, boosting security, and following best practices.

- **Cost Optimization:** Trusted Advisor advises cutting expenses by pinpointing resources and suggesting budget-friendly alternatives. This enables you to optimize the returns on your AWS investment.
- **Best Practices:** The system assesses your AWS setup based on AWS guidelines. Offers best practices for enhancing efficiency, safety, and fault tolerance.
- **Key Features:** It checks for ways to reduce costs, follow security guidelines, enhance performance, improve fault tolerance, and adhere to service limits to optimize your AWS setup and meet industry standards.

AWS X-Ray: Service Debugging and Performance Analysis

AWS X-Ray is a tool that helps developers examine and troubleshoot distributed applications. It offers information on how your applications perform, simplifying the process of pinpointing and resolving any issues that may arise.

- **Service Debugging:** AWS X-Ray tracks requests as they move through services within your application. This visibility assists in locating the root cause of performance problems and recognizing areas of congestion.
- **Performance Analysis:** The system gathers information on how applications perform, allowing you to examine and grasp how your applications behave in different situations. This helps you optimize performance and ensure reliability.
- **Key Features:** The system involves tracking from start to finish for a view of how applications operate, service maps for diagrams showcasing application interconnections, and examining errors to pinpoint and solve problems efficiently.

AWS X-Ray is essential in troubleshooting, assessing, and optimizing the efficiency of serverless and microservices applications. With its distributed tracing, in-depth performance analysis, and visual service mappings, X-Ray aids in unraveling the complexities of your application, pinpointing bottlenecks, and ensuring reliable operations. Regular utilization of AWS X-Ray can result in enhancements in application performance, faster problem resolution, and an enhanced user experience.

By grasping the functionalities of these services in *Table* 8.1 and how they collaborate harmoniously, you can proficiently oversee, automate, and govern your AWS infrastructure to achieve peak performance levels while prioritizing security measures and cost-effectiveness.

Service	**Functionality**
Fleet Management and Automation	AWS Systems Manager: Acts as a central hub for managing and automating tasks across infrastructure, including on-premises and cloud resources. Offers features such as patch management, session manager, automation, and document management.
Command-Line Interface	AWS CLI: Allows direct interaction with all AWS services from the terminal, enabling task automation, script deployments, and infrastructure management programmatically.
Resource Management and Change Tracking	AWS Config: Continuously monitors AWS resources, recording configuration history, tracking changes, ensuring compliance with security standards, and automating remediation actions for configuration drift.
Proactive Monitoring	AWS Health Dashboard: Proactively monitors AWS service health, providing real-time status updates, notifications about potential issues, and planned maintenance activities, and tools for mitigation and troubleshooting.
Software License Management	AWS License Manager: Simplifies software license management for AWS resources, automating license acquisition, tracking, renewal, and ensuring compliance with license agreements, and reducing the risk of violations.

Web-based Management Interface	The AWS Management Console offers a user-friendly interface for managing AWS services. It lets users view and modify resources, configure services, and monitor resource health and performance.
Serverless Development and Management	AWS Proton: Streamlines serverless application development and deployment, offering infrastructure provisioning and environment management for different development stages, and blue/green deployments for risk-free updates.
Self-service Provisioning	AWS Service Catalog allows users to access a catalog of authorized IT resources. Users can allocate resources using a self-service portal, which enhances productivity, ensures adherence to rules and regulations, and minimizes errors during provisioning.
Cost Optimization and Best Practices	AWS Trusted Advisor: Provides real-time recommendations for optimizing AWS costs and enhancing security posture, identifying cost savings opportunities, addressing security best practice gaps, and improving overall performance and efficiency.
Service Debugging and Performance Analysis	AWS X-Ray: Aids in debugging and analyzing the performance of serverless and microservices applications, offering distributed tracing, performance insights, and service maps to identify bottlenecks and optimize code.

Table 8.1: *AWS X-Ray services and functionalities*

Understanding the integration of these services is key to managing, automating, and regulating your AWS configuration to ensure its operation, security, and cost efficiency.

Real-World Use Cases

Let us see some of the real world use cases:

1. **Using DevOps Automation to Deploy Lambda APIs Across Accounts and Environments**

For managing multiple AWS accounts, enterprises adopting serverless technologies need automated release processes. This use case depicts the usage of CloudFormation and cross-account access for building a cross-account code pipeline to automate releases.

Solution Overview: An IAM user can assume a production role via AWS STS using a cross-account pipeline. This lets the user automate deployment across environments while following the least privileged access.

Code pipeline workflow:

1. DevOps team IAM user logs into AWS CLI.
2. IAM users assume pre-production deployment roles in AWS CodeCommit, CodeBuild, CodeDeploy, and CodePipeline.
3. AWS CodeBuild generates the CloudFormation template stack into S3.
4. AWS CodePipeline deploys code from S3 via Amazon API Gateway in pre-production.
5. Code is deployed to production by assuming the STS production IAM role.

This fully automated pipeline switches between pre-production and production accounts, deploying validated builds using CloudFormation templates. The following figure depicts this use case.

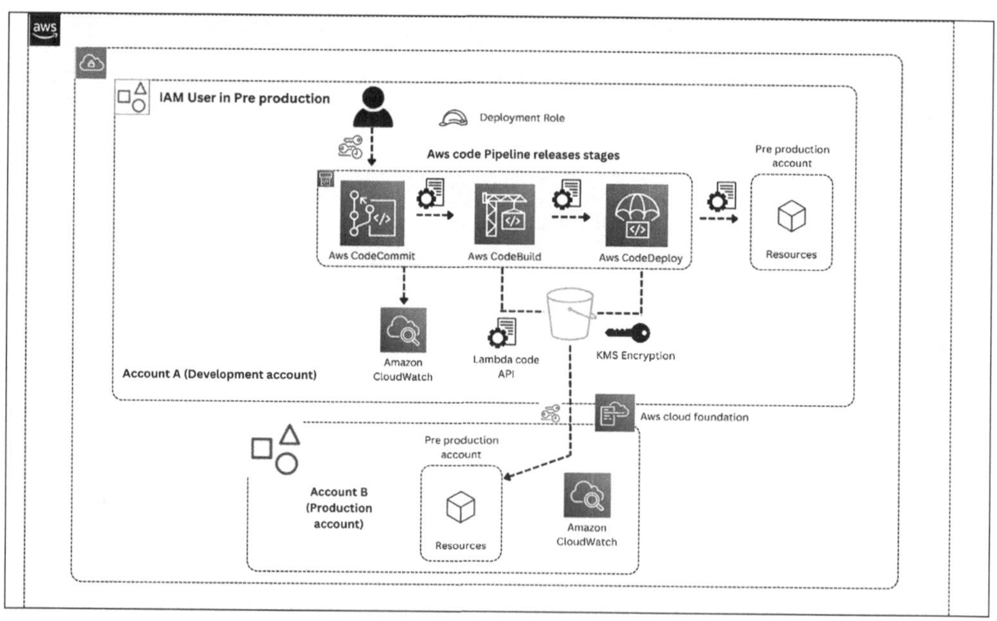

Figure 8.5: *Using DevOps Automation to Deploy Lambda APIs across Accounts and Environments*

2. **Monitoring and Logging with CloudWatch and CloudTrail**

   In today's cloud environments, it is critical to log and monitor events to maintain operational excellence and security. The following use case demonstrates how to integrate AWS CloudWatch and CloudTrail in an organization for comprehensive monitoring and logging across AWS accounts.

   Solution Overview: This solution uses CloudWatch Logs to store log data and CloudTrail to audit AWS API calls. This ensures centralized logging and security best practices.

Steps:

1. Configure CloudWatch to store, monitor, and analyze log files.
2. Enable CloudTrail to log API calls and analyze events to understand user activities.
3. Using AWS organizations, you can manage and consolidate CloudTrail logs from multiple accounts into a single S3 bucket. This allows you to manage logs efficiently.
4. For additional security, use AWS KMS to encrypt CloudTrail log files. Implement least-privilege access controls and multi-factor authentication (MFA) to protect log data.

This integrated approach to monitoring and logging with CloudWatch and CloudTrail enables organizations to maintain high-security standards and operational excellence in their AWS environments. This use case is illustrated in the following figure.

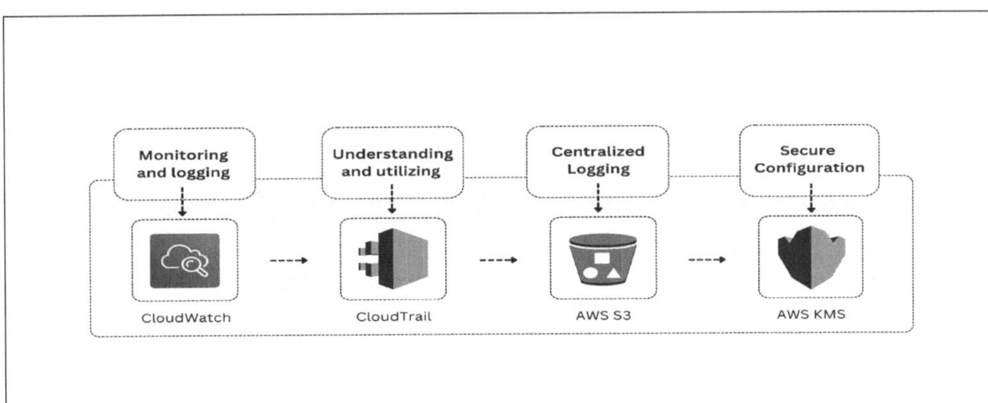

***Figure 8.6**: Monitoring and Logging with CloudWatch and CloudTrail*

3. **Comprehensive Management and Governance with AWS Services**

   It is essential to leverage a suite of AWS management and governance services to maintain operational efficiency, governance, and security in AWS environments. This use case demonstrates the integration of various AWS services for comprehensive management, monitoring, and optimization across AWS accounts.

Solution Overview: This solution integrates AWS Systems Manager, AWS CLI, AWS Config, AWS Health Dashboard, AWS License Manager, AWS Management Console, AWS Proton, AWS Service Catalog, AWS Trusted Advisor, and AWS X-Ray for providing a robust framework to aid resource management, license management, development and optimization.

Steps:

1. Configure Systems Manager to manage and automate your fleet of EC2 instances. Use Run Command to automate common administrative tasks across multiple instances.
2. Install AWS CLI and use CLI commands to launch instances, manage S3 buckets, and operate other resources.
3. Enable AWS Config to track and manage the configuration of AWS resources and detect changes.
4. Access the AWS Health Dashboard to receive personalized alerts. Integrate with Amazon CloudWatch and Systems Manager to automate incident response and ensure high availability.
5. Set up an AWS License Manager to manage your software licenses and define licensing rules to ensure compliance.
6. For an intuitive, web-based interface and to access AWS services, use the AWS Management Console.
7. Use AWS Proton to manage serverless and container-based applications. It streamlines this process.
8. Use AWS Service Catalog to create and manage approved IT services catalogs.
9. Use AWS Trusted Advisor to receive real-time recommendations to improve cost efficiency, security, fault tolerance, and performance.
10. Enable AWS X-Ray to trace and analyze application requests as they travel through your application, for debugging and performance improvements.

This use case is illustrated in the following figure:

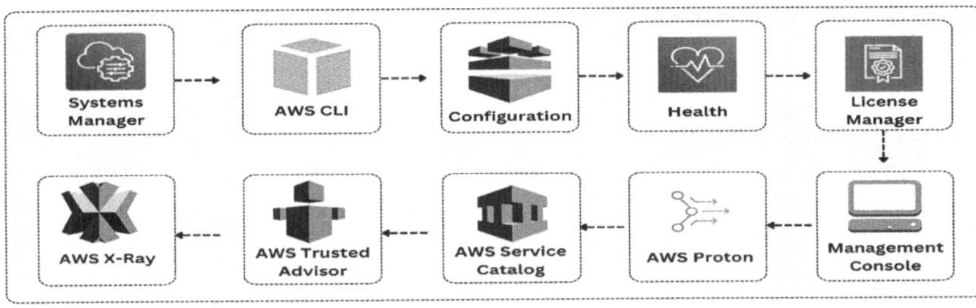

Figure 8.7: *Comprehensive Management and Governance with AWS Services*

Conclusion

Navigating the changing realm of technology and handling cloud infrastructure is not easy. When you have AWS (Amazon Web Services) on your side, you can access various tools to make operations easier and improve efficiency. Adopting Infrastructure as Code (IaC) principles and using Continuous Integration/Continuous Delivery (CI/CD) processes allows you to maintain uniformity and reliability across your setup while expediting project launches.

In conclusion, the architect's workspace is a testament to the importance of creativity and flexibility in dealing with situations. The studio has paved the way for efficiency, uniformity, and safety in its projects by using AWS services.

Through the application of Infrastructure as Code (IaC) and DevOps practices, the studio has reached a level of automation and dependability previously considered unachievable. Incorporating CI/CD pipelines and strong monitoring tools has taken their endeavors to levels guaranteeing speed and excellence, resilience, and adherence to regulations.

As our studio expands and develops, pursuing perfection remains a journey. In this phase, we will delve into cloud security, similar to strengthening the base and framework of a majestic architectural marvel. By grasping the shared responsibility model, implementing data protection strategies, and leveraging AWS security services, our studio will persist in prospering amidst a terrain filled with obstacles, ensuring a future marked by creativity and triumph. The next chapter discusses tools, such as Amazon Macie, Amazon Inspector, GuardDuty, and Security Hub and services, such as Shield, WAF, and KMS to help you secure your cloud environment.

Multiple Choice Questions

1. Which services make it possible to create and manage AWS resources via templates?
   a. AWS CloudFormation
   b. AWS CloudTrail
   c. AWS Config
   d. AWS CloudWatch
2. Which AWS services are used for monitoring and logging purposes?
   a. AWS CloudTrail
   b. AWS CloudFormation
   c. AWS CloudWatch
   d. AWS Trusted Advisor
3. Which services are used to monitor user activities and API calls against one's account?
   a. AWS CloudFormation
   b. AWS CloudTrail
   c. AWS Config
   d. AWS Service Catalog
4. Which service provides real-time data about resource usage and operational well-being?
   a. AWS CloudWatch
   b. AWS CloudFormation
   c. AWS Trusted Advisor
   d. AWS Systems Manager
5. Which AWS services do you use to ensure that resources have the appropriate security policies applied?
   a. AWS Config
   b. AWS CloudTrail
   c. AWS CloudFormation
   d. AWS CloudWatch

6. Which of the following services enables you to centrally govern and manage your environment as you increase the scale of AWS Resources?

    a. AWS Service Catalog

    b. AWS Control Tower

    c. AWS Organizations

    d. AWS Config

7. Which service provides an organization-wide view of compliance and governance in AWS?

    a. AWS Security Hub

    b. AWS Config

    c. AWS Trusted Advisor

    d. AWS CloudTrail

8. Which of the following services would you use to check on the security and compliance status of your AWS environment?

    a. AWS Security Hub

    b. AWS CloudFormation

    c. AWS Systems Manager

    d. AWS CloudTrail

9. Which one of the following AWS services provides you with a unified visibility into your whole AWS environment?

    a. AWS Control Tower

    b. AWS Organizations

    c. AWS Systems Manager

    d. AWS Config

10. Which service will help you automate operational tasks across AWS resources?

    a. AWS Systems Manager

    b. AWS CloudFormation

    c. AWS CloudTrail

    d. AWS Trusted Advisor

Answers

1. a
2. c
3. b
4. a
5. a
6. b
7. a
8. a
9. a
10. a

References

- https://docs.aws.amazon.com/cloudformation/
- https://docs.aws.amazon.com/AWSCloudFormation/latest/UserGuide/template-guide.html
- https://docs.aws.amazon.com/AWSCloudFormation/latest/UserGuide/gettingstarted.templatebasics.html
- https://docs.aws.amazon.com/AWSCloudFormation/latest/UserGuide/best-practices.html
- https://docs.aws.amazon.com/codepipeline/
- https://docs.aws.amazon.com/codecommit/
- https://aws.amazon.com/cloudwatch/
- https://docs.aws.amazon.com/AmazonCloudWatch/latest/monitoring/working_with_metrics.html
- https://docs.aws.amazon.com/AmazonCloudWatch/latest/monitoring/WhatIsCloudWatch.html
- https://docs.aws.amazon.com/AmazonCloudWatch/latest/monitoring/CloudWatch_Dashboards.html
- https://docs.aws.amazon.com/systems-manager/
- https://docs.aws.amazon.com/cli/latest/userguide/getting-started-install.html

- https://docs.aws.amazon.com/config/
- https://docs.aws.amazon.com/health/latest/ug/aws-health-dashboard-status.html
- https://docs.aws.amazon.com/license-manager/latest/userguide/getting-started.html
- https://aws.amazon.com/console/
- https://docs.aws.amazon.com/proton/
- https://docs.aws.amazon.com/servicecatalog/
- https://docs.aws.amazon.com/awssupport/latest/user/trusted-advisor.html
- https://docs.aws.amazon.com/xray/

Chapter 9
AWS Cloud Security

Introduction

Imagine you are an architect designing a secure and safe building. This is the same thing you do with your AWS cloud data. This chapter has the necessary blueprints and tools for constructing a robust and safe cloud environment.

This chapter will cover the required information to guarantee data security in the cloud. We will begin by exploring the shared responsibility model and some common attack types and, later, progress to AWS security services. We will then explore AWS's other security services, such as Shield, WAF, and KMS.

The next half of the chapter briefly touches upon Amazon Macie, Amazon Inspector, GuardDuty, and Security Hub. We will also explore how to manage security with AWS organizations and provide insights into additional security tools.

Brace for landing as we land our infrastructure in a secure environment!

Structure

In this chapter we will cover the following topics:

- Introduction to Cloud Security
- AWS Security Services
- AWS Shield
- AWS Web Application Firewall (WAF)
- AWS Key Management Service (KMS)
- Amazon Macie
- CloudHSM (Cloud Hardware Security Module)
- Amazon Inspector
- Amazon GuardDuty
- Security Hub
- Managing Security Across Accounts with AWS Organizations

- Additional Security Tools
- Real-world use cases

Introduction to Cloud Security

Unlike traditional security practices, cloud security is a shared responsibility between the user and the cloud service provider (CSP).

The Shared Responsibility Model

Imagine you have shifted into a new apartment complex. You are responsible for keeping your house secured and protecting all your valuable stuff by keeping them in the locker. On the other hand, the building staff maintains the security of the entire building. This is analogous to the division of accountability that the Shared Responsibility Model prescribes in the AWS cloud.

- **Your Responsibility:** You are responsible for securing your data, configuring access controls, and implementing security best practices within your cloud environment.
- **AWS's Responsibility:** AWS handles the security of the infrastructure, which includes the physical security of data centers, the security of the network, and the address of any vulnerabilities through patches.

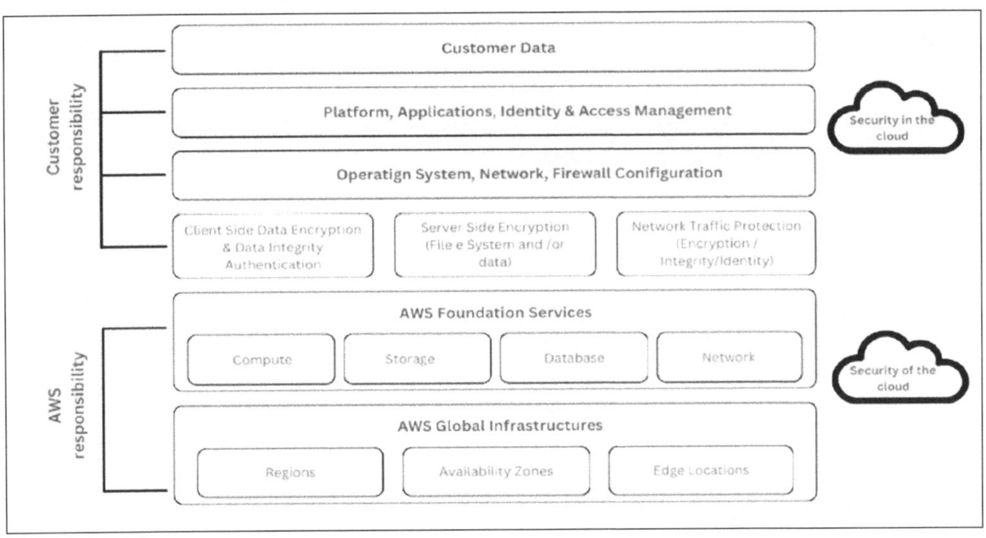

Figure 9.1: *Shared Responsibility Model*

Figure 9.1 depicts the shared responsibility model. This is particularly useful for e-commerce platforms to understand their security responsibilities. Their teams know that AWS secures the cloud infrastructure, and they are responsible for securing their data and applications.

Security of Data at Rest and In Transit

To assure your data is secure and safe when it is at rest and when it is in transit, AWS offers a wide range of services to assist you :

- **Encryption:** Encrypting your data at rest and in transit makes it unreadable to anyone who shouldn't have access.
- **Access Controls:** Implement strong access controls to restrict who can access your data and what they can do.
- **Monitoring and Logging:** Monitor activity and log events to detect foul behavior in your cloud environment.

For example, healthcare providers should secure sensitive transaction data when stored and transmitted by using AWS encryption services to encrypt data at rest in S3 and TLS to encrypt data in transit.

DevSecOps

DevSecOps adds security to the developer/operations symbiosis, which is the foundation of DevOps philosophy. It integrates security measures into each stage of the development cycle rather than considering security a secondary process. This will help developers, security experts, and operations staff collaborate to create secure programs and infrastructure from scratch. A software development firm can ensure the automation of security checks by adopting DevSecOps to integrate security into its CI/CD pipeline. This reduces vulnerabilities in the final product.

Common Attack Types

By understanding common types of attacks like DDoS attacks and SQL injection, you can proactively take steps to protect your data from these vulnerabilities. Some of the most widely known types include:

- **Denial of Service**: Let's imagine a crowded restaurant. A DoS attack is like a group of people pulling pranks by calling in fake reservations, causing the restaurant to lose legitimate business, waste resources on non-paying customers, or provide poor service (or no service) to legitimate customers. Likewise, the attackers flood the system with traffic, causing it to crash or become unresponsive.
- **SQL Injection Attack**: Imagine having a conversation with your librarian. An SQL Injection attack is similar to having a conversation with the librarian, except that you extract sensitive information from the database during the conversation. Attackers exploit weaknesses in the communication link between the website and the database to steal or manipulate data.

- **Phishing Attack**: Imagine receiving a seemingly official email from your bank. But here's the catch! The mail is not official; it has just been designed to look real. The attacker sends such emails or messages that appear legitimate communications from a trusted source(bank, credit card company, and so on.) to extract your personal information or make you click on malicious links.
- **Malware Attack**: Malware is a bunch of bugs that sneak into your computer. Some malicious software includes:
  - Ransomware (restricts the owner's access until ransom is provided)
  - Spyware (this steals personal information)
  - Viruses (these can spread between devices and damage or destroy data and/or hardware)

Knowing these attack methods, you can be more alert and choose tools that help you prioritize security. This will make it harder for attackers to access your data. Any social media platform can use AWS Shield Advanced to mitigate the attack and AWS WAF to block SQL injection attempts, ensuring data protection and applications.

AWS Security Services

AWS has many security options to protect your data, applications, and infrastructure in the cloud. AWS Identity and Access Management (IAM) plays a crucial role by controlling multi-factor authentication, as MFA provides an extra layer of security. Amazon Virtual Private Cloud (VPC) enhances network and infrastructure security by creating network environments, while AWS Shield offers managed DDoS protection. For web applications, AWS Web Application Firewall (WAF) defends against exploits, and AWS Firewall Manager streamlines WAF rule management across accounts and resources.

AWS Key Management Service (KMS) generates encryption keys to ensure data protection, while AWS CloudHSM provides control over operations using cloud-based hardware security modules. Amazon Macie uses machine learning to identify, categorize, and secure data to meet privacy terms and regulations. A startup can build a strong security standing by using various AWS security services, such as AWS WAF, Shield, and GuardDuty.

AWS Shield-Protecting Against DDoS Attacks

A DDoS (Distributed Denial-of-Service) attack is an extreme threat in the digital world. It aims to entirely disturb the regular traffic of a specific server, network or service by flooding it with excessive internet traffic.

AWS Shield is your digital bodyguard against such attacks. It is a controlled service that identifies and minimizes probable DDoS risks, ensuring your application runs uninterrupted and safeguarding your online image. For example, to get enhanced protection, a news website under the threat of DDoS attacks can subscribe to AWS Shield Advanced to ensure the availability of its site.

Think of it like this:

- **DDoS attack:** A group of attackers bombarding your website with traffic, like a swarm of angry bees trying to shut down your store.
- **AWS Shield:** A security guard with a super-powered radar instantly detects the attack and deploys defenses to block the bad traffic, allowing legitimate customers to access your store as usual.

Understanding AWS Shield

- **Always on Guard:** Shield constantly monitors your AWS resources, looking for suspicious traffic patterns that might indicate a DDoS attack.
- **Automatic Response:** When an attack is detected, Shield automatically takes action to mitigate it without you needing to intervene. This can involve filtering out malicious traffic, increasing bandwidth capacity, or redirecting traffic to less affected resources.
- **Two-Tier Protection:**
    - **AWS Shield Standard:** This free service provides basic protection against common DDoS attacks, similar to a basic security system in your store.
    - **AWS Shield Advanced:** This paid service offers more comprehensive protection for sophisticated attacks, including 24/7 access to a specialized DDoS Response Team (SRT) for custom mitigation strategies. This is similar to a professionally trained security team ready to handle any situation.

Benefits of using AWS Shield

- **Peace of Mind:** Knowing your applications are protected from DDoS attacks allows you to focus on your business without worrying about downtime or security breaches.
- **Reduced Downtime:** Shield's automatic mitigation helps minimize the impact of attacks, ensuring your website and applications remain accessible to your users.
- **Cost Savings:** Shield can help you avoid the financial losses associated with downtime and potential data breaches caused by DDoS attack

AWS Web Application Firewall (WAF)

The main purpose of AWS Web Application Firewall (WAF) is to protect web applications from attacks.

AWS WAF, a Web Application Firewall, is a security guard that blocks any potentially harmful traffic from accessing your web application.

Here's how* AWS WAF *works:

AWS WAF checks every incoming request to your website like the security guard checking your identity cards at the college gate. It follows rules to identify hackers trying to steal your data or inject malicious code. If a request triggers a rule, WAF can block it completely!

This helps protect your website from previously mentioned attacks like SQL injection or cross-site scraping (injecting malicious code to steal data). By filtering out these threats, AWS WAF keeps your website safe and smooth.

It can also be configured to allow regular users access while blocking suspicious ones. You can also personalize the regulations to suit your website's requirements. An online retailer, for example, uses AWS WAF to protect its web applications from attacks, such as SQL injection and cross-site scripting (XSS).

AWS Key Management Service (KMS)

AWS Key Management Service (KMS) AWS aids in creating, administering, and supervising encryption keys to secure data. The process begins with the generation of encryption keys, followed by the management of these keys and supervision of key usage. For example, a gaming company can use AWS KMS to create and manage cryptographic keys to encrypt data at rest.

Types of Keys

Let us look at the breakdown of KMS and its different key types:

KMS uses top-notch security hardware to store and protect your encryption keys. These keys are similar to passwords that scramble your data, making it unreadable to anyone without access to the key. Types of keys:

KMS offers different key types, each suited for specific tasks:

- **Symmetric keys**: These are analogous to single keys for a padlock. They work for encryption and decryption and are ideal for daily use cases in AWS.
- **Asymmetric keys:** Imagine a key pair like a combination lock with two keys. The public key encrypts data, and the private key decrypts it. These are useful for digital signatures and secure communication.
- **HMAC Keys:** Consider these as special codes used to verify the authenticity of data. They ensure information hasn't been tampered with during transit.

An enterprise can use symmetric keys to encrypt data and asymmetric keys to secure communications.

KMS vs AWS Secrets Manager: Choose the Right Service for Secrets Management

KMS and Secrets Manager are both AWS services for securing sensitive information, but they serve different purposes.

Use KMS to:

- Generate and manage cryptographic keys for data encryption
- Control access to these encryption keys
- Integrate key management with other AWS services.

Use Secrets Manager for:

- Storing and managing application secrets like passwords and API keys
- Rotating secrets automatically to enhance security
- Granting access to secrets based on IAM roles
- Retrieving secrets securely in your applications without hardcoding them.

Secrets Manager relies on KMS for secret encryption. It uses KMS keys to generate data that encrypt actual secrets before storing them. KMS offers more granular control over key management, whereas Secrets Manager focuses on ease of use and access control for secrets.

Feature	Key Management Service	Secrets Manager
Purpose	To manage encryption keys	Stores and manages secrets
Type of data	Encryption keys (for example,symmetric, asymmetric)	Sensitive data (passwords, tokens, API keys)
Permissions	To control who can use and manage keys	To control who can access and retrieve secrets
Auditing	Logs key usage and management operations	Logs secret access and rotation events
Functionality	Generates, rotates, controls access to keys	Stores secrets securely, retrieves secrets
Versioning	Key versions can be archived and restored	Secrets may have multiple versions for rotation and rollback
Integration	Integrates with various AWS services(for example, S3, and so on)	Integrates with KMS for encrypting secrets at rest

Table 9.1: *KMS vs Secrets Manager*

Table 9.1 compares KMS with Secrets Manager. In essence, KMS is like a vault with the master keys for your encryption needs, and the Secrets Manager is the locker within that vault designed to store and manage sensitive application needs.

Amazon Macie

The main purpose of Amazon Macie is to classify and protect sensitive data. This tool uses machine learning and pattern matching to detect, classify, and protect sensitive data in your Amazon S3 storage buckets. For example, a law firm can use Amazon Macie to discover and protect sensitive data in their S3 buckets.

The following steps can explain this process:

- **Classification**: Macie scans your S3 buckets automatically and analyzes the data they contain. It segregates sensitive information using predetermined patterns and guidelines. These patterns may have Personally Identifiable Information (PII), such as Social Security numbers, credit card information, and Protected Health Information (PHI). Macie can be taught to identify data types specified by your organization as sensitive.
- **Protection**: After Macie has identified sensitive data, it helps you protect it in several ways:
    - **Visibility:** Macie provides detailed reports on the location and type of sensitive data discovered. This helps you comprehend your data landscape and prioritize data security efforts.
    - **Security Findings:** Macie generates alerts whenever it detects sensitive data in S3 buckets with weak or improper security configurations, like public accessibility or unencrypted storage.
    - **Integration with Security Measures:** Macie can integrate with other AWS security services, like AWS Lambda, to trigger automated actions upon finding sensitive data. These actions could involve encrypting the data, restricting access, or sending notifications to security teams.

Benefits of Amazon Macie

- **Automated Discovery of Data**: Machine learning and pattern matching automatically find sensitive information in S3 buckets (like personally identifiable or protected health information). This saves significant time and effort compared to manual search.
- **Reduced Risk of Security Breaches:** Macie reduces the risk of data breaches by identifying and protecting sensitive data. This saves your organization from financial losses and reputational damage.
- **Continuous Monitoring of S3 Buckets:** Macie constantly monitors your

S3 buckets for security issues, such as publicly accessible or unencrypted buckets, so that you can identify and address potential security threats.

- **Cost-effective Solution**: Macie is a managed service, so you need not worry about the overhead of managing your data security solution.
- **Compliance with Data Privacy Regulations:** Macie helps you meet compliance requirements, such as GDPR, PCI-DSS, and HIPAA.
- **Customizable Data Discovery:** Macie helps you define custom data types to identify types of sensitive data important to your company. This helps you ensure your data is protected and identified.

CloudHSM (Cloud Hardware Security Module): Enhanced Key Management in the Cloud

Imagine high security for your encryption keys. That's what a Cloud Hardware Security Module (CloudHSM) is. It provides a secure environment to manage and protect the cryptographic keys used for encrypting sensitive data within the cloud. A government agency can use CloudHSM to store and manage cryptographic keys in hardware security modules, ensuring a high level of security for cryptographic operations.

Let's look at the breakdown of CloudHSM and its benefits:

- **Dedicated Hardware:** CloudHSM utilizes dedicated physical hardware to store and process cryptographic keys. This hardware is designed so that it is difficult for hackers to access.
- **Enhanced Security:** The physical isolation of the keys within the hardware and the robust security features built into the HSM itself significantly reduce the risk of unauthorized access.
- **Cloud Convenience:** While offering hardware-based security, CloudHSM resides within the cloud environment, providing the benefits of scalability, remote access, and easier integration with cloud-based applications.
- **FIPS Compliance:** Many CloudHSM solutions are validated according to FIPS (Federal Information Processing Standards) 140-2, a rigorous government standard for cryptographic modules. This ensures the HSM meets strict security requirements for sensitive data.

Amazon Inspector

This is an automated vulnerability management service offered by AWS. It helps you continuously scan your AWS workloads for software vulnerabilities. For example, an online payment processor can automate security assessments and identify vulnerabilities in their EC2 instances using Amazon Inspector.

Let's look at its key features:

- **Automated Scanning**: Automated scanning is done by Amazon Inspector to find vulnerabilities in operating systems, applications, and libraries of your workloads through regular scans.
- **Detection of Vulnerabilities**: It recognizes vulnerabilities, such as security misconfigurations, outdated software, and common exploits and classifies them according to seriousness to assist in concentrating on critical issues initially.
- **Support with Compliance:** The Inspector can help meet compliance needs for different security standards by pinpointing weaknesses that may lead to violations of these standards.
- **Network Exposure Assessment**: The Inspector also checks for unintended network exposure of your resources. This helps you identify open ports or security groups that allow unauthorized access to your systems.
- **Reporting**: After a scan, the Inspector provides detailed reports that list the vulnerabilities found and offers recommendations for remediation. This helps you understand your environment's security posture and take steps to address any vulnerabilities.

Amazon GuardDuty

This threat detection service monitors your AWS accounts and data in S3 for malicious activity.

Let us look at how it helps you secure your environment:

- **Continuous Monitoring**: GuardDuty constantly monitors your accounts for suspicious activities, including unauthorized access attempts, unusual data downloads, and other events that deviate from normalcy.
- **Alerting and Notification**: GuardDuty sends detailed alerts when it detects a potential threat. This helps you investigate the event and take proper action.
- **Machine Learning and Threat Intelligence**: GuardDuty integrates threat intelligence from AWS and leading security providers to help you identify suspicious activities.
- **Integration with Other Services**: GuardDuty integrates with other AWS security services, such as Amazon Inspector and Amazon CloudTrail. This lets you have a clear picture of your security posture and can take steps accordingly.
- **Threat-detection Capabilities**: GuardDuty can identify various threats,

including unauthorized access attempts, data breaches, malware infections, and denial-of-service attacks.

Security Hub

This provides a centralized view of your security posture. Amazon Security Hub serves as the main security hub in your AWS environment. It offers a consolidated perspective on your security status by combining discoveries from different origins:

- **Compliance Standards**: Security Hub lets you compare your security posture against industry standards and best practices, such as AWS Foundational Security Best Practices (FSBP) standard, CIS Controls, PCI DSS, and NIST. It performs automated checks against these standards and generates findings highlighting gaps.
- **Third-party Security Tools**: Security Hub can also integrate third-party security tools, so you can see findings from these tools alongside AWS security findings.
- **AWS Security Services**: Security Hub collects findings from numerous AWS security services, such as Amazon Inspector, Amazon GuardDuty, Amazon Macie, and more, and provides a consolidated view of security issues across your resources.

Key Benefits of Security Hub:

- **Actionable Insights**: Security Hub provides detailed information about each finding, including its severity and the resources affected. This lets you take targeted actions to address security risks.
- **Security Issues are Prioritized**. Security Hub provides a view of your security posture, helping you identify and address security gaps in your environment.
- **Automation Capabilities:** By integrating Security Hub findings with other tools, you can save time and effort.
- **Centralized View**: Security Hub provides a unified view by consolidating security alerts from multiple sources, thus eliminating the need to manage findings from multiple sources in different formats.
- **Compliance Management**: Security Hub allows you to streamline compliance efforts by checking your environment against industry standards and best practices, such as the CIS AWS Foundations Benchmark, PCI DSS, and NIST.

Managing Security Across Accounts with AWS Organizations

You can enforce consistent security policies and best practices across your entire cloud infrastructure with the ability of AWS Organizations to centrally manage and secure multiple AWS accounts on a single unit.

Let us look at the breakdown of key features:

Organizational Hierarchy: Structuring Your Accounts

Organizational units (OUs): You can simplify management by grouping related accounts into OUs based on function, environment (dev, test, prod), or compliance requirements.

Service Control Policies (SCPs): Enforcing Security Standards

SCPs act as guardrails to ensure accounts adhere to your security guidelines. They define the maximum permissions allowed for IAM users and roles within member accounts of your organization.

Benefits and Automation with Example:

- **Automation-** SCPs can automate security by denying access to prohibited actions automatically.
- **Standardization-** SCPs prevent accidental misconfigurations and improve overall security by enforcement of consistent security policies.
- **Reduced Risk-** SCPs mitigate the risk of unauthorized access by restricting actions or services.

Let us look at an example:

An SCP can deny all S3 bucket creation requests, requiring approval for specific teams needing S3 storage. Here's how it would work:

- **SCP Policy**: An SCP Policy would deny S3 bucket creation requests for all principals (users, roles, or services) within that organizational unit.
- **Limited Permissions:** The IAM policies would not allow S3 bucket creation requests.
- **Approval Process:** Users submit requests through a separate system, which a designated team reviews before the approval.
- **Bucket Creation:** Once approved, the designated team with broader permissions will create a bucket on the user's behalf.

Control Tower

Control Tower simplifies setting up best practices, enforcing compliance, and continuously monitoring your environment. It also helps you automate governance tasks within your organization.

Benefits:

- **Automated Guardrails**: Control Tower can automate both the generation and implementation of SCPs, guaranteeing uniform security measures throughout your company.
- **Compliance Management:** It assists in establishing and upholding compliance regulations throughout your accounts, making audits and certifications easier.
- **Cost-optimization:** Control Tower can assist in optimizing your AWS expenses by avoiding resource mismanagement with SCPs.

By using the hierarchy within the organization, service control policies, and Control Tower, AWS Organizations enables you to oversee security in all your AWS accounts efficiently. A multinational company can use AWS Control Tower to set up and govern multi-account AWS environments.

Additional Security Tools

Let us look at some other security tools in brief.

AWS Artifact: Secure Storage for Infrastructure as Code (IaC)

AWS Artifact safely stores and organizes your infrastructure as code (IaC) templates, like CloudFormation scripts. With this, you can access and download compliance data. The artifacts known by AWS are grouped into two groups: confidential and public. The confidential artifacts need clearance from Amazon. Artifacts and artifact agreements are complementary to AWS. The contracts include the Nondisclosure Agreement (NDA) and the Business Associate Addendum (BAA). You can visit the AWS Artifact portal through the AWS Management Console anywhere and anytime.

Advantages:

- Safeguards your IaC templates
- Prevents unauthorized access and changes
- Lets you download AWS ISO certifications
- Utilizes papers to measure your company's controls

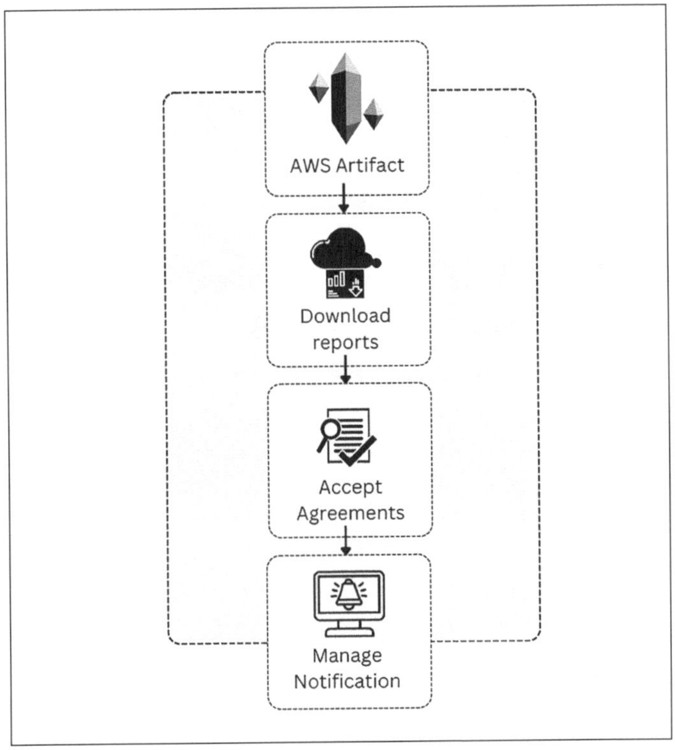

Figure 9.2: *AWS Artifacts*

Figure 9.2 explains some uses of AWS Artifacts. Let us look at its other applications.

- **Backup and Storage:** Amazon's cloud services can propel your business. You can send critical data and images to AWS for backup.
- **Agreement Acceptance:** You can accept agreements for multiple accounts that can legally process restricted information with AWS Artifacts.

AWS Audit Manager

This enhances compliance audits by automating evidence gathering, report generation, and evaluation of security measures. It pulls required data from other AWS services, such as AWS Security Hub, AWS Config, and AWS CloudTrail. It then uses this data as evidence of control implementation and converts it to an auditor-friendly format. AWS Audit Manager facilitates automated evidence gathering, which helps businesses track their compliance continuously. Since it is integrated into the AWS platform, it completes most evidence-gathering without human intervention. The advantages are:

- Reduces the time and energy required for audits
- Streamlines compliance procedures
- Supports a robust security stance.

Frameworks allow users to deploy AWS Audit Manager assessments. Users also get to build custom frameworks. The pre-built frameworks for various compliance standards are:

- ISO/IEC 27001:2013 Annex A
- PCI DSS V3.2.1
- SOC 2
- CIS Benchmark for CIS Amazon Web Services Foundations Benchmark
- General Data Protection Regulation (GDPR)
- FedRAMP Moderate Baseline
- Health Insurance Portability and Accountability Act (HIPAA)

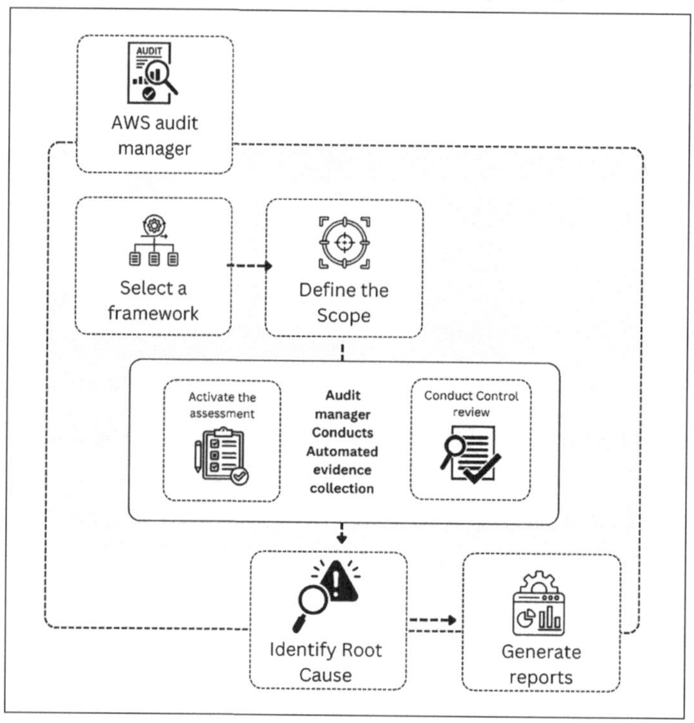

Figure 9.3: *AWS Audit Manager*

Figure 9.3 describes the workflow of using AWS Audit Manager.

Applications:

- **Deployment of internal risk assessments**: Launch an assessment for collecting evidence automatically by customizing pre-built frameworks.
- **Continuous audits for compliance**: Monitor your compliance status, collect evidence, and reduce risk by fine-tuning your controls.

- **The transition from manual to automated evidence collection**: With automated evidence collection, you don't have to manually collect, manage, and review evidence.

AWS Certificate Manager (ACM)

AWS Certificate Manager offers a controlled service for setting up, handling, and distributing SSL/TLS certificates for your AWS services. It provisions, manages, and deploys public and private SSL/TLS certificates for use with AWS services and your internally connected resources. ACM minimizes downtime due to misconfigured, revoked, or expired certificates. ACM also lets you centrally manage SSL/TLS ACM certificates in an AWS Region using AWS Management Console, AWS CLI, or AWS Certificate Manager APIs.

Advantages:

- Removes the need for manual certificate management tasks
- Lowers the chance of security issues related to certificates
- Streamlines HTTPS setup

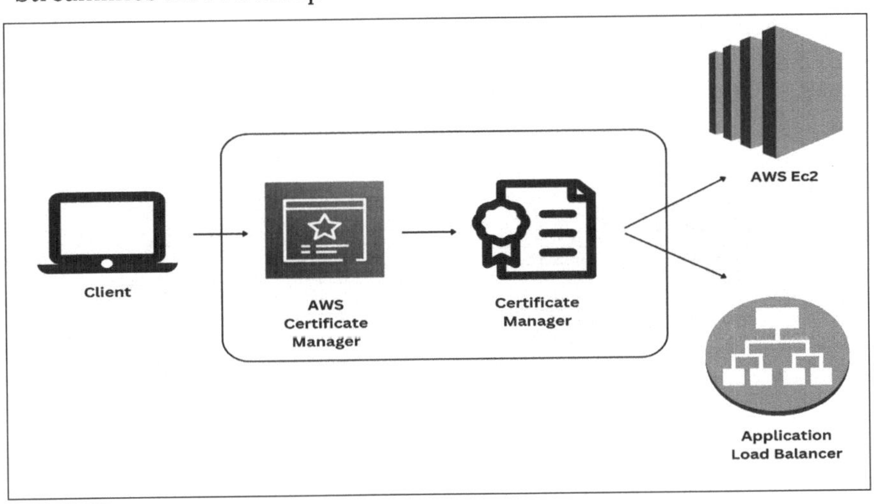

Figure 9.4: *AWS Certificate Manager*

Figure 9.4 gives an overview of the AWS Certificate Manager

The applications of AWS Certificate Manager are:

- Improvement in uptime: Maintain SSL/TLS certificates along with certificate renewals, with automated certificate management.
- Protection of internal resources: You can secure communication between connected resources on private networks, such as servers, mobile devices, and IoT devices.

- Protection and security of your website: We provide and manage certificates that securely terminate traffic to your website or application.

Amazon Detective

Amazon Detective examines security incidents in your AWS resources to pinpoint their main reasons. Amazon Detective can identify potential security issues, such as Amazon GuardDuty, Amazon Macie, and AWS Security Hub. It extracts time-based events, such as API calls, log-in attempts, and network traffic from data sources to create a view of daily resource interactions. A cybersecurity team can use Amazon Detective to investigate security incidents and identify the root cause of suspicious activities in their AWS environment.

Advantages:

- Decreases the time and energy spent on probing security problems
- Aids in determining where and how security breaches occurred
- Allows for quicker resolution

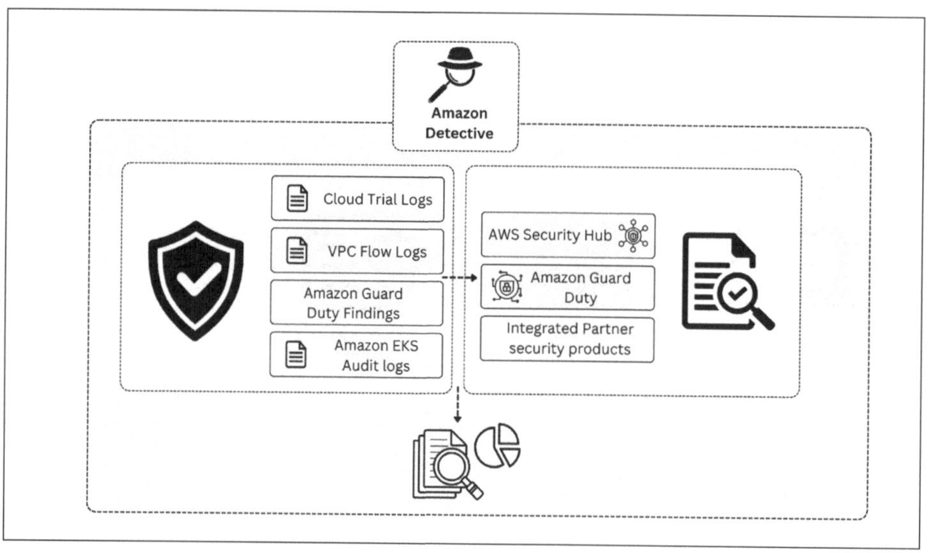

Figure 9.5: *Amazon Detective*

Figure 9.5 describes the workflow of using Amazon Detective to investigate potential security threats.

Some of its applications are:

- **Threat Hunting**: This finds hidden threats based on some clues. Amazon Detective's proactive analysis helps you focus on resources, such as IP addresses, VPCs, and EC2 instances.

- **Investigating Incidents:** When Amazon GuardDuty identifies an incident, you can use Amazon Detective to see the activity related to that incident, identify unusual patterns, and further determine the activity that caused the incident.
- **Triage Security Findings-**:The first stage of the investigation process is Triage. It determines if the discovery is genuine or false. With the help of an Amazon Detective, you can easily determine if the finding is malicious or a false positive by seeing associated IP addresses and resources.

AWS Network Firewall

AWS Network Firewall allows you to centrally define and enforce security policies for your VPC by provisioning a stateful managed firewall service. You can inspect traffic at OSI layers from the network layer to the application layer. AWS Firewall works with Network Firewall, allowing you to build policies based on their rules and then apply those policies across your VPCs and accounts centrally. It also integrates with AWS IAM to add a layer of security and management.

Advantages:

- Offers granular control over traffic flow
- Simplifies network security management
- Protects your resources from unauthorized access

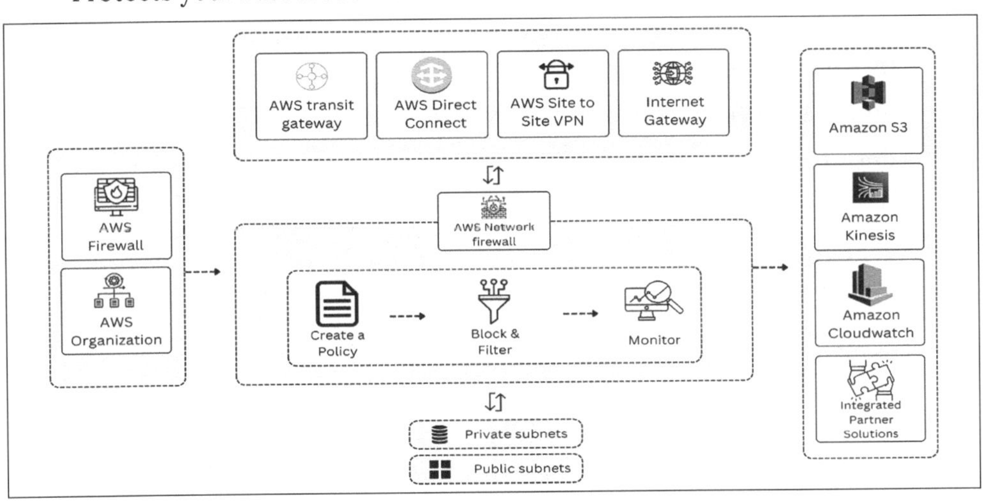

Figure 9.6: *AWS Network Firewall*

Figure 9.6 describes the workflow and integration of AWS Network Firewall within an AWS environment.

Some of its applications are:

- Inspecting inbound internet traffic involves examining encrypted traffic using

SSL/TLS decryption. Stateful inspection keeps track of active connections and makes decisions based on similar criteria. Protocol detection also ensures that only approved protocols are allowed.

- Securing AWS direct connect and VPN traffic protects your resources from unauthorized access and potential threats. It can also include an intrusion detection and prevention system to monitor traffic for suspicious activity.
- Filtering outbound traffic involves monitoring and controlling outbound traffic that can prevent leaks of sensitive information. It also involves blocking connections to known malicious sites.
- Preventing inbound internet traffic intrusion helps to block unauthorized access by monitoring network traffic for suspicious or unusual activity.

AWS Firewall Manager

AWS Firewall Manager centrally controls firewall regulations for multiple AWS accounts and VPCs within your organization. It simplifies your maintenance tasks across multiple accounts and resources. By using Firewall Manager, you need to set up your protections once, and the service can then automatically apply those across your resources and accounts, even if you scale those.

Advantages:

- Guarantees uniform security policies throughout your system
- Streamlines firewall setup for a large scope
- Minimizes the chance of incorrect configurations
- Adds protection automatically to newly added resources

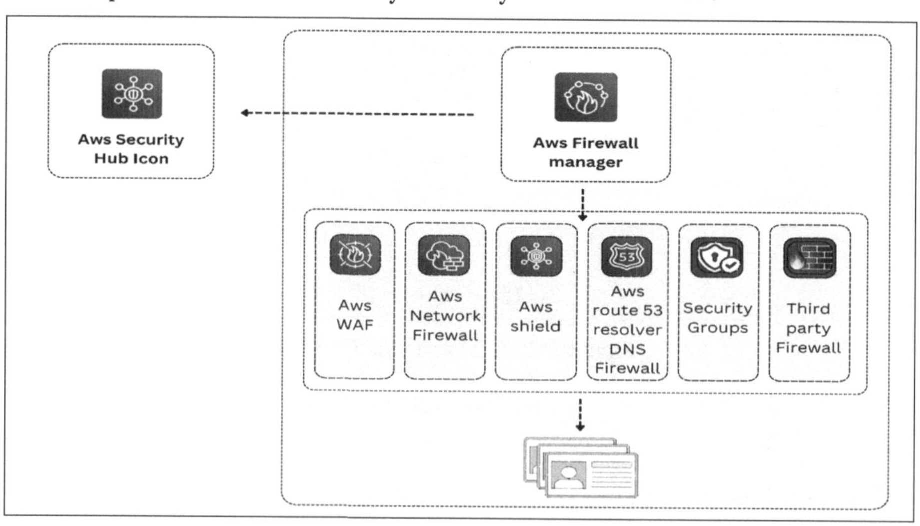

***Figure 9.7**: AWS Firewall Manager*

Figure 9.7 explains how AWS Firewall Manager helps you centrally create and manage account firewall rules.

Some of its applications are:

- **Continuous auditing of resources:** You can audit and control security group rules to identify potentially high risks and clean redundant groups.
- **Protect applications hosted on EC2 instances:**While deploying rules catered to specific applications, enforce a set of security group rules with a common security group policy.
- **Deploy tools at scale to protect data:** Maintain, create, and configure firewalls with common security policies across accounts.

AWS Resource Access Manager (AWS RAM)

AWS RAM allows the safe sharing of AWS resources among accounts in your organization. With RAM, you don't have to create duplicate resources across multiple accounts. In the case of a multi-account system, you can build resources centrally and then transfer those using RAM in these steps:

1. Make a resource share
2. Provide resources
3. Specify accounts
4. Share resources

Table 9.2 gives an overview of services that RAM lets us share:

Service	Resource
AWS CodeBuild	Projects, report groups
Amazon EC2	Capacity reservations, dedicated hosts, subnets, traffic mirror targets, transit gateways
AWS Resource Groups	Resource groups
Amazon Route 53	Forwarding rules
AWS License Manager	License configurations
Amazon Aurora	DB Clusters
Amazon EC2 Image Builder	Components, images(AMI), image recipes

Table 9.2: *Services shared by RAM*

Advantages:

- Streamlines resource sharing while providing detailed control over access permissions
- Decreases the necessity for intricate IAM (Identity and Access Management) regulations

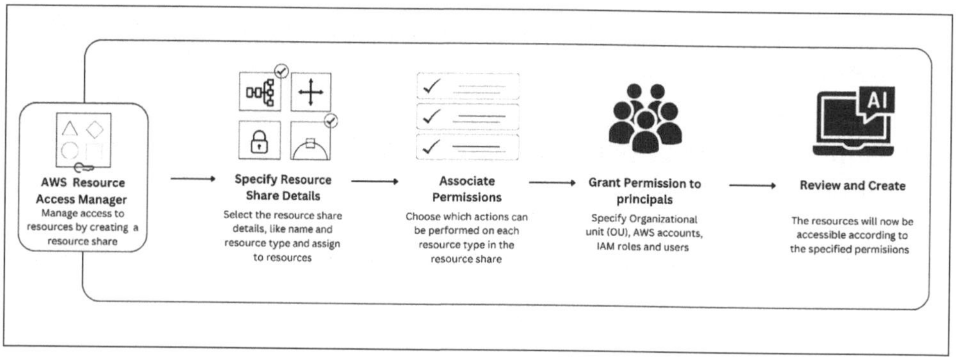

Figure 9.8: AWS RAM

Figure 9.8 depicts the working of AWS RAM

Some of its applications are:

- **Centrally govern access to resources:** You can centrally manage resources like private certificate authorities to reduce operational overhead and costs.
- **Least privilege on shared resources**: Grant only the permissions required to perform tasks using managed permissions.
- **Share resources in multi-account environments:** You can allow multiple accounts to deploy application resources to the same subnet and share foundational infrastructure like Amazon VPC subnets across accounts.

AWS Trusted Advisor

AWS Trusted Advisor is a service that helps AWS customers optimize their cloud infrastructure. Presenting instant best-practice advice on cost optimization, security, performance, and fault tolerance, tools sift through AWS environments to provide insights and recommendations for customers to improve their infrastructure efficiency, security, and reliability.

Some key features of AWS Trusted Advisor are:

- **Cost-optimization:** This tool provides a way to show the potential of reduced spending on AWS by indicating the underused resources and how the costs can be optimized.
- **Security:** AWS Trusted Advisor is your vigilant guardian, identifying security

recommendations to fortify your AWS environment. It also pinpoints security risks and vulnerabilities, providing a roadmap to reduce exposure and ensure peace of mind.

- **Performance:** AWS Trusted Advisor acts as your performance mentor, offering guidance on the efficiency of your AWS resources. It points out instances of over or underutilization, guiding you toward optimal performance.
- **Fault-tolerance:** This gives you insight and suggestions on how the technology can be more robust for the applications being designed, whether it's turning on data replication or suggesting backup strategies.
- **Service Limits:** To prevent disruption, it notifies users when they are near usage limit thresholds.

Trusted Advisor offers detailed recommendations with actionable insights to implement best practices and a dashboard where one can view the status of their checks. The availability of the trusted advisor checks depends on the access level under the AWS Support plan: Basic, Developer, Business, or Enterprise.

Any individual interested in taking the AWS Certified Solutions Architect exam must familiarize themselves with AWS Trusted Advisor in all ways relevant to cost optimization, security best practices, or general infrastructure management.

Real-World Cases

Let us look at some real-world use cases for all sections discussed in this chapter.

1. **Integrated security with AWS Shield and AWS Web Application Firewall (WAF)**

   To protect web applications from cyber threats, AWS Shield and AWS Web Application Firewall (WAF) provide a robust defense against DDoS attacks. The engineers implement these in Unison.

   Solution Overview: This combines AWS Shield for DDoS protection and AWS WAF for application security, thus protecting web applications on AWS.

Steps:

1. Implement AWS Shield to safeguard against Distributed Denial of Service (DDoS) attacks.
2. Protect web applications from common web exploits and vulnerabilities using AWS WAF.
3. Integrate AWS Shield and WAF for comprehensive security coverage. This integration provides robust and layered security for applications.

4. Use Amazon CloudWatch to monitor security events and application performance.
5. Use AWS Security Hub to address emerging threats and vulnerabilities. This helps in mitigating new and evolving threats.

Figure 9.9 illustrates this use case.

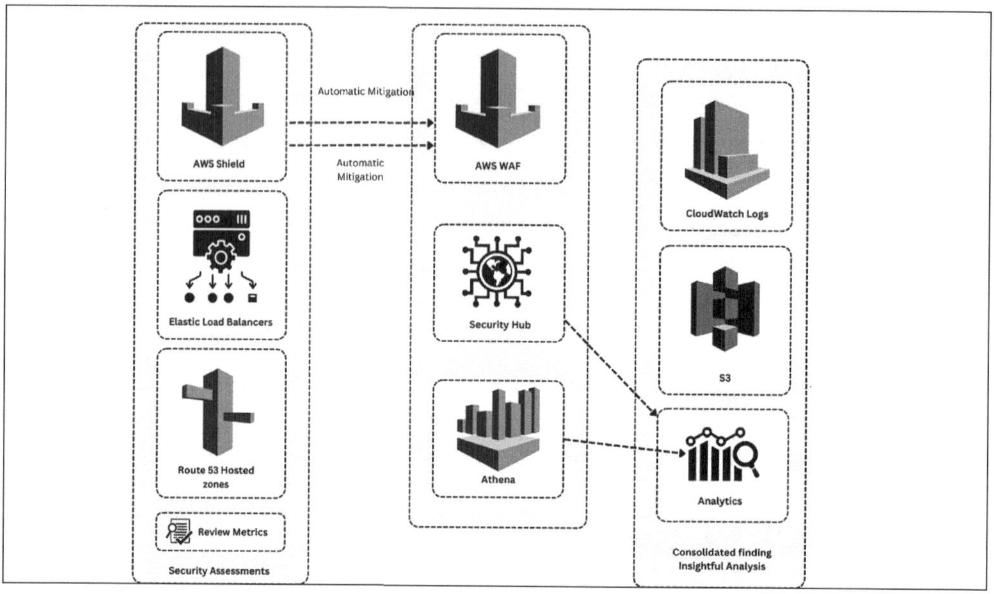

Figure 9.9: *Security with AWS Shield and AWS Web Application Firewall* (WAF)

2. **Managing security across accounts with AWS organizations**

   Centralize security management across multiple AWS accounts using AWS Organizations.

   Solution Overview: In a multinational corporation, AWS Organizations structure accounts hierarchically for centralized security management. Service Control Policies (SCPs) enforce standards, AWS Control Tower automates governance, and centralized logging ensures proactive monitoring. Continuous improvement includes regular audits and policy reviews.

Steps:

1. Structure accounts hierarchically using AWS Organizations. This helps you centrally manage multiple AWS accounts.
2. Enforce security standards across all accounts using SCPs.
3. Automate governance with security guardrails with AWS Control Tower.

4. Use Amazon CloudWatch and AWS CloudTrail to monitor security and account activities.
5. Conduct regular audits and policy reviews to enhance security and compliance adjustments continuously using AWS Security Hub.

Figure 9.10 illustrates this use case.

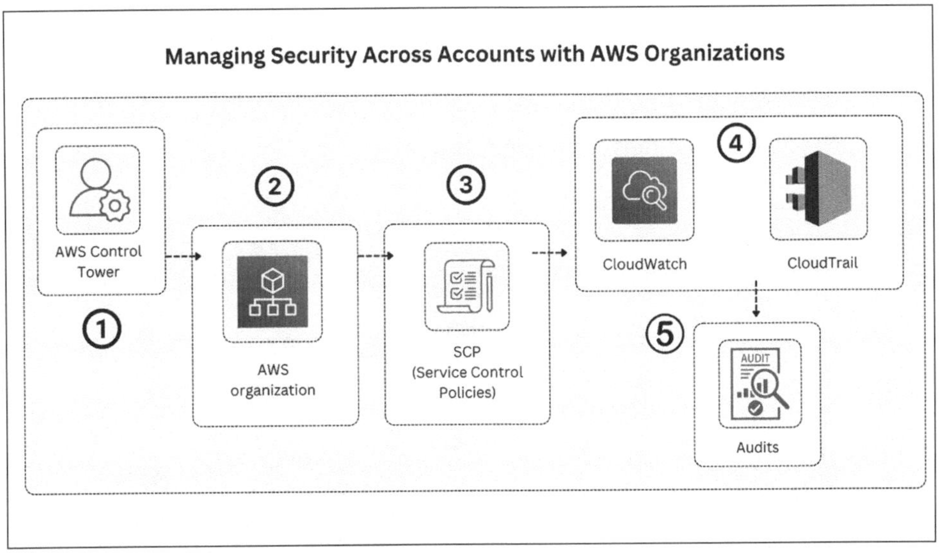

***Figure* 9.10**: *Managing Security Across Accounts with AWS Organizations*

3. **An e-commerce company needs to deploy a secure, compliant application on AWS, managed across multiple accounts**

Solution Overview:

- **AWS Artifact**: Manage compliance documents.
- **AWS Audit Manager**: Automate compliance audits.
- **AWS Certificate Manager (ACM):** Manage SSL/TLS certificates.
- **Amazon Detective:** Analyze security issues.
- **AWS Network Firewall**: Implement stateful firewall rules.
- **AWS Firewall Manager**: Centrally manage firewall rules.
- **AWS Resource Access Manager (AWS RAM):** Securely share resources.

Steps:

1. Access compliance documents via AWS Artifact.
2. Create and configure assessments to automate evidence collection.

3. Request and validate a public SSL/TLS certificate. Attach the certificate to load balancers or CloudFront for HTTPS.
4. Enable Amazon Detective and analyze security data to identify and resolve incidents.
5. Deploy AWS Network Firewall in the VPC. Define and apply stateful firewall rules.
6. Enable and configure AWS Firewall Manager.
7. Create resource shares for VPC subnets and other resources and share them securely with specified AWS accounts.

Figure 9.11 illustrates this use case.

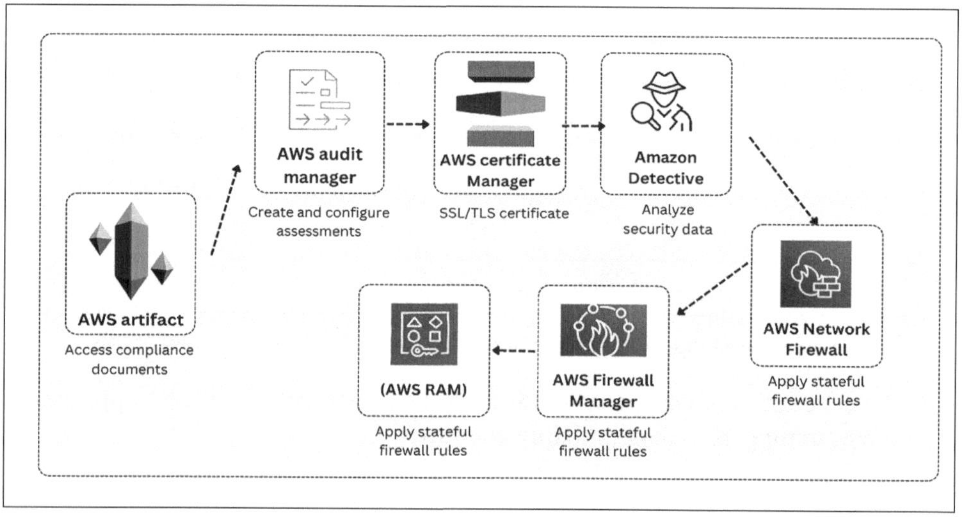

Figure 9.11: *An e-commerce company needs to deploy a secure, compliant application on AWS, managed across multiple accounts.*

Conclusion

We have explored various security services AWS offers, such as Shield, WAF, and KMS, which help you protect your data. We have also explored other tools, such as Macie, Inspector, GuardDuty, and Security Hub, which provide a complete security solution. AWS organizations provide a centralized control center for managing security access across multiple accounts.

With the help of the tools and knowledge you have obtained in this chapter, you can build a secure and reliable cloud environment.

In the next chapter, we will look at the popular cloud architecture patterns.

Multiple Choice Questions

1. What is the primary function of AWS Shield?
    a. Encryption
    b. DDoS Protection
    c. Identity Management
    d. Logging
2. Which services are used for at-rest data encryption within AWS?
    a. AWS Shield
    b. AWS KMS
    c. AWS WAF
    d. AWS Macie
3. What is the purpose of the service: AWS WAF?
    a. Protects web applications from common exploits
    b. Encrypts data in transit
    c. Monitors network traffic
    d. IAM policy management
4. Which services provide discovery, classification, and protection for sensitive data in AWS?
    a. AWS CloudHSM
    b. AWS Macie
    c. AWS KMS
    d. AWS Shield
5. Which of the following manages hardware security modules in the cloud?
    a. AWS CloudHSM
    b. AWS KMS
    c. AWS Macie
    d. AWS Shield

6. Which of the following can assess the vulnerability of AWS resources?
    a. Amazon GuardDuty
    b. AWS Inspector
    c. AWS Security Hub
    d. AWS Macie
7. What is primarily monitored by Amazon GuardDuty?
    a. Network traffic and account behavior
    b. DDoS attacks
    c. Encryption keys
    d. IAM policies
8. Which service provides more insight into security threats to your AWS environment?
    a. AWS Security Hub
    b. Amazon GuardDuty
    c. AWS Inspector
    d. AWS CloudTrail
9. How do AWS Organizations enhance the security management of your AWS resources?
    a. It centralizes the billing
    b. It enforces the policy across accounts
    c. Monitors network traffic
    d. It encrypts data
10. Which of the following is the AWS service that protects against DDoS attacks?
    a. AWS Shield
    b. AWS WAF
    c. AWS Macie
    d. AWS Inspector

Answers

1. b
2. b
3. a
4. b
5. a
6. b
7. a
8. a
9. b
10. a

References

- https://cloudsecurityalliance.org/
- https://docs.aws.amazon.com/whitepapers/latest/introduction-aws-security/data-encryption.html
- https://aws.amazon.com/marketplace/solutions/devops/devsecops
- https://aws.amazon.com/secrets-manager/faqs/#Secrets_Manager_and_AWS_KMS
- https://aws.amazon.com/macie/
- https://aws.amazon.com/products/security/
- https://aws.amazon.com/audit-manager/
- https://intellipaat.com/blog/what-is-aws-artifact/
- https://kirkpatrickprice.com/blog/aws-audit-manager/
- https://k21academy.com/amazon-web-services/aws-certificate-manager-acm/
- https://k21academy.com/amazon-web-services/amazon-detective/
- https://k21academy.com/amazon-web-services/aws-network-firewall-an-overview/
- https://k21academy.com/amazon-web-services/aws-ram/

- https://www.w3schools.com/aws/aws_cloudessentials_sec_securityintroduction.php
- https://aws.amazon.com/controltower/
- https://www.stormit.cloud/blog/what-is-amazon-macie/
- https://docs.aws.amazon.com/waf/latest/developerguide/ddos-overview.html
- https://aws.amazon.com/firewall-manager/
- https://aws.amazon.com/certificate-manager/

CHAPTER 10
Cloud Architecture and AWS Framework

Introduction

This chapter delves into the essentials of popular cloud architecture patterns and the AWS Well-Architected Framework, providing a guide for building robust, scalable, and efficient cloud applications. As architects design buildings to meet safety standards and functionality, we begin with the twelve-factor methodology, ensuring a solid foundation for cloud-native applications.

Next, we explore popular cloud architecture patterns akin to an architect choosing structural designs. These include tiered architecture (2-tier, 3-tier, n-tier), microservices, event-driven architectures, serverless solutions, and data-driven designs like Customer 360 and IoT data event-driven architecture. Each pattern is tailored to specific needs, ensuring the application is functional and efficient.

We then focus on designing highly available and scalable cloud applications, like an architect ensuring a building's durability and capacity. Emphasizing scalability, loose coupling, high-availability, and fault tolerance, we provide real-world examples, such as scalable architectures for millions of users and a social media website. These examples are case studies, much like an architect studying past projects.

Toward the end of the chapter, we will discuss the AWS Architected Framework, highlighting its advantages and delving into its five pillars: cost optimization, reliability, operational excellence, security, and performance efficiency. Each pillar is discussed in detail with practical strategies and tools like Cost Explorer for cost optimization, similar to an architect adhering to building codes and standards.

This chapter equips readers to design and evaluate cloud architectures effectively, leveraging AWS best practices, much like an architect who combines creativity and technical knowledge to create enduring structures.

Structure

In this chapter we will cover the following topics:

- Key Considerations
- 12 (Twelve) Factor Methodology
- Popular Cloud Architecture Patterns
- Designing Highly Available and Scalable Cloud Applications
- Introduction to the AWS Well-Architected Framework
- Deep Dive into the Five Pillars of the AWS Well-Architected Framework

Key Considerations

- **Elasticity**: Utilize cloud services that automatically adjust resources based on demand, such as AWS Auto Scaling or Azure Virtual Machine Scale Sets.
- **Decoupling**: Use messaging queues (like Amazon SQS or Apache Kafka) to decouple services and ensure smooth communication between components.
- **Microservices**: Decompose applications into microservices, allowing each service to scale independently based on its specific load.
- **Fault tolerance**: Implement fault tolerance to ensure the system stays operational even if it fails. Maintain service continuity with data replication, redundant systems, and automated recovery processes.
- **High-availability**: While designing a highly available e-commerce application, if the aim is to make it 99.99% available, it means that out of 10,000 requests, only one is allowed to fail. This is extremely necessary to maintain customers' trust and prevent revenue loss. Unavailability for even a day in a year can result in substantial revenue loss, probably millions. To achieve high-availability, we need robust infrastructure, including:
    - **Load balancing**: Ensure no single server gets overwhelmed by distributing incoming traffic across multiple servers.
    - **Automated failover**: Switch automatically to a standby system in case of a failure.
    - **Backup and restore**: A reliable restore process and regular backups are necessary to recover data quickly.
    - **Redundancy**: Duplicate critical components and systems to prevent single points of failure.
- **Disaster recovery**: In case of unpredictable events, it is important to implement policies that quickly restore the functionality of applications, thus minimizing downtime and data loss. Some strategies include:

- o Implementation of reliable backup and restore processes
- o Ensuring data replication across diverse locations
- o Maintaining automated recovery procedures

With a solid recovery plan, businesses can reduce the impact of unforeseen situations and safeguard their data, ensuring a quick return to normalcy. Best practices for disaster recovery are:

- o Regular testing of your disaster recovery plans using tools such as AWS Elastic Disaster Recovery
- o Automating your deployment using AWS CloudFormation and AWS Elastic Beanstalk
- o Defining RTO and RPO
- o Implementing comprehensive monitoring using Amazon CloudWatch

Recovery Time Objective (RTO) and Recovery Point Objective (RPO) are the essential metrics defining acceptable downtime and data loss in a disruption. They ensure systems can be restored efficiently and with zero to minimal impact on operations. Together, these help businesses maintain high- availability and ensure continuity. Understanding and optimizing these objectives for minimizing downtime and preserving integrity is important.

- RTO is the maximum acceptable time to restore a service after failure. For critical applications, it is often in minutes.
- RPO is the maximum acceptable amount of data loss measured in time. In critical applications, this is often in seconds or minutes.

In the case of a highly available e-commerce platform:

- Short RTOs can be more expensive due to the requirement for faster failover mechanisms. It dictates how quickly the service must be restored after an outage.
- A lower RPO may require more frequent backups and more storage. It determines the frequency of backups.

RTOs and RPOs effectively involve:

- **Regular testing:** Conduction of regular disaster recovery drills ensures that RTOs and RPOs can be met.
- **Continuous improvement:** Improving and updating disaster recovery plans as the business and technology landscape evolves.
- **Defining clear objectives:** Understanding the business impact of downtime and data loss.

Some real-time applications:

- **Security-** To protect against cyber threats that could compromise availability using AWS Shield and AWS WAF.
- **Monitoring and alerting-** To implement comprehensive monitoring with AWS CloudWatch to detect and respond to issues promptly.
- **Latency optimization-** To use AWS CloudFront to reduce latency by caching content closer to users.
- **Scalability-** To ensure the application can handle sudden spikes in traffic with auto-scaling.

12 (Twelve) Factor Methodology

The 12-factor approach guides flexible web application development that excels in cloud settings. Let's look at each factor in the following figure and discuss how AWS offerings can play a role in putting them into practice.

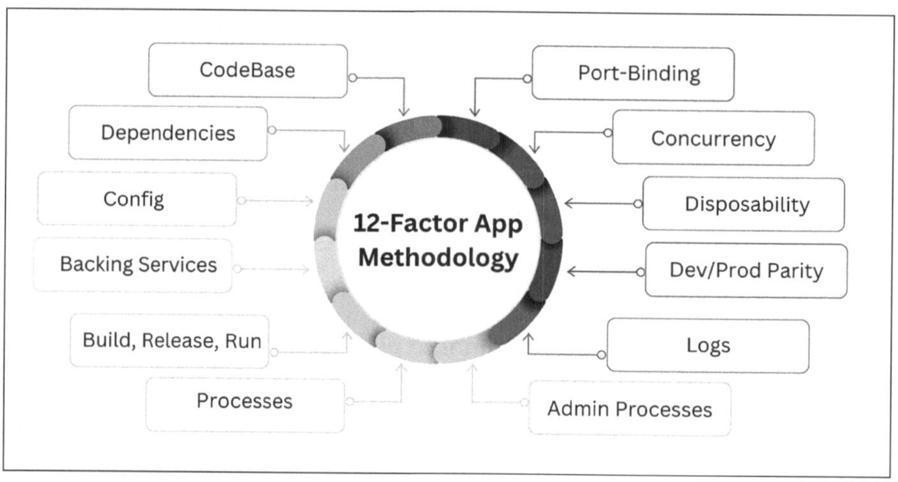

Figure 10.1: *12 Factor Methodology*

1. **Codebase: AWS CodeCommit**

Ensure your software has a code base using a version control system, like AWS CodeCommit. This enables collaboration during development, tracking of changes, and straightforward rollbacks if needed. AWS CodeCommit provides repository hosting services in the AWS cloud. It works seamlessly with AWS tools to facilitate development.

2. **Dependencies: Explicit Management with Package Managers and AWS CodeArtifact**

Ensure to state all the dependencies your application needs. This will help maintain consistency and prevent conflicts between development, staging, and production environments. Use known package management tools, such as npm (Node.js), pip (Python) or Maven (Java) to manage dependencies effectively. To improve security and have control over your dependencies, you might want to explore AWS CodeArtifact. This service lets you securely store and distribute packages privately within your organization.

3. **Config: Environment-Specific Configuration with AWS Secrets Manager and Parameter Store**

It's a practice to keep your configuration settings separate from your application code. This helps keep your code neat and makes handling configurations in different environments easier. To store data securely, such as database credentials and API keys, consider using AWS Secrets Manager. It comes with access control features that allow you to limit access to authorized individuals. The AWS Systems Manager Parameter Store is an option for managing configuration parameters. It serves as a hub for handling configuration variables and ensures easy accessibility for your application across various environments.

4. **Backing Services: Treat External Services as Resources on AWS**

Think of the services that your application relies on, such as databases, caches, and message queues as resources. This approach encourages a design and makes it easier to scale and replace them when necessary.

AWS provides a variety of services that can serve as supporting resources:

- Amazon RDS, Relational Database Service, handles databases, such as MySQL, PostgreSQL, and Aurora.
- DynamoDB is a NoSQL database service designed for applications with data structures.
- ElastiCache provides in-memory caching solutions, such as Redis and Memcached to boost application performance.
- AWS services like SQS (Simple Queue Service) for message queuing or SNS (Simple Notification Service) for pub/sub messaging are worth exploring.

5. **Build, Release, Run: Streamlined Processes with AWS CodeBuild and CI/CD Tools**

Outline the phases for creating, launching, and operating your application. This helps establish a development process and eases deployment. Leverage AWS CodeBuild, a managed building service, to automate the building process. It seamlessly integrates with used source code repositories and building tools for code creation and testing. Integrate Continuous Integration and Continuous Delivery (CI/CD) tools, such as Jenkins, CircleCI, or GitLab CI/CD to automate the pipeline from code submission to deployment.

6. **Processes: Embrace Statelessness with AWS Fargate and Lambda**

When creating your application, consider developing it using one or more processes. This setup ensures that each request and response cycle operates independently without relying on stored information between interactions. This approach enhances scalability and resilience.

AWS provides a range of services tailored for running applications:

- Elastic Beanstalk offers a managed environment for deploying and expanding web applications supporting programming languages and frameworks.
- AWS Fargate enables you to run containerized applications without the need to handle the underlying infrastructure, making it an excellent choice for deploying and scaling stateless microservices.
- AWS Lambda is a serverless computing service that runs code responding to various events, making it perfect for handling short-lived and event-triggered tasks.

7. **Port Binding: Load Balancing with AWS Elastic Load Balancing**

This explains how your app shares services by mentioning the ports it uses for communication with systems. When running a setup with multiple instances or containers, use Elastic Load Balancing to spread traffic evenly among different operational instances of your app. This way, you guarantee that your app is always available and can scale effectively.

8. **Concurrency: Horizontal Scaling with AWS Auto Scaling**

To achieve scaling, you can increase the number of processes used to manage traffic levels. This helps your application handle spikes in demand. With AWS Auto Scaling, EC2 or container instances are terminated automatically based on set scaling metrics. This guarantees that your application always has the resources to accommodate changing requirements.

9. **Disposability: Fast Startup and Graceful Shutdown with Serverless Options**

It ensures that your application is optimized for initialization and smooth termination of instances. This helps reduce any interruptions in service when deploying updates or scaling up. Serverless solutions such as Lambda or Fargate are known for efficiently handling resources and scaling seamlessly. They provide resources and scale automatically, removing the burden of managing server lifecycles.

10. **Dev/Prod Parity: Maintain Consistency with AWS CloudFormation and CDK**

It ensures that your development, staging, and production setups match closely to minimize errors from environment differences and make deployment easier.

AWS Provides services such as:

- AWS CloudFormation or AWS CDK (Infrastructure as Code) to outline your infrastructure. This guarantees uniform infrastructure setup across all environments.
- CloudFormation employs templates to outline your infrastructure resources (such as EC2 instances, databases, and more), whereas CDK enables you to define infrastructure using known programming languages like Python or Java.

11. **Logs: Stream Events with AWS CloudWatch Logs**

Consider logs as streams rather than fixed files. This makes gathering, analyzing, and troubleshooting application activities easier in one location.

AWS Provides services such as:

- Make the most of AWS CloudWatch Logs to gather, aggregate, and save logs from your application and different AWS services.
- CloudWatch Logs offers filtering and search capabilities for logs to simplify troubleshooting tasks and provide information on your application's health and efficiency.

12. **Admin Processes: Leverage Serverless for One-off Tasks**

Performing administrative tasks, such as data backups, migrations or deployments as one-off processes helps eliminate the requirement for specialized servers dedicated to these functions.

AWS Provides services such as:

- Serverless choices such as AWS Lambda or AWS Step Functions to carry out these responsibilities.
- Lambda enables the creation of code executed in reaction to events, which is perfect for brief tasks. Step Functions coordinate processes that involve AWS services.

By adhering to these 12 factors and utilizing the features of AWS, you can develop scalable and sustainable cloud-native applications. The fusion of the 12-factor methodologies recommendations with the range of AWS offerings enables you to craft applications that are:

- **Resilient:** Designed to handle failures and recover quickly.
- **Agile:** Easy-to-deploy, update, and scale.
- **Cost-effective:** Pay only for the resources you use.

This sets the groundwork for developing applications that excel in the changing cloud setting.

Popular Cloud Architecture Patterns

This section will explore tiered, microservices-based, event-driven, data-driven, and serverless architectures to help you design secure, scalable, and cost-effective cloud solutions for your needs.

Tiered Architecture

Tiered architecture, also referred to as layered architecture, stands out as a popular framework in cloud computing. This method involves structuring the application into layers or tiers, each assigned to a role in the application's operation. This division facilitates scalability, maintenance, and deployment. Some of the tiered architectures include:

N-Tier Architecture

The N-tier architecture extends the three-tier model by further breaking down the application tier into additional distinct layers:

- **Presentation Tier**: User interface components.
- **Service Tier**: Provides reusable services.
- **Business Tier**: Enforces business rules and processes.
- **Data Tier**: Manages data storage and retrieval.

The following figure depicts the N-tier architecture.

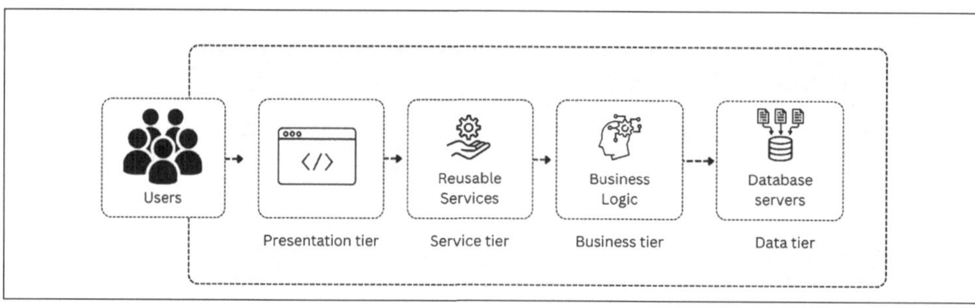

Figure 10.2: *N-tier Architecture*

This architecture can handle a lot of data, is great for managing workloads, and handles different aspects separately, which works well for big and intricate projects.

Real-World Example for N-Tier Architecture

An e-commerce platform employs an n-tiered architecture to enhance scalability, maintainability, and security. This separates the application into distinct layers:

presentation, application, and data, allowing each to be developed, managed, and scaled independently.

Steps:

1. **Presentation Tier:** For delivering web content and distributing traffic efficiently using Amazon CloudFront and AWS Elastic Load Balancing (ELB).
2. **Application Tier**: Deploy Amazon EC2 instances and AWS Lambda for the business logic, handling requests from the presentation tier.
3. **Data Tier**: For relational databases and Amazon DynamoDB, you can store data using Amazon RDS and ensure high availability and performance.
4. **Caching Layer**: To reduce latency and improve user experience, implement Amazon ElastiCache to cache frequently accessed data.
5. **Security and Monitoring**: Amazon CloudWatch, AWS WAF, and AWS Shield are used to monitor performance and secure the architecture.

Figure 10.3 illustrates this use case.

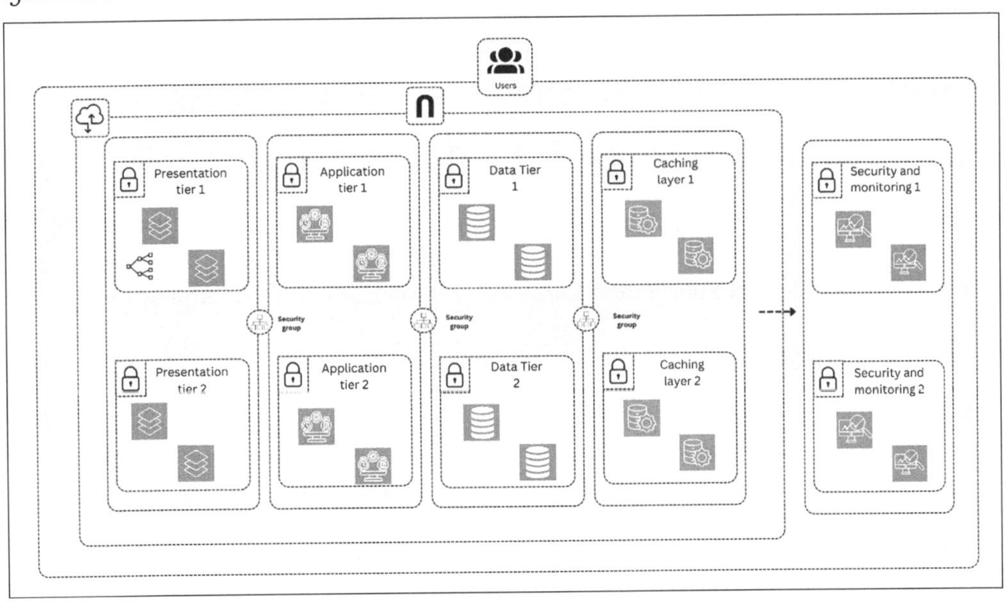

Figure 10.3: *N-tier architecture use case*

This n-tiered architecture allows the e-commerce platform to handle high traffic volumes, ensure a seamless user experience, and maintain robust security.

Three-Tier Architecture

In a three-tier architecture, an extra layer is inserted between the presentation and data tiers:

- **Presentation Tier:** This part refers to the application's front end or user interface(UI).
- **Application Tier:** Also called the business logic or application server, this layer manages data processing and enforces business regulations.
- **Data Tier:** The database or storage layer for data.

This design offers scalability and manageability compared to the two-tier architecture since it segregates business logic from presentation and data handling duties.

Two-Tier Architecture

In a two-tier architecture, the application is divided into two layers:

- **Presentation Tier:** This part is where users engage with the application, such as through web pages, mobile apps, or desktop applications.
- **Data Tier:** Consists of the database or data storage system where the application's information is stored and handled.

The two-tier architecture works well for smaller to medium-sized applications, but it may encounter difficulties handling increased user traffic and maintaining performance as the user community expands.

Microservices-Based Architecture

In the microservices architecture, an application is decomposed into small, loosely connected services, each handling a particular function. These services interact through defined APIs, enabling development, deployment, and scalability.

API Gateway

An API Gateway is the access point for users directing requests to the microservices. It manages load distribution, security measures, request direction, and sometimes caching and altering requests and responses. Some instances include AWS API Gateway and Kong.

Service Discovery

Microservices rely on service discovery mechanisms to locate and interact with each other promptly. Popular tools such as Consul, Eureka, or Kubernetes's built-in service discovery features facilitate this process. By utilizing service discovery, microservices can effortlessly scale up without the need for setup.

Circuit Breaker Pattern

The circuit breaker pattern enhances the systems' fault tolerance and resilience by halting requests for a failing service and offering solutions. This strategy prevents failures and contributes to the system's overall stability. Hystrix is an example of implementing the circuit breaker pattern.

Data Management

In a microservices architecture, each service typically handles its persisted database. This separation enables services to select the data storage technology based on their requirements. However, it necessitates handling data coherence and transactions, which can be attained through consistent and distributed transactions.

Real-World Example

Improve scalability, fault isolation, and deployment agility for a monolithic application, experiencing deployment challenges with growth in the user base.

Solution Overview: An e-commerce platform uses a microservices-based architecture to enhance scalability, flexibility, and resilience. By breaking down the application, the platform can handle high traffic, rapid development, and complex business requirements.

Steps:

1. User Authentication Service manages user registration, login, and authentication processes. Use Amazon Cognito to manage this.
2. Use Amazon DynamoDB to handle product listings, searches, and inventory management.
3. Use Amazon SQS to manage order creation, updates, and status tracking.
4. Use AWS Lambda with Amazon API Gateway to process securely using various payment gateways.
5. Use Amazon SNS to manage shipping options, tracking, and delivery status updates.
6. Use Amazon RDS to allow users to review and rate products.
7. Use Amazon SageMaker to provide personalized product recommendations based on user behavior and preferences.
8. Use Amazon CloudWatch to monitor service health, performance, and security.
9. Use AWS CodePipeline and AWS CodeDeploy to implement CI/CD pipelines for rapid development and deployment of microservices.

Figure 10.4 illustrates the discussed e-commerce use case.

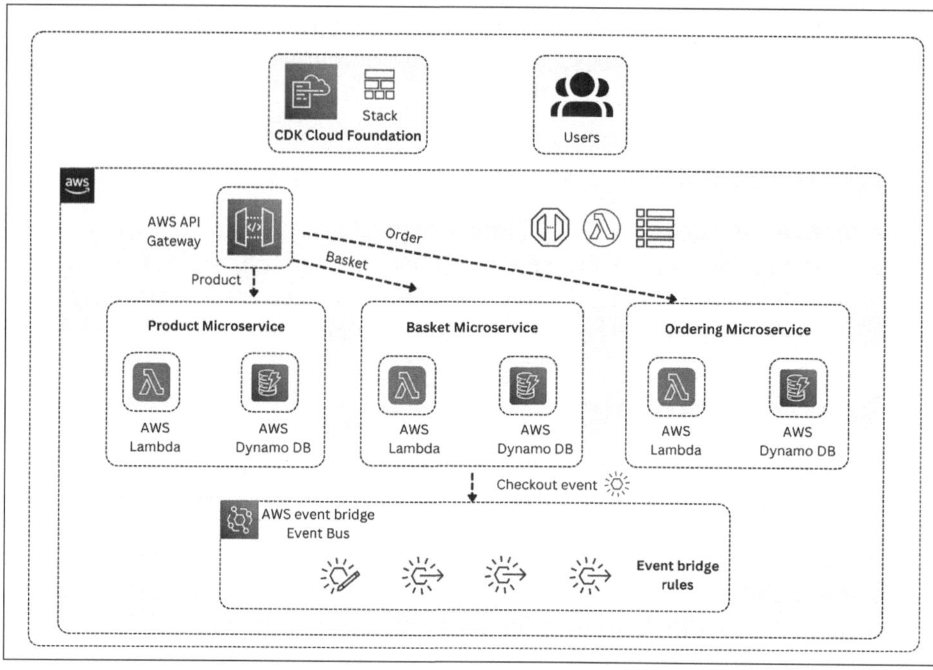

Figure 10.4: *Microservices-based architecture use case*

Event-Driven Architecture

In event-driven architecture (EDA), the progression of the pattern is guided by events like user interactions, sensor data, or software communications. This approach emphasizes coupling and scalability, making it well-suited for real-time processing and swift application responsiveness.

Event Producers and Consumers

In exploratory data analysis (EDA), events are created by event producers and are utilized by event consumers. Communication between producers and consumers occurs via events, which represent the happening of something interesting. This approach enables system components to engage with each other without dependencies.

Event Brokers

Event brokers are responsible for overseeing and directing events from creators to recipients. They serve as go-betweens that store, line up, and transmit events. Some common examples are Amazon SNS, Apache Kafka, and RabbitMQ. Event brokers play a role in enabling separation, dependability, and growth in event-triggered setups.

Event Sourcing

In event sourcing, the system's state is saved as a series of events, each indicating a state change. By replaying these events, the system can recreate its state. This method guarantees that all modifications are recorded and can be reviewed or replayed for troubleshooting or recovery.

Command Query Responsibility Segregation (CQRS)

CQRS separates a system's read and write operations. The command side handles data modifications (writes), while the query side handles data retrieval (reads). This pattern optimizes performance, scalability, and security by allowing read and write operations to be scaled independently and optimized for specific tasks.

Example of Event-Driven Architecture

Solution Overview: An online retail system uses an event-driven architecture to respond to real-time user and system events. This allows the system to be scalable and responsive to changes.

Steps:

1. **Event Producers:** User actions (such as placing orders) and system events (such as new additions) generate events.
2. **Event Router:** Use Amazon EventBridge or AWS SNS to route events to appropriate services.
3. **Order Processing Service:** AWS Lambda processes orders and other services.
4. **Inventory Management:** DynamoDB streams or AWS Kinesis handles real-time inventory updates.
5. **Notification Service:** Use Amazon SNS to send real-time notifications to users (about order status, payments, and so on).
6. **Analytics Service:** Store analytics data in Amazon Redshift or Amazon S3 for further analysis.
7. **Error Handling and Retry Mechanism:** Handle failed event processing with Amazon SQS
8. **Monitoring and Logging:** Use Amazon CloudWatch to monitor event flow and system performance.

Figure 10.5 illustrates the use case for event-driven architecture.

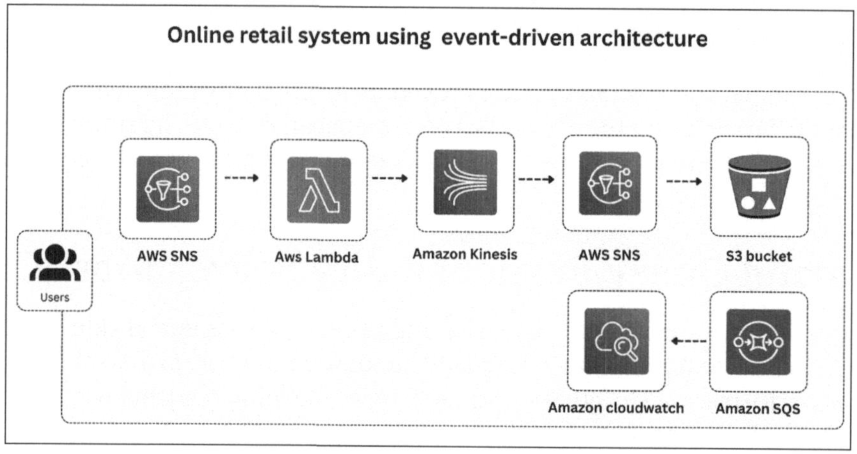

Figure 10.5: *Event-driven architecture use case*

Serverless Architecture

Serverless architecture abstracts server management, allowing developers to focus on code execution. Cloud providers automatically manage the infrastructure, scaling, and maintenance and charge only for the compute time consumed.

Figure 10.6 depicts Serverless architecture.

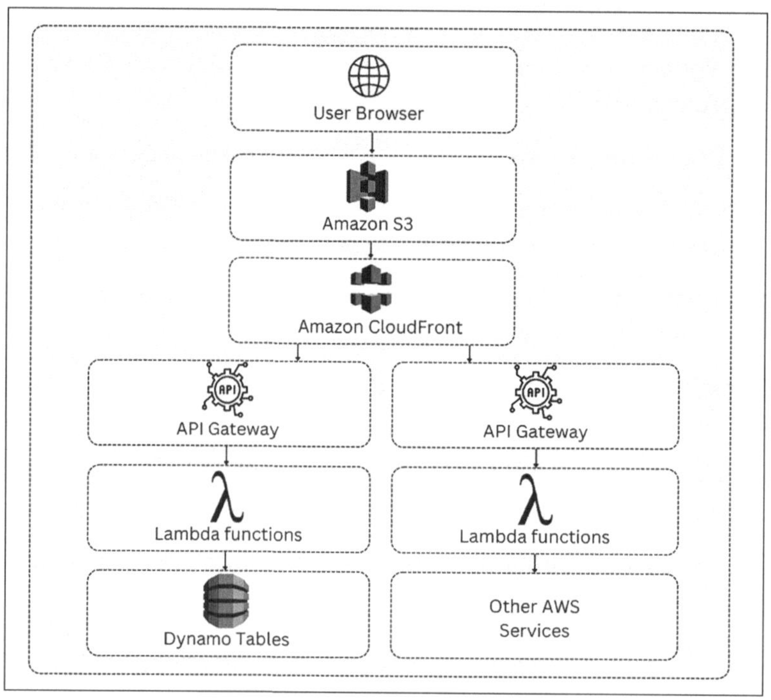

Figure 10.6: *Serverless architecture*

Let's consider a use case where an e-commerce website experiences fluctuating traffic and occasional surges during seasonal sales. In this case, serverless architecture automatically scales up and down based on demand. You only pay for what you use, as AWS Lambda functions run only when triggered, and resources are allocated dynamically.

However, serverless architecture is not useful in cases where the application requires continuous processing of lengthy tasks such as video encoding. This is because AWS Lambda has a maximum execution timeout of 15 minutes. Serverless architecture also cannot be used when the application needs high-performance computing resources as they are limited in memory and CPU power.

Why Serverless Architecture?

- scales based on demand; ideal for applications with unpredictable traffic patterns
- Reduces costs by eliminating the need to maintain servers
- Easily integrates with other AWS services, thus providing a versatile platform

Function-as-a-Service (FaaS)

FaaS platforms such as AWS Lambda, Azure Functions, and Google Cloud Functions allow developers to run individual functions responding to events without provisioning or managing servers. Functions are stateless and can be scaled automatically based on demand.

Problem Statement: To optimize development focus by minimizing infrastructure management overheads.

FaaS is used when the team prefers to focus on developing the data processing logic rather than managing infrastructure. The team can concentrate on writing and deploying code without worrying about server management as AWS Lambda abstracts the underlying infrastructure.

However, FaaS cannot be used in tasks that exceed Lambda's 15-minute execution limit.

Why FaaS?

- Scales automatically while handling varying loads
- Cost-effective
- Lets developers focus on business logic without worrying about infrastructure management.

Let's consider an application that processes user-uploaded images. The user first uploads an image to an S3 bucket, configuring to trigger a Lambda function that processes the image. This processed image is then saved to another S3 bucket or another service.

Backend-as-a-Service (BaaS)

BaaS platforms provide managed backend services, such as databases, authentication, and API management. Examples include Firebase and AWS Amplify. These services allow developers to build and deploy applications quickly without managing the underlying infrastructure.

Serverless architecture is ideal for event-driven, sporadic workloads and can significantly reduce operational overhead and costs.

Let's consider a mobile chat application that requires real-time data synchronization. In this example, Amazon Cognito handles user sign-up, sign-in, and access control. Amazon DynamoDB stores messages and user data. AWS Amplify provides real-time data synchronization between the mobile app and DynamoDB.

Let's look at another example to understand it better.

Solution Overview:

With AWS Lambda, the chat application achieves high scalability, reduced operational overhead, and cost-efficiency. It leverages a serverless architecture to handle dynamic user interactions without the need to manage server infrastructure.

Steps:

1. Manage user sign-up, sign-in, and access control using Amazon Cognito.
2. Implement AWS Lambda functions to process and route messages between users.
3. Use AWS AppSync or Amazon API Gateway with WebSockets to enable real-time message delivery.
4. Store chat history and user data in Amazon DynamoDB for low-latency access and scalability.
5. Use AWS Lambda and Amazon S3 to upload and serve media files, such as images and videos.
6. Use Amazon SNS or AWS Lambda triggers to send real-time notifications.
7. Use AWS X-Ray for tracing and debugging and Amazon CloudWatch to monitor application performance.
8. Implement CI/CD pipelines with AWS CodePipeline and AWS CodeBuild for automated deployment and updates.

9. Automatically scale with AWS Lambda's built-in scaling features and optimize costs by only paying for actual usage.

Data-Driven Architecture

Data-driven architecture focuses on efficiently managing, processing, and analysis of data. This architecture is crucial for applications that rely heavily on data insights and big data processing.

Why data-driven architecture?

- Provides a factual basis for strategic and operational decisions
- Helps identify inefficiencies and areas for improvement within operations
- Scales with growing data volumes

Data Lake

A data lake is a centralized repository that stores all structured and unstructured data at any scale. Tools such as Amazon S3, Azure Data Lake, and Google Cloud Storage are commonly used. Data lakes support storing raw data in its native format until it is needed for analysis.

Data Warehouse

A data warehouse is designed for reporting and data analysis, structured to support query and analysis rather than transaction processing. Examples include Amazon Redshift, Google BigQuery, and Snowflake. Data warehouses store processed and cleaned data optimized for complex queries and reporting.

Real-Time Data Processing

Real-time data processing platforms, such as Apache Kafka, Apache Flink, and AWS Kinesis, enable the processing and analysis of streaming data as it arrives. This allows for immediate insights and actions based on current data.

Batch Data Processing

Batch data processing tools, such as Apache Hadoop and AWS Glue, process large volumes of data in batches. These tools suit ETL (Extract, Transform, Load) jobs and data warehousing, where data is processed in bulk and scheduled.

Example of Data-Driven Architecture

A business intelligence (BI) platform uses a data-driven architecture. This enables insights through comprehensive data analysis and visualization.

Steps:

1. Use AWS Glue or AWS Data Pipeline to collect data from various sources such as databases, APIs, and so on.
2. Store raw and processed data in a scalable data lake on Amazon S3.
3. Use AWS Lambda and AWS Glue to prepare data for analysis.
4. Load processed data into Amazon Redshift for high-performance querying and analysis.
5. Use Amazon Athena and AWS Glue for data preparation and cleaning.
6. Use Amazon QuickSight to create interactive dashboards.
7. Use Amazon SageMaker to apply machine learning models and derive predictive insights.
8. Use AWS Lake Formation to ensure data security, compliance, and quality.
9. Use Amazon CloudWatch to monitor data workflows.

Let us look at another example.

Problem statement: An e-commerce platform struggling with real-time user analysis needs to provide personalized recommendations to users.

Solution Overview: Implement a data-driven architecture. Amazon Kinesis captures and streams real-time data from user interactions on the website. Then, AWS Glue processes and transforms this streaming data, preparing it for analysis. The processed data is further stored in Amazon Redshift. SageMaker further builds and deploys machine learning models and serves recommendations to users.

Steps:

1. Use Amazon Kinesis to capture and stream real-time data from user interactions on the website.
2. Process and transform the streaming data for analysis using AWS Glue.
3. Store the processed data, and enable efficient querying using Amazon Redshift.
4. Build, train, and deploy machine learning models that generate personalized recommendations with SageMaker.

Figure 10.7 illustrates the 'e-commerce platform' use case for event-driven architecture.

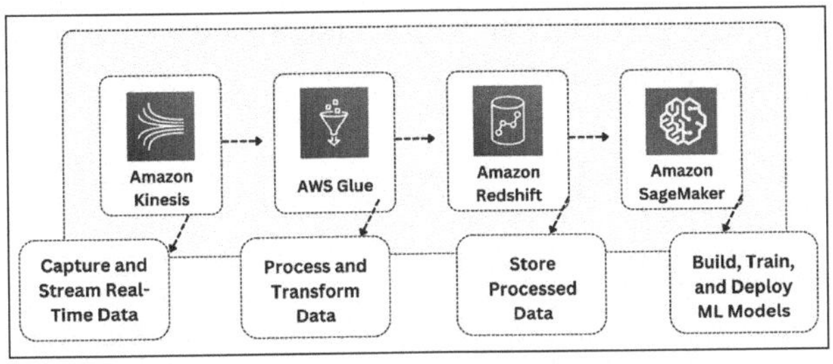

Figure 10.7: *Use case for e-commerce platform*

Overview of All Architectures

Let us now look at a brief overview of all architectures discussed in this chapter in *Figure 10.8*.

Architecture	Main Components	Best Suitable For	Real-World Use Cases	Cloud-Infra Expertise Level	Reason
Tiered Architecture	- Presentation Tier: Web servers, UI components -Application Tier: Application servers, business logic -Data Tier: Databases, storage solutions	- Traditional enterprise applications - Systems requiring clear separation of concerns	- E-commerce platforms - ERP systems	- Intermediate	Requires understanding of networking, load balancing, and tier separation.
Microservices -based Architecture	- Microservices: Independent, loosely coupled services -API Gateway: Central entry point for APIs - Service Registry: Service discovery and registration - Service Mesh: Service-to-service communication - Database per Service: Dedicated databases for each service	- Complex, large-scale applications - Agile development environments	- Netflix - Amazon - eBay	Advanced	Requires expertise in containerization, orchestration (e.g., Kubernetes), and CI/CD.
Event-driven Architecture	- Event Producers: Systems generating events - Event Consumers: Systems processing events - Event Brokers: Message brokers like Kafka, RabbitMQ - Event Routers: Services directing events to consumers	- Asynchronous, decoupled systems - Real-time data processing	- IoT applications - Financial transaction systems	Advanced	Requires understanding of messaging systems, event streaming (e.g., Kafka), and scalability.
Serverless Architecture	- Functions (FaaS): AWS Lambda, Azure Functions - API Gateway: Managed API services like AWS API Gateway - Managed Databases: DynamoDB, Firebase - Event Sources: Triggers such as HTTP requests, file uploads	- Applications with variable or unpredictable workloads - Rapid prototyping	- AWS Lambda for backends - Serverless REST APIs	Intermediate to Advanced	Simplifies infrastructure management but requires understanding of event-driven models and cloud services.
Data-driven Architecture	- Data Ingestion: ETL/ELT pipelines, data streams - Data Storage: Data lakes (e.g., AWS S3), data warehouses (e.g., Redshift) - Data Processing: Big Data tools (e.g., Hadoop, Spark) - Data Analytics: BI tools, machine learning platforms	- Data-intensive applications - Business intelligence and analytics	- Data analytics platforms - Machine learning pipelines	Advanced	Requires expertise in big data tools, data processing frameworks, and data warehousing

Figure 10.8: *Overview of all architectures*

Let us now progress to the next section which discusses the designing of highly available and scalable cloud architectures.

Designing Highly Available and Scalable Cloud Applications

Designing cloud applications that are both highly-available and scalable is crucial for modern businesses, as it ensures reliability, efficiency, and the ability to handle increasing loads. High availability refers to continuously operational systems, while scalability involves the capacity to grow and manage increased demand. This chapter delves into the essential considerations for creating architectures that meet these requirements, discussing design principles for scalable and loosely coupled architectures and providing examples and illustrations of highly-available and fault-tolerant systems.

Let's consider a global news website that needs to be highly available and scalable to handle traffic spikes. Amazon Route 53 directs user traffic to the nearest AWS region for low latency. Then, AWS Elastic Load Balancer distributes incoming traffic across multiple EC2 instances in availability zones within each region. Further, Amazon EC2 Auto Scaling adds or removes instances based on traffic load. Amazon RDS is configured for Multi-AZ deployments, and Amazon CloudFront delivers content globally.

Designing Scalable and Loosely Coupled Architectures

Scalability is the ability of a system to handle a growing amount of work by adding resources. Loose coupling minimizes dependencies between components, allowing them to function independently and scale without affecting the entire system.

Example: An e-commerce platform designed using microservices might have separate services for user authentication, product catalog, order processing, and payment. Each service can be independently scaled according to its load, ensuring increased user traffic to the product catalog does not affect the order processing service.

This ensures high availability by allowing each service to be independently scaled. Increasing product catalog traffic won't affect the order processing service. Suppose the user authentication service handles user registration and login; the product catalog will manage product listings. The payment service handles transactions, and the order processing service tracks and updates customer needs.

Let us look at the services mentioned:

1. **User Authentication Service**: This handles user registration, login, authentication, and authorization.

2. **Product Catalog Service**: This manages the product listings, including product details, categories, pricing, and availability.
3. **Order Processing Service**: Manages creating, updating, and tracking customer orders.
4. **Payment Service**: This handles payment processing, including integration with payment gateways and managing transactions

Figure 10.9 gives an overview of the architecture deployed in this example.

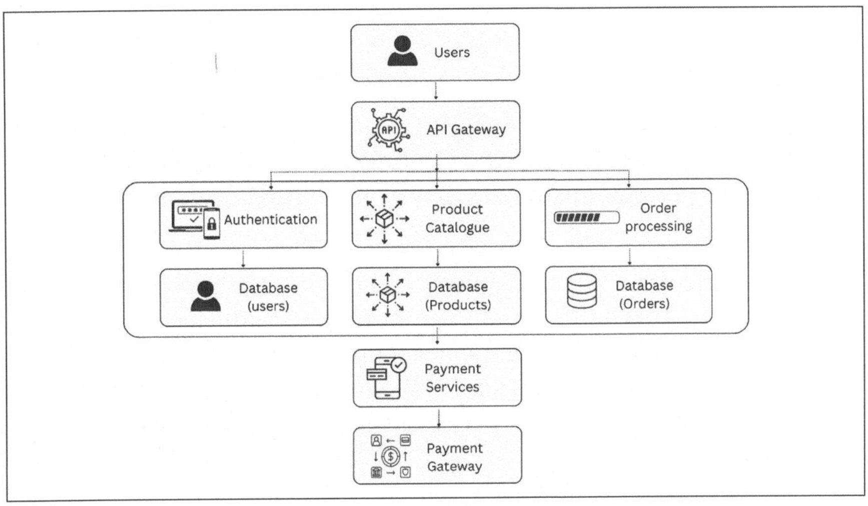

***Figure 10.9**: Microservices*

Designing Highly Available and Fault-Tolerant Architectures

High Availability (HA) ensures a system remains operational during component failures. Fault tolerance allows the system to continue functioning correctly even when part of the system fails.

Key Considerations:

- **Redundancy**: Deploy multiple instances of critical components across different availability zones or regions.
- **Failover Mechanisms**: Implement automated failover systems that detect failures and switch to standby resources without user intervention.
- **Load Balancing**: Use load balancers to distribute traffic evenly across multiple servers, preventing any single server from becoming a point of failure.

Example: A financial services application might use multiple databases in different regions with data replication to ensure that even if one region goes down, the application remains accessible by failing over to the secondary database.

The cost of removing the '9'

If an e-commerce platform is available 99.9% of the time (three nines) instead of 99.99%, it translates to almost 8.76 hours of downtime compared to 52.56 minutes. This is a significant difference. To understand this better:

1. **99.99% Availability (Four Nines):** If the platform is operational at this level, it would be offline for approximately 52.56 minutes a year. This downtime might occur during non-peak hours.

2. **99.9% Availability (Three Nines):** At this level, downtime jumps to roughly 8.76 hours annually. This increased downtime can lead to substantial disruptions. During these periods, customers may be unable to access the platform, leading to losses.

99.9% of the time, the service is available, meaning there is approximately 8.76 hours of downtime annually. This heightened amount of downtime may result in significant disturbances. Although it may not appear significant at first glance, the 8.23 hours (8.76 hours - 52.56 minutes) gap is crucial in the rapidly moving e-commerce industry, where even the slightest downtime can result in substantial financial setbacks. The effects consist of:

- **Decreased profits:** Prolonged periods of inactivity result in limited chances for clients to buy goods or services. Even a short downtime can lead to significant revenue loss for busy e-commerce websites.
- **Customer Trust and Loyalty:** Regular or extended periods of downtime can weaken customer trust. Clients anticipate consistent service and frequent interruptions can push them toward rival companies.
- **Impact on Operations:** Downtime negatively impacts customers and services alike.

Examples of Highly Available Architectures

Let us understand this section with some examples.

Scaling for Millions: Building High-Performance, Resilient Systems

Solution Overview: You need a combination of technologies while scaling a system for millions to manage high traffic, ensure low latency, and maintain performance. This involves using distributed databases, CDNs, and horizontal scaling of application servers.

Steps:

1. **Distributed Databases:** Amazon DynamoDB or Amazon Aurora can be used to provide scalable and high-performance database solutions.
2. **Content Delivery Network (CDN):** Implement Amazon CloudFront to deliver content globally.
3. **Horizontal Scaling:** Scale application servers horizontally with AWS Auto Scaling. Add more instances as demand increases.
4. **Microservices Architecture:** Divide the application into microservices to distribute the load and scale individual components independently.
5. **Event-driven Architecture:** Use Amazon SNS and Amazon SQS for handling asynchronous processing.
6. **Caching:** Use Amazon ElastiCache to implement caching strategies and speed up response times.
7. **API Gateway:** Use Amazon API Gateway to handle and scale API requests.
8. **Serverless Functions:** Use AWS Lambda to run code responding to events, automatically scaling to handle varying loads without provisioning servers.
9. **Monitoring and Analytics:** Use Amazon CloudWatch and AWS X-Ray to monitor application performance, identify bottlenecks, and optimize scaling strategies.

Figure 10.10 shows an illustration of this example.

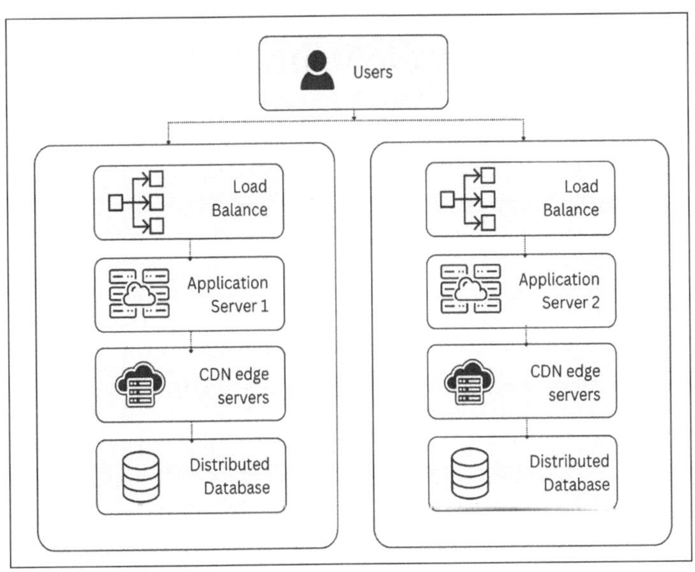

Figure 10.10: *Highly scalable architecture*

This architecture has the following components:

- **Users:** Users from different geographical locations access the system effortlessly.
- **Load Balancer:** This ensures that incoming traffic gets evenly distributed among multiple application servers so that no single server is overwhelmed.
- **Application Servers:** Multiple instances of application servers are horizontally scaled to handle user requests collaboratively.
- **CDN Edge Servers:** These servers in various locations deliver static content (images, videos, and stylesheets) more efficiently.
- **Distributed Databases:** Databases are split into shards or replicas to ensure data availability and reliability.

Example- Amazon Web Services (AWS) Scale: AWS employs a combination of services to achieve high scalability, including Elastic Load Balancing (ELB) for traffic distribution, Amazon RDS for scalable database solutions, and AWS Lambda for serverless compute that automatically scales based on the number of requests.

Social Media Website Example: A social media platform must handle high traffic volumes and ensure data is available and consistent globally. The architecture includes:

- **CDNs** for serving static content rapidly worldwide.
- **Microservices** for different functionalities, such as user management, posts, comments, and likes.
- **Distributed Databases** with data replication across multiple regions for high availability.

End-to-End Cloud Application Architecture Examples

Healthcare App Example: A healthcare application requires high availability, data privacy, and scalability to manage patient records, appointments, and real-time health monitoring.

Key Components:

- **User Interface**: Mobile and web apps for patient and doctor access.
- **API Gateway**: Manages API requests and routes them to appropriate services.
- **Microservices**: Separate services for user authentication, patient records, appointment scheduling, and health data monitoring.
- **Database**: A combination of SQL and NoSQL databases to handle structured patient records and unstructured health monitoring data.
- **Data Analytics**: Real-time analytics services for monitoring and alerting.

- **Security**: Implement strong authentication, authorization, and encryption to ensure data privacy and compliance with regulations like HIPAA.

Procedure:

1. **User Authentication**: Patients and doctors log in through the mobile/web app.
2. **Appointment Scheduling**: Users book appointments, and the request is routed through the API Gateway to the Appointment microservice.
3. **Health Monitoring**: The Health Monitoring microservice sends real-time health data from wearable devices.
4. **Data Storage**: Patient records are stored in an SQL database, while health monitoring data is stored in a NoSQL database.
5. **Analytics and Alerts**: Real-time analytics service processes the health data to detect anomalies and sends alerts if necessary.

Designing cloud applications for high availability and scalability involves a combination of architectural principles and best practices. By leveraging scalable, loosely coupled architectures and implementing high availability and fault tolerance, organizations can ensure their applications are robust, resilient, and capable of handling increasing demands. Examples like the e-commerce platform, financial services application, and healthcare app illustrate how these principles can be applied in real-world scenarios to achieve desired outcomes.

Introduction to the AWS Well-Architected Framework

The AWS Well-Architected Framework is a comprehensive set of best practices that Amazon Web Services (AWS) developed to help cloud architects build secure, high-performing, resilient, and efficient infrastructures for their applications. This framework provides a consistent approach for evaluating architectures and implementing designs that can scale over time. This chapter introduces the AWS Well-Architected Framework, outlines its core principles, and explores the benefits of using it to optimize cloud architectures.

Understanding the AWS Well-Architected Framework

Let's consider you building a house. The AWS Well-Architected Framework serves as the blueprint, built around five pillars, each representing a critical aspect of architectural excellence. These pillars form the framework's foundation, guiding cloud architects through the design, deployment, and management of cloud applications to ensure they are aligned with best practices.

- **Operational Excellence**: This pillar focuses on running and monitoring systems to deliver business value and continuously improve processes and procedures. It emphasizes automating deployments and infrastructure as code and monitoring systems to ensure they perform as expected. This is analogous to regular inspections of houses to fix minor issues before they turn into something major.
- **Security**: Emphasizes protecting information, systems, and assets through risk assessments and mitigation strategies. This includes implementing strong identity and access management, encryption, data integrity measures, and incident response planning. This is similar to focusing on security features such as sturdy locks, CCTV, and so on.
- **Reliability**: Ensures a workload performs its intended function correctly and consistently. This involves designing systems that can recover quickly from failures, have fault-tolerant architectures, and are resilient to accidental and deliberate disruptions. This resembles building a house on a stable foundation, incorporating only high-quality materials.
- **Performance Efficiency**: Focuses on using resources efficiently to meet system requirements and maintaining that efficiency as demand changes and technologies evolve. This pillar involves selecting the right types and sizes of resources, monitoring performance, and making informed decisions to optimize performance. In the house analogy, this can be considered as selecting the right materials to ensure the house functions well with optimal resource utilization.
- **Cost Optimization**: Focuses on avoiding unnecessary costs and making informed decisions to maximize the value of the investment. This involves using the most cost-effective resources, taking advantage of pricing models, and continually reviewing and optimizing expenses. This stage's in-house analogy aims to get the most value from the decided budget.
- **Sustainability:** Focuses on reducing environmental impact by using energy-efficient resources and designing for minimized waste. Utilizing AWS's sustainability effort such as renewable energy investments, aids in decreasing the environmental impact of cloud operations.

Benefits of Using the AWS Well-Architected Framework

The AWS Well-Architected Framework offers numerous advantages, ensuring that applications are designed and managed according to industry best practices. The key benefits include:

- **Improved Operational Efficiency**: The operational excellence pillar encourages automation, monitoring, and optimization of operations. By implementing these guidelines, organizations can enhance their operational processes, reduce human error, and ensure that systems are continually monitored and improved. Automated deployment pipelines and monitoring systems can lead to faster incident response times and more reliable deployments. Tools like AWS CloudFormation enable infrastructure as code, automating the provisioning and management of AWS resources, while AWS CloudWatch provides detailed monitoring and alerting capabilities.
- **Enhanced Security Posture**: Security is a critical architecture component. The security pillar provides comprehensive best practices to safeguard data and systems. This includes identity and access management, infrastructure protection, data protection, and incident response. By adhering to these principles, organizations can better protect their applications from threats and vulnerabilities, ensuring compliance with regulatory requirements, such as GDPR, HIPAA, or PCI DSS. AWS Identity and Access Management (IAM) helps securely manage access to AWS services and resources, while AWS Key Management Service (KMS) provides tools for encryption key management.
- **Increased Reliability**: The reliability pillar focuses on designing systems that recover quickly from failures and maintain their intended functions. By following these guidelines, organizations can build fault-tolerant systems that automatically recover from hardware or software failures. This includes using multiple availability zones for redundancy, implementing robust backup and disaster recovery plans, and monitoring system health to detect and respond to issues promptly. Services such as Amazon Route 53 for DNS failover, AWS Elastic Load Balancing (ELB), and Amazon RDS for database replication contribute to highly reliable architectures.
- **Optimized Performance**: The performance efficiency pillar emphasizes choosing the right resources and technologies for specific workloads. This ensures that applications are scalable and can handle varying loads efficiently. For example, leveraging auto-scaling groups, selecting appropriate instance types, and optimizing storage solutions can help maintain performance as demand fluctuates. Organizations can also use AWS services like Amazon CloudFront for content delivery and Amazon RDS for managed relational databases to enhance performance. AWS offers various instance types and sizes to match workload requirements, ensuring optimal performance.
- **Cost Savings**: Cost optimization is a crucial aspect of cloud architecture, directly impacting the bottom line. The cost optimization pillar provides strategies

for managing costs, such as right-sizing resources, using reserved instances, and leveraging AWS pricing models. By following these recommendations, organizations can avoid over-provisioning and ensure that they only pay for the resources they need. This leads to significant cost savings and better financial planning. Services like AWS Cost Explorer and AWS Budgets help monitor and manage costs effectively.

- **Comprehensive Evaluation and Improvement**: The AWS Well-Architected Framework includes the Well-Architected Tool, which allows organizations to review their workloads against AWS best practices. This tool provides a consistent way to measure architectures and identify areas for improvement. By regularly reviewing and updating their architectures, organizations can ensure they are always aligned with the latest best practices and technological advancements. The Well-Architected Tool offers insights and recommendations, helping organizations continuously improve their cloud applications.

  The AWS Well-Architected Framework is an invaluable resource for cloud architects seeking to build robust, secure, and efficient applications on AWS. Organizations can ensure their architectures are optimized for performance, reliability, and cost-efficiency by adhering to its principles and leveraging the Well-Architected Tool. The framework helps design and deploy cloud applications and provides a continuous improvement process to adapt to evolving business and technological needs.

Deep Dive into the Five Pillars of the AWS Well-Architected Framework

The AWS Well-Architected Framework is designed around five key pillars: Cost Optimization, Reliability, Operational Excellence, Security, and Performance Efficiency. These pillars represent essential aspects of building and maintaining robust, scalable, and efficient cloud architectures. This chapter provides an in-depth exploration of each pillar, detailing its significance, practical strategies, and implementation tools. By understanding and applying these principles, cloud architects can ensure their AWS environments are well-architected and optimized for success.

Cost Optimization Pillar

The Cost Optimization pillar focuses on strategies and tools for managing and reducing costs in the cloud. Effective cost management ensures that resources are used efficiently and that spending aligns with business objectives.

Using Cost Explorer and Billing Tools

AWS provides several tools to help organizations track and manage their costs:

- **AWS Cost Explorer**: This tool allows users to visualize, understand, and manage their AWS costs and usage over time. It provides detailed reports and insights into spending patterns, helping identify areas for potential savings. Users can create custom reports to analyze specific cost drivers and forecast future costs based on historical data.
- **AWS Budgets**: AWS Budgets lets users set custom cost and usage budgets, which can trigger alerts when thresholds are exceeded. This proactive approach helps prevent overspending by providing timely notifications and enabling corrective actions.
- **AWS Cost and Usage Report (CUR)**: The CUR offers comprehensive cost and usage data. It provides detailed information about AWS resource consumption and costs, allowing for in-depth analysis and allocation.

Strategies for Cost Optimization

Several strategies can help optimize costs in the cloud:

- **Right-Sizing Resources**: Continuously monitor and adjust the size of your resources to match the workload requirements. This prevents over-provisioning and under-utilization of resources. Tools like AWS Trusted Advisor can provide recommendations for right-sizing instances.
- **Use of Reserved Instances and Savings Plans**: Commit to using AWS services over a one- or three-year term to receive significant discounts compared to on-demand pricing. AWS Savings Plans offer flexible pricing models for EC2 and other services, providing savings based on usage patterns.
- **Auto-scaling**: Implement auto-scaling to adjust the number of running instances based on current demand. This ensures that you only pay for what you need, scaling down during low-demand periods.
- **Leveraging Spot Instances**: Spot instances can be used for flexible workloads that can tolerate interruptions. They offer substantial cost savings compared to on-demand instances.
- **Monitor and Optimize Storage**: Regularly review and optimize storage usage by archiving infrequently accessed data and deleting unnecessary data. Use lifecycle policies for S3 to automatically transition data to lower-cost storage classes.

Reliability Pillar

The Reliability pillar ensures that workloads perform their intended functions correctly and consistently, even when failures occur. This involves designing systems that are resilient, fault-tolerant, and capable of recovering quickly from disruptions.

Questionnaire for Evaluating Reliability

To assess the reliability of an architecture, consider the following questions:

- How are you managing service limits and quotas?
- How are you backing up your data?
- How are you monitoring and managing system health?
- How do you handle failures, and what are your recovery strategies?
- How are you planning for disaster recovery and continuity of operations?

Importance of Reliability in Cloud Architecture

Reliability is crucial for maintaining the availability and integrity of applications and data. Reliable architectures minimize downtime, ensure data consistency, and maintain the trust of users and customers. Key practices include:

- **Design for Failure**: Anticipate and plan for failures by implementing redundancy and failover mechanisms. Use multiple Availability Zones (AZs) to distribute workloads and protect against localized failures.
- **Automate Recovery**: Automate systems to detect and respond to failures quickly. AWS CloudWatch can monitor the health of resources and trigger automated recovery actions.
- **Regular Backups and Testing**: Perform regular backups and test the recovery process to ensure data can be restored during a failure. Services like AWS Backup automate and centralize backup tasks.

Operational Excellence Pillar

The Operational Excellence pillar focuses on running and monitoring systems to deliver business value and continuously improve processes and procedures. This involves automation, monitoring, and effective operations management.

Questionnaire for Assessing Operational Excellence

To evaluate operational excellence, consider the following questions:

- How do you manage and document operational procedures?
- How do you monitor workloads and handle operational events?
- How do you improve and optimize operations over time?

- How do you ensure compliance and security during operations?
- How do you train and support your operations team?

Importance of Operational Excellence in the Cloud

Operational excellence ensures that cloud environments are well-managed, efficient, and continuously improving. Key practices include:

- **Infrastructure as Code (IaC)**: Use IaC tools like AWS CloudFormation to automate the provisioning and management of cloud resources. This ensures consistency and reduces the risk of manual errors.
- **Continuous Monitoring and Feedback**: Implement monitoring and logging to gain insights into system performance and operational health. AWS CloudWatch and AWS X-Ray provide detailed metrics and tracing capabilities.
- **Proactive Operational Practices**: Develop and implement operational procedures, runbooks, and incident response plans. Review regularly and update these documents to reflect environmental changes and best practices.

Security Pillar

The Security pillar emphasizes protecting information, systems, and assets through risk assessments and mitigation strategies. It involves implementing strong security practices and controls to safeguard data and applications.

Questionnaire for Evaluating Security Posture

To assess security posture, consider the following questions:

- How do you manage identity and access management (IAM)?
- How do you protect data at rest and in transit?
- How do you detect and respond to security incidents?
- How do you enforce compliance with security policies?
- How do you secure the network infrastructure?

Importance of Security in Cloud Architecture

Security is critical to protect sensitive information, maintain privacy, and comply with regulations. Key practices include:

- **Identity and Access Management**: Implement robust IAM policies to control resource access. Use AWS IAM to define permissions and roles and enable multi-factor authentication (MFA) for added security.
- **Data Encryption**: Encrypt data at rest using AWS Key Management Service

(KMS) and encrypt data in transit using SSL/TLS. This ensures that data is protected from unauthorized access and tampering.

- **Security Monitoring and Incident Response**: Use AWS security services like Amazon GuardDuty for threat detection and AWS Security Hub for a centralized view of security alerts. Develop and test incident response plans to address security breaches quickly.

Performance Efficiency Pillar

The Performance Efficiency pillar focuses on using resources efficiently to meet system requirements and maintaining that efficiency as demand changes and technologies evolve. This involves optimizing resource use and staying up-to-date with the latest AWS services and features.

Questionnaire for Assessing Performance Efficiency

To evaluate performance efficiency, consider the following questions:

- How do you select the appropriate instance types and sizes for your workloads?
- How do you monitor and optimize resource performance?
- How do you ensure scalability and elasticity in your architecture?
- How do you stay current with AWS innovations and best practices?
- How do you balance performance and cost considerations?

Importance of Performance Optimization in the Cloud

Performance optimization ensures that applications run efficiently, meet user expectations, and scale seamlessly with demand. Key practices include:

- **Right-sizing Resources**: Monitor and adjust resource sizes based on performance metrics and workload requirements. Use AWS Trusted Advisor for recommendations.
- **Auto-scaling**: Implement auto-scaling to adjust the number of instances based on demand. This ensures optimal performance during peak times and cost savings during low-demand periods.
- **Regular Performance Reviews**: Review performance metrics regularly and optimize configurations accordingly. Use AWS CloudWatch and AWS X-Ray for detailed monitoring and tracking.

Sustainability Pillar

The Sustainability pillar is dedicated to the company's environmental responsibility, which means using only necessary resources and avoiding waste. This includes sustainable strategies, improving resource consumption efficiency, and using eco-friendly technology.

Questionnaire for Assessing Sustainability

For evaluating sustainability, consider the following questions:

- How is the environmental impact assessed and monitored in your organization?
- How can you save resources when executing this particular activity?
- How do you incorporate sustainability into your cloud solutions?
- What mechanisms do you put in place to abide by environmental legal requirements?
- How do you communicate sustainability and ensure your team learns what you want them to know?

Importance of Sustainability in the Cloud

Sustainability helps to offer services in an environmentally sustainable way without implying long-term dangerous effects. Key practices include:

- **Efficient Resource Utilization:** Other services, such as AWS Auto Scaling, allow users to pay only for the resources humans need, and services, such as AWS Lambda, provide services only when required. Lay down right-sizing and scheduling techniques to address the organization's resource management issue.
- **Energy-efficient Infrastructure:** Select hardware and infrastructure options from the cloud service providers with energy-efficiency functionality. Another essential component of AWS's architecture is its relative energy efficiency, partly used by renewable energy.
- **Sustainable Design Principles:** Approach your architecture design for sustainability by embracing the great rule of thrift, avoiding over-provisioning components, and choosing the right services and regions. Adhere to AWS's Well-Architected framework to meet best practice standards concerning sustainability.

Conclusion

Congratulations! You have successfully grasped the concepts of the 12-factor methodology and the various cloud architectural patterns. The real-world use cases have also assisted you in understanding how to implement these architectural patterns in daily scenarios. Understanding and implementing the principles of the AWS Well-Architected Framework's five pillars–Cost-optimization, Reliability, Operational Excellence, Security, Performance Efficiency, and Sustainability–is crucial for building robust, scalable, and efficient cloud architectures.

By leveraging AWS tools and best practices, organizations can optimize their cloud environments, ensuring they meet business objectives while maintaining high security, performance, and cost-efficiency standards. The next chapter will prepare you for AWS SAA C-03 Certification with helpful insights, questionnaires, and tips.

Multiple Choice Questions

1. What key things should you remember when designing scale cloud architecture?
   a. Cost
   b. Redundancy
   c. Load Balancing
   d. Encryption
2. The 12-factor methodology is used mainly for which of the following?
   a. Scaling applications
   b. Designing microservices
   c. Monitoring cloud resources
   d. Encrypting data
3. Which pattern distributes loads across several services to improve availability?
   a. Monolithic Architecture
   b. Microservices Architecture
   c. Three-Tier Architecture
   d. Serverless Architecture
4. What does the AWS Well-Architected Framework assist one in attaining?
   a. Cost Optimization
   b. Data Encryption
   c. Automated Deployments
   d. Multi-Region Redundancy

5. Which pillar of the AWS Well-Architected Framework focuses on ensuring a workload resists disruptions?
    a. Security
    b. Reliability
    c. Performance Efficiency
    d. Operational Excellence
6. Which architecture pattern should be used for applications requiring event-driven compute services?
    a. Serverless Architecture
    b. Microservices Architecture
    c. Monolithic Architecture
    d. Multi-Region Architecture
7. How is a highly available cloud application best supported?
    a. Single-Region Deployment
    b. Redundant Infrastructure
    c. Manual Scaling
    d. On-premise backups
8. Which of the following pillars of the AWS Well-Architected Framework covers the capability to run and monitor systems delivering business value?
    a. Operational Excellence
    b. Security
    c. Performance Efficiency
    d. Reliability
9. In a 12-factor methodology, what is configuration separated from code for?
    a. To enhance scalability
    b. Ease of Deployments
    c. Enhance security
    d. Reduction in costs

10. What is the benefit of microservices architecture in Cloud-based applications?
    a. Centralized Management
    b. Better fault isolation
    c. Greater horizontal scalability
    d. Better debugging

Answers

1. c
2. b
3. b
4. a
5. b
6. a
7. b
8. a
9. b
10. b

References

- https://d0.awsstatic.com/whitepapers/architecture/AWS_Well-Architected_Framework.pdf
- https://aws.amazon.com/?nc2=h_lg
- https://docs.aws.amazon.com/wellarchitected/latest/framework/welcome.html
  https://medium.com/@bijit211987/cloud-architecture-considerations-framework-427a08e5c646
- https://tutorialsdojo.com/aws-well-architected-framework-six-pillars/
- https://www.equinix.sg/?_gl=1*1w5fyl4*_up*MQ..&gclid=CjwKCAjw65-zBhBkEiwAjrqRMNsAeUbG8_FDV6LxJuJ4V__jNwFjrvanfwaRo-FjmInrnYlV8vW-0BoCL58QAvD_BwE

CHAPTER 11

AWS SAA C-03 Certification Preparation

Introduction

In cloud services, candidates ascend to a realm where scalability and resource optimization reign supreme. Amazon EC2, akin to digital clay, allows architects to sculpt compute capacity to fit any workload, while AWS Lambda promises serverless computing paradigms. From containerization with Amazon ECS to batch processing via AWS Batch, the array of compute services empowers architects to craft solutions that seamlessly adapt to fluctuating demands.

With AWS's storage services, storage becomes a versatile landscape. From the vast expanse of Amazon S3's infinite object storage to the sturdy blocks of Amazon EBS and the nimble file systems of Amazon EFS, architects wield a palette of solutions to create robust, scalable, and secure data repositories. Networking serves as the connective tissue binding architectures together. Amazon VPC forms isolated enclaves for digital ecosystems, Amazon Route 53 excels in DNS routing, and Elastic Load Balancing ensures smooth application traffic across distributed landscapes. Amazon CloudFront delivers content with speed and reliability, enhancing digital experiences with unparalleled acceleration.

Databases are the repositories of wisdom in the AWS ecosystem. Amazon RDS offers managed databases, Amazon DynamoDB caters to NoSQL enthusiasts, Amazon Redshift shines in data warehousing, and Amazon Aurora stands out as a top-tier database performer. Security and compliance are crucial for safeguarding data and assets within AWS. Candidates delve into IAM, encryption methods, and regulatory adherence to upholding confidentiality, integrity, and availability.

Application integration is orchestrated with tools, such as Amazon SQS and SNS for message routing, Amazon MQ for managed message brokering, and Amazon SWF for coordinating distributed workflows. Monitoring and management are essential for maintaining control and insight. Amazon CloudWatch provides unparalleled visibility into AWS resource health and performance, AWS CloudTrail audits every action for compliance, and AWS Config ensures resource configuration sanctity. AWS Systems Manager centralizes operations management, empowering architects to control sprawling digital landscapes easily.

This final chapter is your ultimate guide to mastering the AWS SAA C-03 Certification. We will start with an overview of the certification, providing insights into its significance and the competencies it validates. You'll find a comprehensive guide on how to book the exam, along with practical tips on approaching it to maximize your success. We have included sample exam questions to help you gauge your preparedness and understand the exam format better. Additionally, we will address frequently asked questions (FAQs) to clear any lingering doubts. Finally, we will share best practices crucial for passing the exam and excelling in your role as an AWS Solutions Architect. Prepare to consolidate your knowledge and take the final step toward certification success.

Structure

In this chapter we will cover the following topics:

- Introduction to AWS SAA C-03 Certification
- Certification Guide
- Book the Exam
- Tips on Taking the Exam
- Sample Exam Questions
- FAQs
- Best practices

Introduction to AWS SAA C-03 Certification

Essentially, earning this certification involves delving into the fundamentals of AWS. Candidates traverse the landscape of Regions and Availability Zones, grasping the very fabric upon which AWS's distributed architecture is woven. These foundational concepts are the cornerstone for architects to sculpt solutions that meet and exceed performance, reliability, and compliance standards.

AWS SAA C-03 Certification

The AWS Certified Solutions Architect - Associate (SAA C03) certification represents expertise in the changing field of cloud computing within Amazon Web Services (AWS). It signifies not skill but excellence in designing, implementing, and optimizing cloud solutions customized for business requirements.

Achieving the AWS SAA C03 certification goes beyond passing a test; it showcases a comprehension of how AWS's extensive ecosystem operates. Every aspect of cloud architecture is thoroughly examined and perfected, from the principles supporting AWS's infrastructure to the skilled use of its diverse services.

Ultimately, achieving the AWS SAA-C03 certification isn't just about acquiring a badge; it's about ascending to the zenith of cloud architecture mastery. Entering the realm of the IT industry unlocks a plethora of possibilities in the era dominated by cloud computing.

Benefits of Earning the AWS SAA C-03 Certification

Earning the AWS Certified Solutions Architect - Associate (SAA C03) certification goes beyond being an accomplishment; it catalyzes your career growth. In today's job landscape, marked by technological advancements that reshape various industries, employers seek individuals well-versed in cloud computing, particularly within AWS. This certification not only showcases your expertise but also positions you as a valuable asset within the IT industry.

Career Advancement

As businesses progressively embrace cloud technologies to foster innovation, enhance flexibility, and streamline their operations, the demand for AWS specialists steadily rises. AWS empowers organizations to develop, deploy, and scale applications seamlessly, efficiently, and easily. As more enterprises transition from infrastructures to cloud-based systems, professionals increasingly need to craft, implement, and oversee cloud solutions on the AWS platform.

The AWS SAA C03 certification validates your capacity to architect solutions on AWS and your grasp of AWS services, industry best practices, and design principles. Successfully clearing this exam demonstrates your ability to construct cost solutions tailored to meet business requirements.

Skill Validation

The AWS Certified Solutions Architect–Associate (SAA C03) certification elaborates on your architecture skills by working on the AWS platform. It is more than a mere certificate; it validates your capabilities to design and implement systems that meet current computing challenges.

In the realm of cloud technology, adaptability is key. Systems need to handle changes in workload without sacrificing performance or dependability. The AWS SAA C03 certification confirms your ability to create architectures that scale effortlessly, utilizing tools like Amazon EC2 for flexible compute capacity allocation and auto-scaling to adjust to varying demands.

By planning and executing solutions, certified professionals exhibit their proficiency in crafting systems that can expand and adapt alongside business needs, ensuring resource utilization and user satisfaction. Professionals who master this demonstrate their ability to design systems that can handle failures and maintain access to essential services, building trust among employers and clients.

Access to AWS Community

Achieving AWS certification as an AWS Certified Solutions Architect Associate (SAA C03) offers more than proving your skills. It grants access to a group of cloud computing experts dedicated to maintaining standards in their field. Let's delve deeper into how being part of the AWS community can greatly boost your career:

Being a certified AWS professional comes with perks, like attending AWS events, such as AWS Summits, Re-Invent, and specialized webinars. These gatherings provide insights and offer excellent networking opportunities like meeting certain AWS experts, such as developers, solution architects, and other certified professionals from around the globe. These connections often lead to collaborations, mentorship opportunities, and knowledge-sharing sessions that can significantly boost your career growth.

Getting involved with the AWS community can open up career opportunities. Building connections with industry leaders and potential employers at AWS gatherings and on-platforms could lead to job offers, consulting gigs, and collaborations. Moreover, actively participating and gaining recognition within the community can improve your reputation, making you a respected expert in your field.

Potential for Higher Salaries

One of the advantages of obtaining the AWS Certified Solutions Architect – Associate (SAA C03) certification is the potential for increased earnings. Not only does this certification confirm your abilities and expertise in AWS, but it also boosts your value in the competitive IT field.

Earning the AWS SAA C03 certification demonstrates your proficiency in designing and implementing highly reliable and fault systems on AWS. It showcases your understanding of AWS services practices in architecture and your ability to apply these skills to address real-world business challenges. Employers appreciate that certified professionals possess a skill set beyond knowledge, including practical experience and problem-solving skills.

The demand for cloud computing experts with AWS expertise has steadily increased. As businesses move more of their operations to the cloud, there is a growing need for solutions architects who can create dependable and cost-effective cloud infrastructures. Various salary surveys and industry reports indicate that professionals certified in AWS consistently earn better salaries than their certified counterparts.

Target Audience for the AWS SAA C-03 Exam

The AWS Certified Solutions Architect – Associate (SAA C03) test aims to confirm the abilities and expertise needed to create and implement structured solutions on AWS. It is intended for various individuals in the IT and cloud computing sectors. Listed here are the groups that benefit from this certification along with an explanation of how it is beneficial for them.

- **Solutions Architects:** The AWS SAA C03 certification is mainly aimed at solutions architects who create scalable and secure solutions using AWS services. This certification confirms their capability to grasp and implement principles to craft solutions that align with business needs. By earning this certification, solutions architects showcase their proficiency in AWS, boosting their credibility and career opportunities. Moreover, the certification equips them with the expertise to design systems that guarantee business continuity and durability.
- **Cloud Practitioners:** Cloud professionals, including individuals in roles like cloud consultants and engineers, form a target group for the AWS SAA C03 exam. These experts often focus on setting up and overseeing cloud infrastructures. The certification equips them with the expertise to create and implement solutions that effectively utilize AWS services. For cloud practitioners, achieving the AWS SAA C03 certification demonstrates a grasp of AWS cloud architecture, opening doors to career growth and enhanced earning prospects. It also ensures they are proficient in the recommended approaches for cloud deployment, security measures, and cost control, which is an important aspect of executing cloud projects.
- **IT Professionals with Experience in AWS:** IT professionals with experience working with AWS services who want recognition for their skills can greatly benefit from obtaining the AWS SAA C03 certification. This group typically includes system administrators, network engineers, and software developers who regularly work in AWS environments. By acquiring this certification, IT professionals can transition into roles, such as architects, cloud engineers, or DevOps engineers, thus advancing their career prospects.
- **Individuals Looking to Validate their AWS Architecture Skills:** The AWS SAA

C03 certification is great for people looking to showcase their AWS architecture skills, whether they've learned independently or through work experience. This includes those changing careers, recent graduates, and professionals in software development or IT consulting. Getting certified sets a standard for their skills, making it simpler to showcase their skills to employers. It also gives them a way into the expanding world of cloud computing, which is highly sought after in many industries. With this certification, individuals can demonstrate their ability to create and implement AWS solutions, boosting their chances of finding work and exploring career paths.

Certification Guide

Let us look at the breakdown of the certification guide.

Exam Overview

The AWS Certified Solutions Architect - Associate (SAA C03) test is a certification that aims to confirm the abilities and knowledge needed to create and implement structured solutions on AWS. This certification is highly valued by IT experts, cloud specialists, and architects looking to showcase their expertise in AWS cloud design. It shows that an individual can utilize AWS services effectively to create scalable and efficient cloud solutions that meet business needs. Here is a detailed summary of the exam structure, length, scoring system, and additional insights from sources to help candidates understand what to anticipate and how to get ready.

Format

The AWS SAA C03 test includes questions such as multiple choice and multiple responses. Multiple-choice questions have four or more possible options with one correct answer. On the other hand, multiple-response questions have more than five possible answers, with two or more correct choices. This format aims to assess a candidate's ability to identify the solutions and strategies for various real-world situations they might face while working with AWS. These questions test a candidate's knowledge of AWS services and ability to apply best practices in various scenarios.

A mix of questions ensures that candidates memorize information and demonstrate thinking and practical skills. These questions cover various topics, from queries to complex scenario-based challenges that require deep understanding and decision-making abilities. This comprehensive approach guarantees that certified individuals are well-equipped to tackle real-world issues.

Duration

Candidates are given 130 minutes to finish the exam. This time constraint emphasizes the need for time management to ensure that all questions can be read, understood, and answered within the given timeframe. To handle this pressure, candidates must be well prepared and familiar with the types of questions that could appear on the test. It is recommended that candidates practice with timed mock exams to develop effective time management skills.

Managing time during the exam is vital as it enables candidates to allocate time for each question, especially those that are more challenging or require deeper thinking. Practising with timed mock exams helps candidates build the endurance and pacing needed to stay focused and efficient throughout the 130-minute test. It also assists in pinpointing areas where they may need to enhance their speed or approach in responding to questions.

Scoring

The grading system for the AWS SAA C03 test is based on a scaled score ranging from 100 to 1000 with a passing threshold set at 720. This scaling method is in place to ensure fairness and consistency across exam iterations that may differ slightly in complexity. Achieving a score of 720 signifies the knowledge and competencies required by AWS for performance in an AWS solutions architect role. Familiarizing oneself with how the scoring works can help candidates establish goals and assess their preparedness through practice tests and evaluations.

With a scaled scoring system, scores (the number of answers) are transformed into a standardized score that considers differences in difficulty among different exam versions. This guarantees that all candidates are assessed fairly. To reach the minimum passing mark of 720, candidates must showcase a grasp of AWS services and architectural principles.

Exam Content Breakdown

The AWS Certified Solutions Architect – Associate (SAA C03) test includes subjects categorized into sections to evaluate a person's skills in creating and implementing strong, safe, and efficient solutions on the AWS platform. Each section is assigned a value based on its significance in the exam. The following figure gives the weightage of these sections:

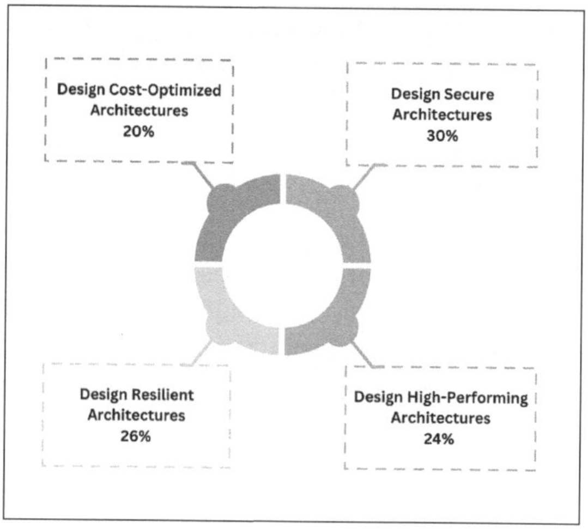

Figure 11.1: *Exam content breakdown*

Domain 1: Design Secure Architectures (30%)

This domain focuses on creating and setting up structures on AWS. With a weight of 30%, it is significant in the exam. Security is a priority for any cloud solution. This section evaluates the candidate's skill in implementing strong security measures. The key topics are:

- **Identity and Access Management (IAM):** Knowing IAM roles, policies and recommended methods to manage access to AWS resources.
- **Network Security:** Developing network designs using Virtual Cloud (VPC) security groups and network ACLs.
- **Data Protection:** Applying encryption for data at rest and in transit utilizing AWS Key Management Service (KMS) and overseeing data access.
- **Security Monitoring and Logging**: Use services, such as AWS CloudTrail and AWS Config to monitor activities and ensure compliance.

Candidates should excel in creating environments that safeguard data integrity, confidentiality, and availability while allowing only authorized users to access resources.

Domain 2: Design Resilient Architectures (26%)

Resilient structures can bounce back from issues and keep working. This area, which makes up 26% of the test, assesses how well a person can create systems that can keep running. The key topics are:

- **Fault Tolerance:** Setting up plans and strategies to keep things running.
- **Disaster Recovery**: Creating and implementing disaster recovery plans, such as performing backups and restoring data.

- **Scalability and Flexibility**: Designing systems that can adjust in size based on need using tools, such as Auto Scaling and Elastic Load Balancing.

The candidates must prove they are skilled at designing architectures that can withstand different problems and bounce back independently with as little downtime as possible.

Domain 3: Design High-Performing Architectures (24%)

Efficiency in performance entails the utilization of resources to fulfill system needs and sustain this effectiveness amidst shifting demands and advancing technologies. This area, which accounts for 24% of the exam, evaluates candidates' ability to create high-performing systems. The key topics are:

- **Optimizing Performance:** Selecting the compute storage and database solutions for effectiveness.
- **Advanced Computing Efficiency (ACE):** Crafting structures that manage demanding operations
- **Monitoring Performance:** Utilizing tools like Amazon CloudWatch to track and enhance performance.

Applicants should know AWS services and functionalities that enhance performance and guarantee that the structure meets specified performance standards.

Domain 4: Design Cost-Optimized Architectures (20%)

Optimizing costs plays a role in maximizing the advantages of cloud computing. This area, which holds a weightage of 20%, focuses on creating structures that offer cost solutions while maintaining performance and scalability. The key topics are:

- **Cost-Effective Resources:** Choosing budget-friendly services like appropriate EC2 instance types and storage options.
- **Cost Monitoring and Management:** Utilizing tools, such as AWS Cost Explorer, AWS Budgets, and others to monitor and manage expenses.
- **Economies of Scale:** Using pricing strategies, such as Reserved Instances and Savings Plans to cut expenses.

Individuals should be able to devise architectures that prioritize cost optimization alongside fulfilling performance and operational needs.

Learning Resources

Adopting a well-rounded study strategy is crucial to excel in the AWS Certified Solutions Architect – Associate (SAA C03) test. This includes utilizing authorized study materials, online classes, hands-on practice, and practice exams. Let's delve into the tools that can support the candidates in fully grasping the exam material:

Official Study Guide- AWS Certified Solutions Architect

The official study guide for the AWS Certified Solutions Architect – Associate exam is a resource that thoroughly covers all exam objectives. This guide offers:

- Thorough Explanations: Each topic provides in-depth explanations of AWS services, architectural principles, and best practices.
- Real-World Scenarios: Candidates are presented with real-world scenarios and case studies to enhance their understanding of how AWS concepts are applied in situations.
- Practice Questions: Each chapter wraps up with practice questions to help candidates evaluate their comprehension and readiness for the exam.
- Online Access: Online resources like videos and extra practice questions enhance the learning experience.

AWS Training and Certification

AWS provides a range of training and certification options designed specifically for preparing for the SAA C03 exam. These options include:

- Instructor-led Training: Training sessions led by AWS professionals that cover an understanding of AWS services and architectural principles in classroom and virtual settings.
- Self-paced Labs: Hands-on labs to give candidates experience working with AWS services in real-world scenarios.
- Exam-readiness: Workshops to help candidates understand the exam format, key concepts, and effective test-taking strategies.

AWS Whitepapers and FAQs

AWS whitepapers and FAQs are invaluable references, delving into specific AWS services and industry best practices. Notable resources include:

- Designing for the Cloud: Tips for Success on AWS: This guide offers recommendations for creating solutions on AWS emphasizing security, dependability, speed, and cost efficiency.
- AWS Architected Framework: Offering a range of practices and guidelines, this framework helps develop and manage dependable, secure, efficient, and budget-friendly AWS systems.
- White Papers on Security and Compliance: Addressing AWS security and compliance facets, these papers are crucial for studying for exams.

Online Courses (A Cloud Guru, Coursera, Udemy)

Numerous online platforms provide courses specifically designed for preparing for the AWS SAA C03 exam. Some known platforms include;

- **A Cloud Guru:** Known for its range of AWS certification courses; It offers video tutorials, hands-on labs, and practice exams.
- **Coursera:** This platform features AWS courses from institutions and industry experts and offers video lectures, interactive quizzes, and peer-reviewed assignments.
- **Udemy**: Offers various AWS certification courses–video materials, quizzes, and downloadable resources at affordable prices.

Practice Exams and Quizzes

Preparing for exams through practice exams and quizzes is crucial to evaluate your readiness and pinpoint areas where you can improve. Some valuable resources to consider are:

- **Whizlabs:** Whizlabs offers a variety of practice exams designed to mirror the AWS SAA C03 exam environment, accompanied by explanations for each question.
- **Official AWS Practice Exam:** AWS provides a practice exam that gives candidates a preview of the exam format and question types they can expect.
- **Other Online Learning Platforms:** Platforms like A Cloud Guru and Udemy often incorporate practice exams as part of their courses, allowing candidates to get acquainted with the structure and content of the exam.

By using these materials alongside study and practice, individuals can effectively prepare for the AWS SAA C03 exam and improve their skills in AWS cloud architecture, setting the stage for a successful certification achievement.

The AWS Certified Solutions Architect – Associate (SAA C03) assessment is an evaluation that confirms a person's capacity to create resilient, high-performing, and cost-efficient architectures on AWS. By grasping the exam content breakdown and utilizing study materials, individuals can adequately prepare for the test and enhance their proficiency in AWS cloud architecture. This certification showcases competence and unlocks plentiful career prospects in the fast-expanding realm of cloud computing.

Book the Exam

Do you aspire to be a cloud architect? In this guide, we'll cover everything you need to know about booking the AWS Certified Solutions Architect–Associate (SAA C03) exam. This includes eligibility requirements to ensure you are ready to undertake the exam, scheduling options to fit your needs, and step-by-step instructions for registering through your account.

Eligibility Requirements

To excel in the AWS Certified Solutions Architect–Associate (SAA C03) certification, candidates should have at least one year of experience designing systems on AWS. This emphasizes the significance of hands-on expertise in AWS cloud architecture, enabling candidates to succeed in the certification exam and apply AWS services effectively in real-world situations.

- **Practical Experience on AWS**

  To excel in the AWS SAA C03 certification test, it's essential to have exposure to creating systems on AWS. This hands-on experience helps learners grasp the nuances of AWS services, architectural guidelines, and design concepts. It equips them to handle situations, make well-thought-out choices, and devise scalable, dependable, and budget-friendly solutions.

- **Understanding of AWS Services**

  Candidates should grasp the services provided by AWS and how they work. This encompasses computing, storage, networking, databases, security, and other key services available on AWS. A thorough understanding of AWS services allows candidates to create architectures that combine services to fulfill business needs and performance goals.

- **Familiarity with Architectural Concepts**

  Candidates preparing for the AWS SAA C03 exam must grasp scalability, availability, fault tolerance, and cost optimization principles. Candidates must apply these principles when designing architectures that align with business requirements and follow AWS's recommended practices and design patterns.

- **Problem-Solving Skills**

  Applicants need problem-solving abilities to tackle issues and limitations that arise while designing. This includes analyzing needs, finding solutions, weighing options, and making informed choices. Problem-solving skills play a key role in creating architectures that are not only technically sound but also in line with business goals.

- **Continuous Learning and Development**

  While it's not mandatory, candidates pursuing the AWS SAA C03 certification should prioritize learning and growth. The field of cloud computing is constantly changing, with new services, features, and best practices emerging frequently. Candidates must keep up with the developments in AWS and continually improve their skills and knowledge to stay competitive.

Though there are no pre-requirements for obtaining the AWS SAA C03 certification, it is beneficial for candidates to have hands-on experience designing systems on AWS. Knowledge of AWS services and architectural principles showcases a candidate's strong problem-solving abilities, which are important for success in the certification exam. Furthermore, dedication to learning ensures that candidates remain updated on the advancements in AWS and are well-prepared to tackle the challenges of developing solutions on the AWS cloud platform.

Scheduling and Cost of the Exam

The AWS Certified Solutions Architect – Associate (SAA C03) exam provides candidates with options for scheduling and cost, making the certification process more accessible and convenient.

- **Cost: $150 USD**

  The AWS SAA C03 exam costs $150 USD, which includes the exam fee. It enables candidates to showcase their expertise in AWS cloud architecture. While it is considered a more expensive certification than others in the field, achieving the AWS SAA C03 certification carries weight and respect within the IT industry, offering valuable career advancement opportunities.

- **Scheduling Options**

  You can schedule your AWS SAA C03 certification exams through AWS Training and Certification. Based on their preferences and convenience, candidates can choose between online proctoring or taking the test at a Pearson VUE

  - **Online Proctoring**: This choice enables candidates to complete the exam from their homes or offices, offering flexibility in scheduling and removing the need to travel to a testing center. Online proctoring maintains security and integrity by monitoring candidates via webcam during the exam duration.
  - **Test Centers**: AWS SAA C03 exams are available worldwide at Pearson VUE for individuals who prefer a testing setting. These centers provide a controlled environment for focusing and concentration, with trained proctors overseeing the examination process to ensure fairness and compliance with testing regulations.

- **Additional Considerations**

  When planning to take the AWS SAA C03 exam, candidates should consider their knowledge of the subject, preparedness for certification, and preferences for testing conditions. To increase the likelihood of success, it's recommended that they set time for studying and rehearsing before booking the exam.

Registering for the Exam Through the AWS Account

To register for the AWS Certified Solutions Architect - Associate (SAA C03) exam, you can easily do so through your AWS Certification Account. Here are the steps to help you with the registration process;

1. **AWS Certification Account- Log in**
    a. Log in to the AWS Certification portal using your AWS account details. If you don't have an AWS account, you'll need to create one.
2. **Choose the exam you wish to schedule**
    a. Go to the **"`Schedule New Exam`"** section or a similar option on your AWS Certification Account dashboard.
    b. Select the AWS Certified Solutions Architect - Associate (SAA C03) exam from the certification list.
3. **Select your testing center or online proctoring method**
    a. Depending on your preference and availability, decide whether to take the exam at a testing center or opt for online proctoring.
    b. If you prefer a testing center, pick a location from the options provided.
    c. If you go for proctoring, ensure that you meet all requirements and choose a suitable date and time for your exam.
4. **Make payment for the exam fee and confirm your booking**
    a. Finalize your registration by paying the exam fee.
    b. The price for the AWS SAA C03 exam amounts to $150. Double-check your booking information, such as the exam date, time, and location (if to guarantee accuracy). Once you've reviewed everything, confirm your booking to complete the registration procedure.

Additional Considerations

a. Make sure you're fully prepared and confident before scheduling the AWS SAA C03 certification exam.

b. Consider your preferences and any logistical considerations when choosing between a testing center or online proctoring for the exam and setting the date and time.

By following these guidelines and going through the registration process on your

AWS Certification Account, you'll be ready to book your spot for the AWS SAA C03 exam. This will bring you closer to reaching your certification goals in AWS cloud architecture.

Tips on Taking the Exam

In this section, you will find some tips that will prove useful for the exam.

Developing a Study Plan

Studying for the AWS Certified Solutions Architect – Associate (SAA C03) test demands an organized approach to thoroughly address all exam areas and guarantee a grasp of the material. Here are guidelines to assist in creating a study schedule:

- **Set aside a time each day for studying**

  Make it a habit to study at the set time every day, whether in the morning, afternoon, or evening. A routine helps you stay on track and progress toward your certification goal.

- **Divide the exam topics. Focus on each one separately**

  Break down the exam topics, such as Design Secure Architectures, Design Resilient Architectures, Design High Performing Architectures, and Design Cost Optimized Architectures, into parts. Concentrate on mastering one topic before moving on to the next. This method allows for a grasp of the material and better retention.

- **Utilize learning methods like reading, videos, and hands-on practice**

  Use resources such as study materials, AWS documentation, instructional videos, and online courses to reinforce your understanding of important concepts. Read AWS whitepapers and FAQs related to each topic for insights into practices and real-world examples. Watch tutorials and educational content from sources, such as A Cloud Guru, Coursera, or Udemy, to complement your learning process and visualize subjects. Gain hands-on experience by creating AWS accounts, trying out AWS services, and completing exercises and lab tasks.

  By following these steps and incorporating a mix of study methods, you can develop an effective study plan tailored to your learning style and schedule, ultimately increasing your chances of success in the AWS SAA-C03 exam.

Time Management Strategies During the Exam

Managing your time while preparing for the AWS Certified Solutions Architect – Associate (SAA C03) exam is the key. Follow these tips to maximize your time:

- **Plan your time according to the number of questions you have**

  Before starting the test, assess the questions and the time allotted for the exam.

  Divide the time by the number of questions to determine the time needed for each question. This approach helps to prioritize tasks and manage your time effectively.

- **Identify questions that you are uncertain about and come back to them later**

  When faced with a challenging question, avoid spending too much time on it then.

  Instead, mark it for review and move on to the next question. This saves your time and also allows you to attempt as many questions as possible within the given timeframe.

  After completing all other questions, revisit those marked for review and answer them.

- **Monitor your time so that you can review your answers**

  Keep track of time left during the exam by checking the clock or timer.

  Strive to finish the exam with a few minutes remaining to review your answers.

  During this review period, check your responses, particularly focusing on questions, ensuring no instructions or details have been missed.

These time management tips can enhance your performance on the AWS SAA C03 exam and increase your likelihood of success.

Best Practices for Selecting Answers

When approaching questions on the AWS Certified Solutions Architect – Associate (SAA C03) test, using tactics to choose answers is crucial for accuracy and achieving good results. Keep these few tips in mind while selecting answers:

- **Eliminate incorrect answers**
  - Start by identifying and eliminating incorrect choices. This may include options that are irrelevant to the question, contradictory to AWS best practices, or contain factual errors.
  - Narrowing down the choices increases your chances of selecting the correct answer by reducing the options to consider.
- **Consider the best practices of AWS and the context of the question**
  - Get familiar with the guidelines, design principles, and suggested strategies for different scenarios within AWS.
  - Assess each option based on how it fits the scenario presented in the question.

  - Choose the option that closely aligns with AWS practices and meets the requirements or limitations outlined in the scenario.
- **Double-check your answers if time permits**
  - After finishing the exam, go through your answers again.
  - Revisit each question-and-answer option to ensure your choices make sense, adhere to AWS standards, and fully meet the scenario requirements.
  - Pay attention to challenging questions or posed challenges during your attempt.

By following these guidelines for selecting answers, you can confidently approach the AWS SAA C03 exam, improving your chances of identifying solutions and achieving an outcome.

Importance of Practice Tests

Studying with practice exams is vital when getting ready for the AWS Certified Solutions Architect - Associate (SAA C03) test. Here are a few reasons for their importance:

- **Identify knowledge gaps**
  - Practice tests can help you determine how well you grasp AWS concepts, services, and best practices.
  - Reviewing your performance on practice questions can help you pinpoint areas for improvement in your knowledge and skills.
  - Recognizing these gaps enables you to concentrate on the topics that you need to focus on, making your preparation more effective.
- **Understand the exam format**
  - Practice tests mimic the layout and design of the SAA C03 exam, including question types and time constraints.
  - Getting familiar with the exam interface and question formats reduces stress on exam day and boosts your confidence.
  - Exposure to practice questions also helps you develop strategies for handling multiple-choice and multiple-response questions.
- **Build confidence and time management skills**
  - Taking practice tests builds confidence in your ability to tackle exam questions efficiently.
  - These tests allow you to assess how quickly and accurately you can answer questions within the specified time limit.
  - Practicing under timed conditions helps refine your time management abilities so that you can pace yourself effectively during the exam.

Including practice exams in your preparation for the AWS SAA C03 test is crucial. They help you evaluate your understanding, get used to the exam structure, boost your confidence, and improve your time management abilities. Taking practice tests can enhance your preparedness and optimize your likelihood of success on the actual exam day.

Maintaining Test Day Focus

During your AWS Certified Solutions Architect - Associate (SAA C03) exam day, it is important to stay composed and attentive to give your best performance. Here are some suggestions to help you maintain concentration on the day of the test:

- **Make sure you get a good night's sleep before the exam**
    - It is important to have a relaxed and stressless night's sleep to wake up refreshed and energetic on the exam day.
    - Avoid staying up late; it can cause sleep deprivation and lead to impaired cognitive function and memory recall.
- **Eat a healthy meal before the test**
    - Kickstart your day with a breakfast containing complex carbs, protein, and good fats to sustain your energy levels during the exam.
    - Steer clear of caffeine or sugar, which might cause energy crashes and disrupt your focus.
- **Arrive early to avoid last-minute stress**
    - Plan to arrive at the testing center on time to allow check-in processes and acquaint yourself with the exam environment.
    - Getting there early helps reduce the chances of delays or disturbances that could cause stress and anxiety before the exam.
- **Keep calm and composed during the test**
    - Practice relaxation methods like breathing or visualization to handle test jitters and maintain a composed mindset.
    - Stay focused on the moment. Keep a positive attitude, reminding yourself of your preparation and belief in your capabilities.
    - When faced with challenging questions, remember to breathe, stay calm, and tackle them one step at a time without getting too stressed out.

Using these techniques and keeping a positive attitude can make the most of your test day experience. Do your best on the AWS SAA C03 exam. Have faith in your preparation. Take the exam with self-assurance and concentration.

Sample Exam Questions

Multiple Choice Questions

1. Which AWS service can you use to set up a network within the AWS cloud?

   Options: a. Amazon VPC, b. Amazon Route 53, c. AWS CloudTrail, d. Amazon S3

   Answer: a. Amazon VPC

   Explanation: With Amazon VPC, you can create a portion of the AWS cloud to deploy resources in a network you define.

2. Which AWS service is recommended for a managed NoSQL database?

   Options: a. Amazon Redshift, b. Amazon DynamoDB, c. Amazon RDS, d. Amazon Aurora

   Answer: b. Amazon DynamoDB

   Explanation: Offering management of NoSQL databases, Amazon DynamoDB ensures consistent performance and effortless scalability.

3. Which AWS service aids in monitoring and overseeing billing and usage?

   Options: a. AWS CloudTrail, b. AWS Config, c. AWS Cost Explorer, d. Amazon CloudWatch

   Answer: c. AWS Cost Explorer

   Explanation: Utilize AWS Cost Explorer to visually analyze and manage your data on costs and usage within the AWS environment.

Multiple Response Questions

1. What advantages does using AWS CloudFormation offer?

   Select two benefits from the options: a. Infrastructure as code, b. Automated code deployment, c. Resource tagging, and d. Template management.

   Answer: a. Infrastructure as code and b. Template management.

   Explanation: AWS CloudFormation allows you to utilize infrastructure as code and manage templates for creating and provisioning AWS resources.

2. What advantages does Amazon CloudFront offer?

   Choose two from the Options: a. Content delivery, b. Data warehousing, c. Reduced latency, d. Managed NoSQL database.

Answer: a. Content delivery, c. Reduced latency

Explanation: Amazon CloudFront is a content delivery network (CDN) service that ensures content delivery and minimizes delays when accessing that content.

3. Which advantages does Amazon RDS offer?

   Please select two options: a. Automated backups, b. Scalability, c. Serverless computing, or d. Data warehousing.

   Answer: a. Automated backups, b. Scalability

   Explanation: The advantages include automated backups and scalability provided by Amazon RDS.

FAQs

1. An app behind NLB with EC2 Auto Scaling has undetected HTTP errors. It requires restarts but no custom scripts. How can a solutions architect improve its availability?
   a. Enable HTTP health checks on the NLB using the company's application URL
   b. Implement a cron job on EC2 instances to monitor application logs for HTTP errors and restart if detected
   c. Swap the NLB with an Application Load Balancer, enable HTTP health checks with the company's application URL, and set Auto Scaling to replace unhealthy instances
   d. Establish an Amazon CloudWatch alarm monitoring UnhealthyHostCount for the NLB, with Auto Scaling replacing instances in an ALARM state

   Answer: c

2. How should a solutions architect provide secure access to an Amazon S3 bucket from an application tier on Amazon EC2 instances inside a VPC? (Choose two.)
   a. Configure a VPC gateway endpoint for Amazon S3
   b. Create a bucket policy to make objects in the S3 bucket public
   c. Create a bucket policy limiting access to the application tier in the VPC
   d. Create an IAM user with an S3 access policy and copy IAM credentials to the EC2 instance
   e. Create a NAT instance for EC2 instances to access the S3 bucket

Answer: a. and c.

Explanation:

Using a combination of a VPC endpoint for S3 (Option A) and a bucket policy restricting access to the VPC (Option C) provides the most secure method for the application tier running on EC2 instances to access the S3 bucket with sensitive user information. This approach keeps data traffic entirely within the private VPC network and minimizes the attack surface.

3. How should a solutions architect improve metadata load times for a mobile game using Amazon RDS?

    a. Migrate to Amazon Aurora with Aurora Replicas

    b. Migrate to Amazon DynamoDB with global tables

    c. Add Amazon ElastiCache for Redis

    d. Add Amazon ElastiCache for Memcached

    Answer: c

    Explanation: Adding ElastiCache for Redis reduces load times by caching frequently accessed metadata.

4. Which AWS service can help you migrate a large on-premises Oracle database to Amazon RDS with minimal downtime?

    a. AWS DataSync

    b. AWS Snowball

    c. AWS Database Migration Service (DMS)

    d. AWS Direct Connect

    Answer: c

    Explanation: AWS Database Migration Service (DMS) helps you migrate databases to AWS with minimal downtime. It supports various database engines, including Oracle, and enables continuous data replication to keep the source and target databases synchronized during migration.

5. Which storage solution is MOST cost-effective for a company that stores critical business data in Amazon S3, requiring immediate access and 4 years of retention?

    a. Move files from S3 Standard to S3 Glacier after 30 days, and delete after 4 years

b. Move files from S3 Standard to S3 One Zone-IA after 30 days, and delete after 4 years

c. Move files from S3 Standard-IA after 30 days, and delete after 4 years

d. Move files from S3 Standard to S3 Standard-IA after 30 days, and move to S3 Glacier after 4 years

Answer: c

Explanation: Immediate accessibility is crucial, and S3 Standard-IA balances cost-effectiveness with retrieval speed for frequently accessed files.

6. How can a company encrypt and replicate data stored in S3 across two AWS Regions with the LEAST operational overhead?

   a. Use SSE-S3 with replication between S3 buckets in each Region

   b. Create a customer-managed multi-region KMS key, use client-side encryption, and replicate between S3 buckets

   c. Use SSE-S3 with customer-managed KMS keys, which are replicated between S3 buckets

   d. Use SSE-KMS with customer-managed KMS keys, which are replicated between S3 buckets

   Answer: b

   Explanation: A multi-region KMS key ensures consistent encryption across regions with minimal management overhead, which is ideal for data replication between S3 buckets.

7. Which service will you use for load balancing in an n-tier architecture?

   a. AWS CloudFront

   b. Amazon Route 53

   c. AWS Elastic Load Balancing (ELB)

   d. AWS WAF

   Answer: c

   Explanation: AWS Elastic Load Balancing (ELB) distributes incoming application traffic across multiple targets, making it ideal for load balancing in n-tier architectures.

8. Suppose your company has a two-tier architecture for a customer relationship management (CRM) application. This application is facing performance issues

and is struggling with scalability. How would you modernize this architecture on AWS?

a. Migrate the application to a single large EC2 instance

b. Transition to a three-tier architecture with Amazon CloudFront, AWS Elastic Beanstalk, and Amazon RDS

c. Implement a serverless architecture using AWS Lambda

d. Use AWS Elastic Load Balancer with multiple EC2 instances

Answer: b

Explanation: Transitioning to a three-tier architecture improves scalability and performance by separating the presentation, application, and data layers, which is ideal for modernizing applications.

9. With the compliance team managing the encryption keys, How should a hospital store patient records in Amazon S3 to ensure PHI is encrypted in transit and at rest?

   a. Use ACM for SSL/TLS, SSE-KMS for encryption, and have the compliance team manage KMS keys

   b. Use `` `aws:SecureTransport` `` policy for HTTPS, SSE-S3 for encryption, and have the compliance team manage SSE-S3 keys

   c. Use `` `aws:SecureTransport` `` policy for HTTPS, and SSE-KMS for encryption, and have the compliance team manage KMS keys

   d. Use `` `aws:SecureTransport` `` policy for HTTPS and Amazon Macie for data protection

   Answer: c

   Explanation: The `` `aws:SecureTransport` `` policy ensures encryption in transit, and SSE-KMS with compliance team-managed keys ensures encryption at rest.

10. How can a company centrally manage security group rules for multiple AWS accounts and offices?

    a. Create security groups in the management account and update as needed

    b. Use a VPC customer-managed prefix list shared via AWS RAM for security groups

    c. Use an AWS-managed prefix list with Security Hub and Lambda for updates

    d. Use Firewall Manager with central security groups

    Answer: b

Explanation: A customer-managed prefix list shared via AWS RAM allows centralized and efficient management of security group rules.

11. A company needs to monitor data in customer AWS accounts by calling AWS APIs for EC2 and CloudWatch. What is the most secure way to access customer accounts?

    a. Have customers create an IAM role with read-only EC2 and CloudWatch permissions and a trust policy to the company's account

    b. Create a serverless API that provides temporary AWS credentials for a role with read-only EC2 and CloudWatch permissions

    c. Have customers create an IAM user with read-only EC2 and CloudWatch permissions and store the access keys securely

    d. Have customers create an Amazon Cognito user with read-only EC2 and CloudWatch permissions and store the credentials securely

    Answer: a

    Explanation: Using an IAM role with a trust policy allows the company to temporarily assume the role in customer accounts, following the principle of least privilege and avoiding long-term access keys.

12. A company wants to query and visualize observability data across multiple AWS accounts using CloudWatch. What is the best solution?

    a. Enable CloudWatch cross-account observability and deploy a CloudFormation template in each account to share data

    b. Set up service control policies (SCPs) for CloudWatch access in the monitoring account

    c. Create a new IAM user in the monitoring account and configure IAM policies in each account to access CloudWatch data

    d. Create cross-account IAM policies and attach them to a new IAM user in the monitoring account

    Answer: a

    Explanation: Enabling CloudWatch cross-account observability and deploying a CloudFormation template ensures data sharing with minimal setup and centralized management.

13. What is the primary function of AWS Identity and Access Management (IAM)?

    a. To manage EC2 instances

    b. To enable secure access to AWS services and resources for users

c. To create databases

d. To manage network traffic

Answer: b

Explanation: IAM allows you to securely manage access to AWS services and resources. Using IAM, you can create and manage AWS users and groups and use permissions to allow and deny their access to AWS resources.

14. Which service is used for migrating databases to AWS?

a. AWS Lambda

b. AWS Database Migration Service (DMS)

c. Amazon S3

d. AWS CloudFormation

Answer: b

Explanation: AWS DMS helps you migrate databases to AWS easily and securely. The source database remains fully operational during the migration, minimizing downtime for applications that rely on it.

15. What is the purpose of Amazon RDS Read Replicas?

a. To enhance security features

b. To offload read traffic and improve application scalability

c. To manage user access controls

d. To store backup copies of data

Answer: b

Explanation: Amazon RDS Read Replicas provide enhanced performance and durability for RDS database instances. They allow you to offload read traffic from your primary database instance, thus improving the performance and scalability of your applications.

16. You want to migrate your company's on-premises data center to the cloud. Which factors should you consider for this migration?

a. Enhanced security, fixed costs, limited scalability, single point of failure

b. Scalability, cost-effectiveness, reliability, wide range of services

c. High initial investment, limited services, complicated management, fixed infrastructure

d. Custom hardware, manual scaling, high maintenance, restricted access

Answer: b

Explanation: AWS provides a broad range of services and a scalable, reliable, cost-effective infrastructure that scales with your business needs. You should consider your data migration strategy, IT infrastructure, security, compliance, and cost management.

17. How would you set up IAM policies to create a secure environment, and what steps would you take?
    a. Grant all users full access to all resources.
    b. Create IAM groups with policies for specific tasks, restrict sensitive data access, and enable MFA.
    c. Use a single IAM user for all developers, disable logging, and share passwords
    d. Allow developers to create their policies, do not monitor activities

    Answer: b

    Explanation: To secure your AWS environment, create IAM groups for developers, enable MFA, enforce the principle of least privilege, and regularly review permissions and monitor access.

18. Which specific AWS services would you use to develop a machine learning model to predict credit card fraud?
    a. Amazon EC2, Amazon S3, AWS Lambda
    b. Amazon SageMaker, AWS Glue, Amazon S3
    c. Amazon RDS, AWS CloudFormation, Amazon DynamoDB
    d. AWS Lambda, Amazon Redshift, AWS IAM

    Answer: b

    Explanation: Amazon SageMaker provides tools for building, training, and deploying machine learning models. AWS Glue can be used for data preparation, and Amazon S3 can store the data.

19. How would you configure your Amazon RDS database for an e-commerce application that experiences periodic spikes in write operations to provide durability?

a. Use a single RDS instance with standard storage
b. Configure RDS with Multi-AZ deployments and Provisioned IOPS storage
c. Set up RDS Read Replicas
d. Use Amazon S3 for storing database logs

Answer: b

Explanation: Multi-AZ deployments provide high availability, while Provisioned IOPS (PIOPS) storage delivers high, consistent, and predictable I/O performance

20. Which service will you use for simplifying deployment and management of applications in the cloud?

    a. Amazon EC2

    b. AWS Elastic Beanstalk

    c. Amazon S3

    d. AWS Lambda

    Answer: b

    Explanation: AWS Elastic Beanstalk abstracts much of the underlying infrastructure and automatically handles application deployment, load balancing, scaling, and monitoring.

Best Practices

Let us look at the best practices that need to be followed(domain-wise):

Design Resilient Architectures

- Deploy essential resources in different availability zones to ensure high availability and fault tolerance.
- Use services like Amazon RDS along with Multi-AZ setups for automatic failover.
- Distribute incoming application traffic among various targets, like EC2 instances, in different Availability Zones.
- Utilize infrastructure as code (IaC) to consistently and predictably provision and manage AWS resources.
- Ensure health checks to route traffic only to healthy instances.
- Use Auto Scaling groups to automatically add or remove instances based on demand, ensuring the right number of instances are running to handle the load.
- Implement dynamic scaling policies for real-time responsiveness.
- Design applications to be stateless to ensure that any instance can handle any request.
- Use external data stores like DynamoDB or S3 for session data and state information.

- Isolate critical components to prevent failures from propagating across the system.
- Use different accounts, VPCs, or subnets to separate workloads.
- Regularly backup data using services like AWS Backup.
- Automate backups and ensure they are stored in different locations.
- Extend AWS infrastructure and services to on-premises locations for hybrid architectures.
- Implement DR strategies such as pilot light, warm standby, or multi-site active-active.
- Regularly test DR plans to ensure effectiveness.
- Utilize AWS Step Functions or application logic to avoid chain reaction failures.
- Use services like Amazon S3 Cross-Region Replication to copy data to another region automatically.
- Consider global services like Amazon Route 53 for DNS failover.

Design High-Performing Architectures

- Distribute incoming traffic across multiple targets to ensure even load distribution and high availability.
- Scale-out and scale-in EC2 instances automatically based on demand.
- Use predictive scaling for better forecasting of traffic patterns.
- Utilize CloudFront to distribute content to edge locations by caching content, decreasing users' latency worldwide.
- Select the appropriate EC2 instance type based on the specific workload requirements, such as compute-optimized, memory-optimized, and other options.
- Use Amazon EBS with provisioned IOPS for high-performance storage requirements.
- Use Amazon S3 for expandable object storage with lifecycle policies for organizing data into different tiers.
- Utilize Amazon RDS Read Replicas for tasks with high read volume.
- Implement AWS X-Ray for tracing and analyzing the performance of distributed applications.
- Consider Amazon Aurora for high performance and availability.
- Utilize Amazon VPC to establish segregated networks with precise control over network setups.
- Utilize VPC endpoints to establish private connections to AWS services without relying on the internet.

- Utilize VPC Flow Logs and AWS Network Firewall to monitor and manage network traffic within your VPC.
- Utilize Amazon ElastiCache for enhanced application performance by caching commonly accessed data.
- Implement application-level caching strategies.

Design Secure Applications and Architectures

- Utilize AWS Identity and Access Management (IAM) to oversee permissions and AWS resource access.
- Apply the least privilege concept by establishing roles with only the necessary permissions.
- Enforce multi-factor authentication (MFA) for all users, especially IAM roles and root accounts.
- Utilize security groups and network ACLs to manage incoming and outgoing traffic for both instances and subnets.
- Utilize dedicated hardware security modules (HSMs) for key management to comply with strict regulatory standards.
- Use AWS Control Tower to set up and govern a secure, multi-account AWS environment.
- Set up VPC peering, VPN, or AWS Direct Connect for secure connectivity.
- Encrypt data at rest using services like AWS KMS.
- Encrypt data in transit using SSL/TLS.
- Use AWS CloudTrail for API call logging and AWS Config for configuration monitoring.
- Implement Amazon CloudWatch to monitor and alert in real-time.
- Use AWS Shield for DDoS protection and AWS WAF for web application firewalls.
- Implement Amazon GuardDuty for continuous threat detection.
- Use AWS Artifact to access AWS compliance reports.
- Implement security frameworks and controls based on GDPR, HIPAA, and PCI DSS standards.
- Rotate, manage, and retrieve database credentials, API keys, and other secrets throughout their lifecycle.
- Apply resource-based policies for controlling access to specific resources, such as S3 buckets and IAM roles.
- Perform regular security assessments and vulnerability scanning.
- Use AWS Trusted Advisor for security best practice recommendations.

Design Cost-Optimized Architectures

- Regularly review and adjust instance sizes to match the workload requirements.
- Use AWS Cost Explorer to identify underutilized resources.
- Purchase Reserved Instances for predictable workloads to save up to 75% over On-Demand pricing.
- Automatically start and stop EC2 instances based on a schedule to save costs.
- Use Compute Savings Plans for flexibility across instance families and regions.
- Utilize Spot Instances for non-critical and flexible workloads to take advantage of unused EC2 capacity at reduced costs.
- Implement Auto Scaling to ensure you pay only for the resources you need.
- Use predictive scaling for optimizing resource allocation.
- Use S3 lifecycle policies for transitioning data to cheaper storage classes (for example, S3 Glacier).
- Delete unnecessary snapshots and data to reduce costs.
- Use AWS Lambda for pay-as-you-go pricing, where you pay only for the compute time you consume.
- Using AWS Direct Connect or AWS VPN can reduce data transfer costs between your on-premises data center and AWS services.
- Implement serverless databases like Amazon Aurora Serverless for scaling automatically based on demand.
- Set up AWS Budgets and Anomaly Detection to monitor and alert on cost and usage.
- Use AWS Compute Optimizer to get recommendations for optimal EC2 instance types.
- Use Cost and Usage Reports for detailed cost analysis and forecasting.
- Tagging can be used to allocate costs to different departments or projects for better cost tracking.
- Minimize data transfer costs for content delivery and caching by using Amazon CloudFront.
- To reduce data transfer charges between VPCs and AWS services, use VPC endpoints.

Conclusion

The certification for AWS Certified Solutions Architect - Associate (SAA-C03) is valuable proof of skills in creating and implementing scalable, highly accessible systems on AWS. It provides various career advantages, such as enhanced professional reputation and increased earning potential, making it perfect for solutions architects and cloud engineers. Preparing for the test includes grasping its structure and material, using AWS tools, and honing exam tactics. Achieving this certification boosts skills and marketability in the competitive cloud computing field!

References

- https://aws.amazon.com/blogs/training-and-certification/how-to-pass-the-aws-certified-solutions-architect-associate-exam/
- https://aws.amazon.com/certification/certification-prep/
- https://acloudguru.com/
- https://docs.aws.amazon.com/
- https://aws.amazon.com/training/
- https://aws.amazon.com/certification/certified-solutions-architect-associate/

Index

Symbols

A

B

C

D

E

M

N

O

P

R

S

T

V